The Wound and the Dream

WITHDRAWN

The American Poetry
Recovery Series

*A list of books
in the series appears
at the end of this book.*

The
Wound
and the
Dream

Sixty Years of American Poems

about the Spanish Civil War

EDITED BY

CARY NELSON

UNIVERSITY OF ILLINOIS PRESS

Urbana and Chicago

© 2002 by the Board of Trustees
of the University of Illinois
All rights reserved
Manufactured in the
United States of America
1 2 3 4 5 C P 5 4 3 2 1
(∞) This book is printed on acid-free paper.

Pages 321–26 constitute an
extension of the copyright page.

Library of Congress
Cataloging-in-Publication Data
The wound and the dream :
sixty years of American poems
about the Spanish Civil War /
edited by Cary Nelson.
p.   cm. — (American poetry recovery series)
ISBN 0-252-02747-7 (cloth : acid-free paper)
ISBN 0-252-07070-4 (pbk. : acid-free paper)
1. Spain—History—Civil War, 1936–1939—Poetry.
2. American poetry—20th century.
3. War poetry, American.
I. Nelson, Cary. II. Series.
PS595.S768W68   2002
811'.54080358—dc21   2001006453

CONTENTS

PREFACE

Veterans of the Abraham Lincoln Brigade and scholars specializing in left-wing American culture have long known there was an outpouring of American poetry devoted to the Spanish Civil War while the war ran its course from 1936 to 1939. A few wartime poems by Americans have also been included in Spanish Civil War anthologies published in Argentina, Spain, France, Italy, Mexico, and the United States, though British anthologies have tended to ignore American poetry. An anthology devoted exclusively to American poetry about the Spanish Civil War has never been published. Thus the full range of the work American poets did has never been readily available to readers.

Perhaps that is why a still more interesting fact has never been acknowledged: there has been a continuing sixty-year tradition of American poetry about the Spanish Civil War, not just a notable body of American poetry during the war itself. American poets turned to the example of Spain repeatedly during the continuing antifascist struggle of World War II. They turned to it again as a resource and counterexample during the heyday of McCarthyism. And poets interested in progressive culture have written about it periodically ever since. This book establishes and makes available that sixty-year tradition for the first time. It offers an opportunity to see the different ways American poets have responded to a major historical event; it also offers a snapshot of progressive American poetry as a whole.

Perhaps no other conflict in this century has combined the drama, the historical importance, and the ethical clarity of the struggle between democracy and fascism. Spain was its first major phase. The 1936–39 Spanish Civil War was, in effect, the opening battle of World War II; it was also the first time the world experienced saturation bombing of civilian targets. For these reasons and others, the struggle had immense ideological importance across the world. It has continued to hold a special place in modern history partly because forty thousand volunteers from fifty-two countries rallied to the defense of the Spanish Republic and joined the International Brigades. Those volunteers included four contributors to this book—Alvah Bessie, William Lindsay Gresham, James Neugass, and Edwin Rolfe.

Only a few months before international volunteers began arriving in Spain in substantial numbers, the country had held democratic elections that installed a new progressive coalition government. The losing conservative parties decided they would not accept the people's vote. They began to plot a coup, and in July 1936 their allies among the most reactionary military leaders attempted to take control of the country. In the major cities of Spain the people rose up to crush the revolt. But Europe's fascist dictators—Germany's Hitler, Italy's Mussolini, and Portugal's Salazar—offered the rebel generals military assistance at the moment their cause seemed lost.

Had Hitler and Mussolini not rapidly offered Spain's rebel generals men and arms, the Spanish Civil War would have remained a short-lived internal conflict instead of a war lasting over two and a half years with broad international implications. The people of Spain would have crushed the military rebellion against their democratically elected government, and the fascist powers would not have had so decisive an opportunity to test the resolve of the Western democracies. Unfortunately, the test did take place, and the West failed it when it adopted a policy of appeasement, refusing to sell arms to the Republic while Germany and Italy generously armed the rebel leader Francisco Franco. The foreign governments had signed a nonintervention pact, but Germany and Italy simply broke their word. Only Mexico and the Soviet Union sold arms to the Republic, but those arms, which had to travel great distances at considerable peril, were no match for the fascists' supplies. Especially in the second half of the war, in 1938 and 1939, the Republic was often overwhelmed by superior equipment. In the retreats of March and April 1938 and again during the fascist counterattack in August, the internationals were often on foot facing mechanized forces. Had the West stood firm against fascism in Spain, the history of our century might read somewhat differently. As this anthology shows, the legacy of that experience haunted American poets through the rest of the century.

This is not a comprehensive anthology of American poems about the war; such a book would have to be twice as long. It is rather a collection of what I have judged to be the best poems on the subject. Yet the book embodies a model for evaluation that will be unfamiliar to many readers and that thus deserves to be stated clearly. Many poetry anthologies use only one major aesthetic standard as a principle for selection, but our literary history has been too rich and varied to be fairly represented by only one standard. I have therefore included what I take to be the best poems of several types—lyrical, agitational, elegiac, topical, political—categories that often overlap. The result is a book that gives a reasonably full account of the ways the Spanish Civil War has occupied our poets for more than half a century, a book that also shows the different ways poets have appealed to readers and the varieties of cultural work poems can do.

INTRODUCTION

The International Context for American Poetry about the Spanish Civil War

A poet takes the sudden bayonet gleam to paper,
Waking hurried echoes in the huddled hills. . . .
—Thomas O'Brien

and all the walls decay and all the world stands bare
until the world is a field of the Spanish War
—Muriel Rukeyser

For this is the act, the chorus argument,
This is the work we have said is to do.
—Ewart Milne

and poetry is a Chinese game that will never be more,
until, like the Greeks' it is action.
—Byron Vazakas

I want to begin not with a poem but with a novel, or rather a novel turned into an historical memento. The novel is *Don Quixote,* in Samuel Putnam's anno- tated translation, published by Viking in 1949. Its singular historical character comes, for my purposes, not from the text itself but from circumstances of ownership and use. My interest is in one particular copy of Cervantes's novel. This copy, which is now in my library, once belonged to Alvah Bessie, a veter- an of the Abraham Lincoln Battalion—a group of Americans who volunteered to fight in the 1936–39 Spanish Civil War as a part of the International Bri- gades—who was himself a novelist, screenwriter, and poet. His use of this copy of the book has been commemorated, as it were, by the federal prison system. The front and back endpapers are marked with the same purple stamp: "INSPECTOR No. 1 / Dec 22 1950." Pencilled in is the censor's signa- ture of approval, "Ok / RGS"; in the nomenclature of the prison he is the "ed- ucational supervisor." These imprints of federal authority and power tell us the book had been inspected for contraband or hidden weapons and that the contents were not deemed subversive.[1] The book could now be passed on to the appropriate inmate. How little the prison knew, for in the aftermath of all that had passed since the last great cause of the 1930s it was subversive to remember Spain and all it stood for.

On the title page the owner had signed his name in the way required, given his circumstances, namely with his federal prisoner identification number: "Alvah Bessie / 5853-TT / Xmas 1950." "TT" refers to the federal prison in Texarkana, Texas. The text is unmarked, so I must mostly look to myself to understand what it meant to read *Don Quixote* as one of the Hollywood Ten, in prison for choosing to defend the First Amendment to the Constitution and defying the House Committee on Un-American Activities (HUAC). Whether Bessie had heard the suggestion that *Don Quixote* itself was written in prison I do not know, though it is certainly one of the relevant ironies we may contemplate. In any case two pages of Bessie's copy of the novel have their corners folded, and these creases mark the moment when one pair of hands registered the onset of the nightmare of McCarthyism. The first fold marks the narrative prologue to chapter 29, which "treats of the amusing artifice and means employed in extricating our enamored knight from the extremely harsh penance he had inflicted on himself." As a matter of principle the Hollywood Ten had willingly, if unhappily and angrily, accepted prison; they refused to invoke the Fifth Amendment. Bessie's brief unpublished poem "Technicality" captures some of the attendant ironies:

It seems, if we had said: "The Fifth Amendment!"
We would never have passed a day in jail.

Instead we cried: "The Bill of Rights!"
And we have spent, now, seven months inside.

Euclid would be stunned to learn, today,
The whole no longer equals all its parts.[2]

Taking the Fifth, as it became known, would not have kept them off the blacklist and saved their careers, but it would have kept them out of jail. In subsequent years many called to testify did just that, but in 1947, when HUAC came to Los Angeles, collective resistance still seemed possible. And so the Hollywood Ten stood their ground and were swept away, much as the Spanish Republic had been a decade earlier.

One later page in Bessie's copy of the novel is also turned down, the notes to chapter 29, which remind us that "the great Complutum" refers to Alcala de Henares, Cervantes's birthplace. That was a town that members of the International Brigades would come to know well. The town acquires addition-

al meanings nearly four centuries after Cervantes's birth, as does *Don Qui-*
xote, for fascists burn books, and to stand in defense of Cervantes's birth-
place—and now to remember that moment on the world stage—was to recall
everything absent from 1950s politics. To read Cervantes behind bars was, of
course, to feel a certain irony. Premature antifascists, the volunteers in Spain
had tilted against the windmills of Hitler's Condor Legion. For all that Bessie's
compatriots understood or valued the stand the volunteers had taken, even
after World War II had overtaken the world and fifty million had died in a
struggle they had tried to end at its outset, the whirlwind might well have
been but a windmill.

Bessie also no doubt felt a certain pride. If Cervantes marked an indelible
chapter in Spanish history and culture, so, too, did the International Bri-
gades. The towns on the map of Spain had new histories to supplement the
classical ones, and though no monuments could be raised to that history
now, it could be commemorated as he raised *Don Quixote* to his eyes in a
prison cell. The Putnam translation also carried with it another set of coded
meanings, for not every Lincoln Brigader could have read it happily. Putnam,
like Bessie himself, had attacked Ernest Hemingway when *For Whom the Bell
Tolls* appeared a decade earlier; this particular translation thus also invoked
an antifascist alliance politics now fractured and under assault.

All this was at stake when Bessie decided to write poetry in his prison
cell. He assembled the poetry into an unpublished book-length manuscript
entitled "The *Free* World and Other Captive Verse." "Poetry," he wrote in the
preface "is generally the concise expression of emotion under pressure. A
man in prison for whatever reason, lives under one of the most extreme
forms of pressure humanity has ever devised—the loss of liberty. When he
is in prison unjustly, or for reasons he believes to be unjust, the pressure is
likely to be extreme."[3]

In a larger sense, of course, the country as a whole—at least for those on
the left—was well on its way to becoming a virtual prison by 1950. Bessie's
sonnet "Buried Alive," unpublished until now, has some of that character:

If you have wondered what it would be like
To live in prison as a prisoner
Then find yourself a former prisoner
And ask him. He will tell you it is like
A room dug only one foot underground.
You listen there to what occurs above;
You hear the people hurry, bustle, shove;
You are the prisoner of every sound.
You feel that if you only reach your hand
A foot above your head, then you can touch

The living world, its living people; such
Is the illusion and it leaves a brand
On mind and body. To the world, your head,
Your heart and body all are buried; dead.[4]

People's lives and livelihoods were being destroyed. The postwar inquisition
had become a purge, first of federal, state, and local government jobs and
then of industry. The policing of thought had become a national preoccupa-
tion. Soon the Communist party would decide it needed to send people un-
derground in order to preserve some structure and membership in the midst
of the witch hunts. People left their homes and families, assumed false
names, and roamed the country like forest partisans under Nazi occupation.

The parallels were not lost on the Left. "Madrid to Washington," Bessie
wrote in "September 23, 1950," his poem commemorating the passage of the
McCarran Act against subversive activities, "is but a step / in hob-nailed
boots / or Washington to Rome or to Berlin."[5] After writing a poem for the
American volunteer Aaron Lopoff, who died trying to take a hill in Spain, he
wrote one for Edward Dmytryk, the one member of the Hollywood Ten who
abandoned his comrades and gave in to the committee. "'And Then There
Were Nine,'" in effect a companion piece to Edwin Rolfe's "Political Prisoner
123456789," treats Dmytryk's defection in a parable about ten men who take
a hill in Spain only to find that one loses courage and abandons his position.
Other poems, such as "Memory of Battle" or "For My Dead Brother," are fo-
cused entirely on the experience of Spain, though always from the vantage
point of a time when all Spain represents seems out of reach.[6]

I came across the manuscript of Bessie's book of prison poems among his
private papers in the course of a search for the repressed poetry of the 1950s.
Bessie was not known as a poet, but for a moment, behind bars for the of-
fense of standing up for his constitutional rights in a country that had demon-
ized most of the commitments that mattered to him, poetry seemed the right
form to use to call forth the mixed emotions he felt: anger at the present mad-
ness and faith in an earlier cause. There was no place to publish a book of
such poems at the time, but several of the poems appeared in *Masses and
Mainstream* and the *National Guardian* over the next two years. Two of the
poems he published were about Spain, a country he had left at the end of
1938 when the International Brigades were disbanded. A few months later
Franco was victorious, and Spain entered its decades-long night of fascism.
The sixty-year tradition of American poems about the Spanish Civil War not
only encompasses the moment of the 1950s but in some ways pivots on it, for
the 1950s is central to understanding why the tradition—not only the wartime
poems of 1936–39—might still matter to us.

There are many Spains we remember, many we have forgotten. Some of them overlap, and some seem to have almost no points of correspondence. The Loyalist Spain of 1951, however, twelve years after the fall of the Republic, the Spain preserved within the American inquisition as a counterpointing resource and reference point, that Spain we have largely forgotten. Indeed, I do not think we as a culture ever knew its existence; it was real only for the subculture of the embattled Left. That Spain is midway through the story I want to tell. But I have decided to begin with it, for the reasons stated above. Here is Bessie's "For My Dead Brother," a poem written in prison in 1951 and addressed to to his fellow American volunteer Aaron Lopoff, mortally wounded in the struggle for Hill 666 in the Ebro campaign of the summer of 1938:

The moon was full that night in Aragón . . .
we sat in the black velvet shadow
of the hazel (called *avellano* there);
the men lay sleeping, sprawled on the packed earth
in their blankets (like the dead). . . .

With dawn we'd move in double files
down to the Ebro, cross in boats,
and many lying there relaxed
would lie relaxed across the river
(but without their blankets).

He said: "You started something, baby—"
(I was thirty-four; he ten years less;
he was my captain; I his adjutant)
"—you started something, baby," Aaron said,
"when you came to Spain."

Across the yellow river
there was a night loud with machine guns
and the harmless popcorn crackle
of hand grenades bursting pink and green,
and he was gone and somehow Sam found me in the dark,
bringing Aaron's pistol, wet with blood.
He said:
        "The last thing Aaron said
        was, 'Did we take the hill?'
        I told him, 'Sure.'"

Aaron, we did not take the hill.
We lost in Spain. Aaron,
I know, finally, what you meant that night
under the black shadow of the *avellano,*
sitting here in prison twelve years later.
We did not take the hill, *mi commandante,*
but o! the plains that we have taken
and the mountains, rivers, cities,
deserts, flowing valleys, seas!
You may sleep . . . sleep, my brother, sleep.

The "we" of Bessie's poem is, of course, the we of the Lincoln Battalion and the International Brigades, and the we that was Loyalist Spain and its allies who joined the army in the years 1936–38. In a larger sense, however, that "we" also refers to the Popular Front of 1936–39, which might have taken the hill if it had succeeded in persuading the allied governments to sanction arms shipments to Spain and if it had been able to hold the various factions in the Spanish Republic in a workable alliance. Many still believe that sufficient arms to balance more fully the men and weapons Hitler and Mussolini provided Franco would have been enough support to turn the war in favor of the elected government and ensure a defeat, rather than a victory, for fascism in 1939. We will never know for certain. But the Loyalists did not take the hill; that much we do know. By extension, then, the vast literature of support for Spain—poems, plays, journalism, novels, broadsides, letters, essays, speeches—that swept the West for those few years failed as well. At least it failed in achieving the practical political effect that was one of its inescapable aims. Did it succeed, however, in other ways? Did it give to successive generations a resource worth drawing on and thus potentially still vital today? That is one, but only one, of the questions a reflective literary history can ask today, though there is also one that it must ask: what is our interest in a past we recover now? It may also ask, as I intend to do here, what the literature of the Spanish Civil War, specifically its poetry, offered to its own time. I am not, I should make clear, attempting a full survey of Spanish Civil War poetry here, something not even a book-length manuscript could hope to achieve. My main aim is rather to begin describing the collective and almost choral nature of the poetry of the Spanish Civil War. In the process I will highlight a few poems from *The Wound and the Dream* and put them in their proper international context. Establishing that context leads me to propose a new choral paradigm for understanding the poetry of this watershed moment in twentieth-century history.[7]

The outpouring of support for the people of Spain and the working alliances it made possible for those few years of 1936–39 are two of the hallmarks of

internationalism and coalition politics of the twentieth century. It was a poli-
tics that embodied both losses and gains, to be sure. One of the most obvious
losses was the more thoroughgoing revolutionary spirit of the first half of the
1930s. The broad alliance against fascism, however necessary it was—and it
would be irrational to claim we did *not* need such an alliance in the late
1930s—displaced the more aggressively class-conscious revolutionary art and
politics of the preceding seven or so years, though it also facilitated broad
public support for the U.S. effort once the United States finally entered World
War II. Yet that same broad alliance disintegrated in the face of the anticom-
munist hysteria of the postwar decade, so whatever resources we feel it may
offer now need to be critiqued in the light of how little it did for the Left in the
late 1940s and throughout the 1950s. Alvah Bessie's poem "For My Dead
Brother" and the poem "To Spain" by Olga Cabral that is printed next to it in
the June 1953 issue of *Masses and Mainstream* may be seen in part as late
flowerings of Popular Front politics. Only a year earlier, the Veterans of the
Abraham Lincoln Brigade had brought out its anthology *Heart of Spain* in an
effort to revive the alliances of the 1930s when they were most needed. The
dominant culture's most succinct response came on June 19, 1953, when Julius
and Ethel Rosenberg were executed. For those in power in the United States
the hard revolutionary Communist stance of the Third Period and the more
liberal democratic policies of the Popular Front were not worth distinguishing.

Of course, this distinction was partly overturned during the Spanish Civil
War as well, most notably when Stalin's secret police collaborated with the
Spanish Communist party in suppressing the revolutionary Marxist POUM
and the Spanish anarchists in the Barcelona area in May of 1937. There was a
sound basis for considering POUM and anarchist policies a threat to the Re-
public, since both groups resisted the government's commitment to a tradi-
tional, hierarchically organized, and centrally controlled army. The indepen-
dent militias had proven highly effective in urban skirmishes in 1936, but
they were no match for Franco's mechanized forces in the open field. Yet a
negotiated, rather than murderous, solution to differences among the Span-
ish Left would have benefited everyone. Meanwhile, the assassination of
POUM leaders and the wholesale suppression of the radical Left, at the very
least, amounted to a violent Comintern (Communist International) betrayal of
the very Popular Front alliance politics it was espousing elsewhere.

The Comintern did, however, organize the International Brigades. Even
George Orwell, whose account of the events in Barcelona in *Homage to Catalo-
nia* has become virtually canonical, repeatedly credits the International Bri-
gades as a genuinely antifascist force. The International Brigades (IB), of
course, played no role in suppressing the POUM. Moreover, even though the
IB received orders from the Comintern, its leaders often objected to those
commands they deemed ill-advised or impractical. The International Brigades

were also subject to Spanish army orders. Moreover, firsthand accounts suggest that Soviet military advisers working with the International Brigades were straightforwardly seeking a victory over fascism. We are therefore left with a complex history that requires us to make a large number of distinctions.

The effect of May 1937 and other Left disputes on Spanish Civil War poetry, however, was minimal, partly because early in the war poetry was established as a place where such differences were either overcome through Popular Front ideology or could coexist within it. Among the poems of *El mono azul* (The blue overalls or The blue monkey), the literary journal of Madrid's Alliance of Antifascist Intellectuals, we can find an homage to the anarchist martyr Buenaventura Durruti (Luis Perez Infante's "La muerte de Durruti," published on February 11, 1937) and an homage to the Communist heroine Lina Odena (Lorenzo Varela's "Romance de Lina Odena," published on October 15, 1937). Most Spanish Civil War poems show few traces of particular Left positions; they most often voice a generalized antifascism. As Stephen Hart has pointed out, however, there are more polemical poems, especially anticapitalist ones, in some of the trade union and militia publications.[8]

Some poets refused to accept the accounts of what had happened in Catalonia. Others were poorly informed. Some simply felt they could best support the cause of Spanish freedom by promoting the Popular Front despite its betrayal by Soviet and Spanish Communists. Years later, in a 1978 interview published when Kenneth Rexroth reissued his Spanish Civil War poems in a beautiful limited edition, he acknowledged he was relatively well informed about events during the war. He corresponded with people who had been in Spain and read an anarchist newspaper published in London. "The twists and turns of the Stalinists in Spain," he remarked forty years later, "were one of the reasons for the Republican defeat." Nonetheless, his poems "Requiem for the Spanish Dead" and "Autumn in California" embody a Popular Front stance.[9]

It is reasonable to conclude that the Popular Front acquired a cultural force of its own that included effects outside Communist control. The Popular Front helped prepare the ground for America's belated entry into World War II. For that matter the Communist commitments of many international volunteers in Spain were not the same as those of Joseph Stalin. There were, in effect, numerous communisms and more than one set of Popular Front beliefs at work in the 1930s. For some scholars, the Popular Front was a "Faustian bargain" struck with international communism;[10] for others, including myself, it promoted the commitment to an alliance antifascism that was necessary to democracy's survival.

None of these issues has much impact on the stories we tell most often about modern literature. Canonical American modernism has its international moments, to be sure, most notably when Ezra Pound and T. S. Eliot were in England or when various American expatriates were in Paris in the 1920s.

Those international moments are comfortable to recall for several reasons. First, they involve many of the canonical figures of modern art and literature. Second, they seem reassuringly aesthetic and personal episodes. Even the sense of distaste for American culture that led many writers to Europe seems individually inflected, a generational phenomenon that has to be understood in terms of personal temperament. No problematic political issues seem centrally at stake in those decisions to travel abroad. Of course, a considerable number of writers from the United States and elsewhere traveled to the Soviet Union in a far more politically charged cultural interaction in the same decade, but we tend not to retell those stories. Spain was, however, the focus of one of the more remarkable international literary interchanges in our history. The case of Spain also suggests that the effort to move beyond the limitations imposed by studying national literatures in isolation might well work less with broad generalizations than with specific historical conjunctures; indeed, we might first open our eyes to the key sites of internationalization we have long ignored. This introduction shows what contributions American poets made to an international phenomenon.

The literary component of the Spanish Civil War is so deeply and intricately international that any effort to read it exclusively in national terms seems seriously misguided. We can properly ask, as does *The Wound and the Dream,* how writers from a given country responded, what contributions a given national literature made to this global conversation, and even what place Spain played in individual careers. It was British and American poets, such as Barrows Dunham in his 1938 poem "Neutrality," not Spanish poets, for example, who were most likely to attack the hypocritical nonintervention policy pursued by the Allies. We can also try to discover what impact writers hoped to have on the particular audiences reached by the books and journals in which they published, audiences that were sometimes—but also often not—focused on a particular country. But any sense of the rhetoric of particular poems, any effort to read them closely or to identify related poems to which particular writers were responding, certainly requires looking widely at the international literature of the war and perhaps necessitates recasting our sense of what a national literature means. For several modern American poets, the period of the Spanish Civil War was a period when they were no longer primarily *American* writers; they were part of an international political struggle and an international community of writers. Part of what is important about American poets' contributions to the dialogue about Spain, therefore, is that a number of them figuratively gave up nationhood as the ground of their being. It is the very reverse of such projects as Hart Crane's poem sequence *The Bridge* (1930) and William Carlos Williams's critical book *In the American Grain* (1925). If a number of American poets had earlier wondered how to give modernist experimentalism an American inflection, how to interleave collage with American sights and sounds, how to construct a myth that would enable uniquely American identities, now in the shadow of fascism the challenge was to enter the international arena seamlessly.

The collective, interactive, and international rhetoric, identity, and motivation of Spanish Civil War poetry do not exhaust its meaning, but they are part of what brought the poems into existence and established and sustained their historical identity. For too long we have thought of these poems exclusively as separate *responses* to shared historical conditions. Whatever commonality of experience, conviction, intention, and meaning is pertinent, or so we imagine, precedes the poem and somehow drops out of contention once the poem itself is under way. Even when we acknowledge that the historical context is central to each poem's meaning, we tend to treat the history as "background" and to assume that various poems' relations to one another and to other cultural forces are at best a minor part of their meaning.

The Spanish Civil War is not simply a historical context that enriches and complicates the poems written under its influence. It is a historical conjuncture that reshapes the very activity of reading and writing poetry, making poems into something they had not been before and would not be afterward. The postwar poems reprinted here are partly memorials to that earlier conjunction. Our twin habits of treating history as background and reading poems in radical isolation from one another prevent us from understanding how these poems came to be and how they functioned in their historical moment. That does not make immanent formal or rhetorical analysis of the poems illicit—indeed I am doing some here—but it does make such analysis impoverished and misguided when it is taken to be a sufficient mode of understanding. Certainly any account with claims to historiography has to take up the collective nature of what has, perhaps deceptively, been called the "literary response" to the war. When Loyalist poets read their work aloud in the trenches, when Republican planes scattered poems over enemy troops, when soldiers from numerous countries tacked their poems up on the battlefield or training area bulletin boards known as wall newspapers, when political groups reprinted poems from earlier periods to give them new meaning (see figure 1), when editors put poems in political journals here or in battalion newspapers in Spain, when Americans read translations of Spanish wartime romances to audiences here and helped build support for the Spanish Republic, they were not *responding* to the war; they were part of it. When poets wrote or translated poems for collective projects, they were engaged not only in solitary creation but also in group activity.

That poetry should have direct bearing on the war, that it should seek to shape attitudes and events, was not taken for granted. It was a result actively sought, a relationship writers and editors worked to ensure and intensify. When Manuel Altolaguirre issued a new printing of his poetry collection *Las*

Figure 1. One side of a flier issued by the British Communist party on March 17, 1938, to protest Neville Chamberlain and the British government's inaction on Spain. A photograph of a dead child in Spain is illustrated with Elizabeth Barrett Browning's "The Cry of the Children." The reverse of the flier extends the argument for supporting the Spanish Republic. Author's collection.

"WE CAN'T BURN OUR FINGERS"

Chamberlain in the House of Commons, March 16, 1938.

This statement of Chamberlain's should fill every British citizen with horror and contempt.

That same night thousands of men, women and children in Barcelona were being torn, mangled and burned alive by bombs from Hitler's and Mussolini's planes.

"WE CAN'T BURN OUR FINGERS," says Chamberlain, as innocent babies' flesh and blood stains Barcelona's streets. When Elizabeth Barrett Browning wrote "The Cry of the Children," it was the Chamberlains she had in mind.

"'How Long,' they say, 'how long,' O cruel nation,
Will you stand, to move the world, on a child's heart,—
Stifle down with a mailed heel its palpitation,
And tread onward to your throne amid the mart?
Our blood splashes upward, O gold heaper,
And your purple shows your path!
But the child's sob in the silence curses deeper
Than the strong man in his wrath."   [SEE OTHER SIDE

islas invitadas on July 31, 1936, he added a new dedication: "Printing this new edition in these dramatic days of conflict, I dedicate it with complete enthusiasm and gratitude to the heroic defenders of liberty and democracy. It is but a small tribute to those who offer every poet a fount of inspiration and a mirror of sacrifice. May my future work embody the nobility awakened by the people's conduct."[11] When the editors of *El mono azul* at the Alliance of Antifascist Intellectuals assembled a two-page spread of poems about the defense of Madrid, they underlined the status of the poems by including reduced versions of two posters from the *Disciplina del fuego* series that gave advice on proper firing practice for rifles and machine guns. If the poems urge the defense of Madrid and grant its defenders heroic status, the *Disciplina del fuego* posters detail how that defense can be carried out. Nor was this information superfluous; Madrid was being defended by volunteer militias with no military background. Across the country, the propaganda ministry in

Catalonia issued small flier versions of the same posters with poems and songs—among them "Hijos del pueblo," "Els segadors," "La joven guardia," and "La internacional"—on the reverse side (see figure 2).

As this suggests, the poetry of the war saw multiple means of distribution and reproduction. Not only books and pamphlets but also broadsides and cards were common means of reproduction. Poem cards were typically issued to commemorate special occasions, while broadsides helped build public consensus and strengthen convictions. The International Brigades printed a stanza by the British volunteer Miles Tomalin—written at the Battle of Brunete—on their 1937 Christmas card, which was then mailed throughout the English-speaking world; in Britain, an illustrated card with Eleanor Farjeon's poem "Christmas in Spain" reminded people of the Republic's needs; the government of Catalonia issued a series of nine-by-twelve-inch poetry broadsides, with an illustration on one side and a poem on the other (Rafael Alberti's "Defensa de Madrid" is number forty-one in the series; see figure 3); and when the International Brigades marched through Barcelona in October of 1938, a series of commemorative three-by-six-inch poem cards—including Miguel Hernández's "Al soldado internacional caido en España" and Rafael Alberti's "A las Brigadas Internacionales"—were distributed among the crowds. Meanwhile, not only literary journals but also mass-circulation newspapers in Spain, Britain, France, and the United States published Spanish Civil War poetry. In all these countries, people often heard poems read aloud before they were published anywhere. Jack Lindsay's "On Guard for Spain!—A Poem for Mass Recitation" was given group performances throughout Britain.[12] Some 346–65 lines in its longest versions, it was apparently shortened for some occasions. One three-page version that has survived from the 1930s—typed in red and annotated for performance in pencil—is cut to 132 lines. There were at least five people scheduled to read the text, with some passages marked for one, two, or three voices and some marked "all."[13] "The effect," wrote Lindsay later, "of a multiple set of individual voices, now and then brought together in a collective outburst, was given a dramatic effect by continual movement among the group—again a movement of individuals which at moment[s] came together in a collective pattern."[14] The technique was at once aesthetic and political; it suggested that a natural interchange could occur between individual and collective action, that people could flow into and out of an appropriate group identity. The poem itself, like the other poems here, simultaneously marked its own and its collaborative being. Recalling one such wartime performance in a 1943 essay, R. Vernon Beste wrote that when the name of Malaga was called out from the stage, "it was a deep growl of fury rather than a name, not just a place in Southern Spain, but a word to give vengeance a sharper meaning, a banner rallying the defenseless and shaming the cynical."[15] Meanwhile, foreign visitors to Spain were astounded by mass poetry readings attended by soldiers and working people.

LA INTERNACIONAL
(Himno de los trabajadores de todos los países)

I

¡Arriba, parias de la tierra!
¡En pie, famélica legión!
Atruena la razón en marcha;
es el fin de la opresión.
El pasado hay que hacer añicos.
¡Legión esclava, en pie, a vencer!
El mundo va a cambiar de base,
los nadie de hoy todo han de ser.

Agrupémonos todos
En la lucha final,
el género humano
es la Internacional.

Agrupémonos todos, etc.

II

Ni en dioses, reyes ni tribunos
está el supremo salvador,
nosotros mismos realicemos
el esfuerzo redentor.
Para hacer que el tirano caiga
y el mundo siervo libertar,
soplemos la potente fragua
que al hombre libre ha de forjar.

Agrupémonos todos, etc.

III

La Ley nos burla, y el Estado
oprime y sangra al productor;
nos da derechos ilusorios;
no hay deberes del señor.
Basta ya de tutela odiosa,
que la igualdad ley ha de ser:
"No más deberes sin derechos,
ningún derecho sin deber."

Letra y música de *De Degaiter.*

Figure 2. One of a series of two-sided fliers issued by the propaganda ministry in Barcelona; each has military instructions on one side, and a number have poems or songs on the other. The Alliance of Antifascist Intellectuals in Madrid issued poster-sized versions of the military instruction panels and used them to illustrate poems in El mono azul. *Author's collection.*

DISCIPLINA DEL FUEGO

¡TIRADORES!
Es necesario que guardéis las vainas disparadas.

¡BATALLONES!
Formad grupos de hombres que recojan las vainas.
Después de una defensiva el equipo de recuperación debe recoger los casquillos caídos.
En la ofensiva ocuparán los equipos de último escalón del orden de combate para recoger los casquillos de los que hayan avanzado, y, especialmente, de las armas automáticas.
¡Premios para los mejores equipos de recuperación!

Cuidado con los sembradores de alarma
La cobardía se parece mucho a la traición

COMISSARIAT DE PROPAGANDA — GENERALITAT DE CATALUNYA

DEFENSA DE MADRID

MADRID, corazón de España,
late con pulsos de fiebre.
Si ayer la sangre le hervía,
hoy con más calor le hierve.
Ya nunca podrá dormirse,
porque si Madrid se duerme,
querrá despertarse un día
y el alba no vendrá a verle.
No olvides, Madrid, la guerra;
jamás olvides que enfrente
los ojos del enemigo
te echan miradas de muerte.
Rondan por tu cielo halcones
que precipitarse quieren
sobre tus rojos tejados,
tus calles, tu brava gente.
Madrid: que nunca se diga,
nunca se publique o piense
que en el corazón de España
la sangre se volvió nieve.
Fuentes de valor y hombría
las guardas tú donde siempre.
Atroces ríos de asombro
han de correr de esas fuentes.
Que cada barrio, a su hora,

si esa mal hora viniere
— hora que no vendrá — sea
más que la plaza más fuerte.
Los hombres, como costillos;
igual que almenas, sus frentes,
grandes murallas, sus brazos,
puertas que nadie penetre.
Quien al corazón de España
quiera asomarse, que llegue.
¡Pronto! Madrid está lejos.
Madrid sabe defenderse
con uñas, con pies, con codos,
con empujones, con dientes,
panza arriba, arisco, recto,
duro, al pie del agua verde
del Tajo, en Navalperal,
en Sigüenza, en donde suenen
balas y balas que busquen
helar su sangre caliente.
Madrid, corazón de España,
que es de tierra, dentro tiene,
si se le escarba, un gran hoyo,
profundo, grande, imponente,
como un barranco que aguarda...
Sólo en él cabe la muerte.

Rafael ALBERTI

Figure 3. An illustrated, two-sided broadside version of Rafael Alberti's "Defensa de Madrid," no. 41 of a series of illustrated poem broadsides issued by the government in Catalonia. The opening line calls Madrid "corazón de España," the heart of Spain. Author's collection.

Here, for example, is an account—written on October 23, 1937—of a poetry reading Langston Hughes gave in Spain the previous day. It is from a letter written by Fred Lutz, an American who had volunteered for service in the Abraham Lincoln Battalion and became a political commisar in Spain:

> Heard Langston Hughes last night; he spoke at one of our nearby units—the Autoparque, which means the place where our Brigade trucks and cars are kept and repaired. It was a most astonishing meeting; he read a number of his poems; explained what he had in mind when he wrote each particular poem and asked for criticism. I thought to myself before the thing started "Good God how will anything like poetry go off with these hard-boiled chauffeurs and mechanics, and what sort of criticism can they offer"? Well it astonished me as I said. The most remarkable speeches on the subject of poetry were made by the comrades. And some said that they had never liked poetry before and had scorned the people who read it and wrote it but they had been moved by Hughes's reading. There was talk of "Love" and "Hate" and "Tears"; everyone was deeply affected and seemed to bare his heart at the meeting, and the most reticent (not including me) spoke of their innermost feelings. I suppose it was because the life of a soldier in wartime is so unnatural and emotionally starved that they were moved the way they were.[16]

It is a remarkable story, as poetry for a moment becomes an occasion for a working-class oral community—not, as literary studies has often held it to be, the sign of an isolated and self-contained subjectivity but a discourse opening a space for sharing experiences and developing collective agency. Exactly what poems Hughes read the letter does not say, but it is fairly safe to assume he would have read some of the poems about the war he had just written. But part of the meaning of those texts derives from their performance before such audiences as these "hard-boiled chauffeurs and mechanics."

Public readings, of course, were available to only a small percentage of the potential audience. Perhaps the most obvious forms that this international poetic activity took were in translation, in international anthologies, and in the broad exchange of the wide range of poems about the Spanish Civil War. There were literally dozens of journals in Britain, France, Spain, Latin America, and the United States publishing poems about the war, and many of these journals issued translations of poems from other countries as well. Some were then collected in books and pamphlets. The most obvious evidence that these poems should be grouped together and read in relation to one another and to their historical moment is the large number of times they have been (and continue to be) anthologized in collections. Although most North American academic modern poetry specialists have no more knowledge of them than they do, say, of lunar geography, anthologies devoted all or in part to Spanish Civil War poetry were important during the war and in subsequent decades. Such American poets as Edna St. Vincent Millay, Muriel Rukeyser, Genevieve Taggard, Ruth Lechlitner, and William Carlos Williams realized that one of the more important things they could do was give Spanish poets a voice in English and a broad American audience; all were among the writers who contributed translations to the 1937 New York anthology *And Spain Sings: Fifty Loyalist Ballads Adapted by American Poets.* Across the ocean, Stephen Spender and John Lehman's 1939 anthology, *Poems for Spain,* mixed original poems with translations, many of which had already been published in newspapers and journals.[17] As Peter Monteath astutely puts it, "In effect these anthologies were the Popular Front in aesthetic form."[18] Meanwhile a number of Spanish poets wrote poems about the international volunteers who had come to the aid of their country. Some were published in journals, some printed as cards and broadsides for mass distribution, and a small anthology of them, *Homenaje de despedida a las Brigadas Internacionales,* was issued in Barcelona in the final months of the war. English translations of collections of works by individual poets—from Alberti to García Lorca—were also published throughout the war years. From 1937 to 1938 the English language magazine of the International Brigades, *Volunteer for Liberty,* published in Madrid and Barcelona and distributed in Europe and the United States, regularly printed both poems translated from the Spanish and original poems in English, most of them written in Spain.

In the United States the publications that turned toward Spain ranged from *Poetry* magazine to the *Daily Worker,* the Communist party's newspaper. The international character of the results can be gauged just by recalling the Spanish Civil War poems the *Daily Worker* printed during the first year of the war. Within a week of the war's onset it opened with an illustrated version of Harrison George's translation of Pla Y Beltran's "Girl Fighter of Spain" (July 26, 1936), a Spanish poem that commemorates the Asturian revolt of 1934. Two months later, Martha Millet responded with "Women of Spain," a poem honoring the women on the barricades in the current conflict. They also published Gene Gordon's "Directives" (August 18, 1936); A. M. Stephen's "Madrid" (October 25, 1936); Rafael Alberti's "Dawn as Street-Crier" (January 10, 1037); the anonymous Irish satire "Off to Salamanca" (January 31, 1937); a cheerful bit of Mike Quin's anti-Franco doggerel (February 14, 1937); Louis Boby's "Defenders of Madrid" (February 14, 1937); Joseph Kehoe's full-page illustrated poem about the bombing of Madrid, "No Need Now" (February 21, 1937); Ted Benson's "Words of Flame," honoring the American pilot Ben Leider after he was shot down and killed (March 2, 1937); the words to the Spanish composer Leopoldo Gonzalez's song "No Pasaran" (March 21, 1937); "Yankee Battle Songs in Spain" (April 4, 1937); Arthur Coyle's "I Awoke in the

Country" (April 17, 1937); the anonymous "Bombers" (May 7, 1937); Pablo Neruda's "To the Mothers of the Dead Militia" (May 8, 1937); Nick T's "They Come for Liberty" (May 24, 1937); Henry Jordan's "Photo-Montage" (June 1, 1937); Ruth Marx's "Young America Speaks" (July 27, 1937); Arthur Coyle's "From the Spanish" (July 28, 1937); and Rafael Alberti's "To the International Brigades" (July 30, 1937).

"They Come for Liberty" was written in Spain by a volunteer and first published in *Mobile Front,* the newspaper of the transport regiment. Of course, most of the English language poems written about the war were composed in England and the United States. For a variety of reasons that I talk about shortly, it was not always easy, especially for American poets or novelists at this distance, to write successfully about Spain. Some of those who did—Hemingway being the most famous case—spent substantial time there and made the commitment to Spain a central fact of their lives thereafter. Others had at least some Spanish experience and combined that with long histories on the left to make a coherent and specific stand possible. Genevieve Taggard spent a year in Spain before the war on a Guggenheim fellowship and thus retained strong images of the Spanish people and Spain's landscape and culture. Muriel Rukeyser was there at the opening of the war in 1936 to cover the antifascist Olympics and was among those foreign nationals evacuated from Barcelona at the time. Her long poem "Mediterranean" is a collage of images from the first days of the war, with an undercurrent of concern about what role poetry should serve in the conflict. It regularly violates grammatical rules within apparent syntactic units to force shifts in perspective that make the collage both material and perspectival.[19] Langston Hughes spent half a year there in 1937 visiting troops, talking with people in Madrid, and acquiring extensive wartime knowledge. His wartime poem "Letter from Spain," published in *Volunteer for Liberty* in November 1937, is a splendid example of the way he uses colloquial language to put the struggle between democracy and fascism in Spain in a broad context of international racism and imperialism:

Dear Brother at home:

We captured a wounded Moor today.
He was just as dark as me.
I said, Boy, what you been doin' here
Fightin' against the free?

He answered something in a language
I couldn't understand.
But somebody told me he was sayin'
They nabbed him in his land

And made him join the fascist army
And come across to Spain.
And he said he had a feelin'
He'd never get back home again.

He said he had a feelin'
This whole thing wasn't right.
He said he didn't know
The folks he had to fight.

And as he lay there dying
In a village we had taken,
I looked across to Africa
And seed foundations shakin'.

Cause if a free Spain wins this war,
The colonies, too, are free—
Then something wonderful'll happen
To them Moors as dark as me.

I said, I guess that's why old England
And I reckon Italy, too,
Is afraid to let a workers' Spain
Be too good to me and you—

Cause they got slaves in Africa—
And they don't want 'em to be free.
Listen, Moorish prisoner, hell!
Here, shake hands with me!

I knelt down there beside him,
And I took his hand—
But the wounded Moor was dyin'
And he didn't understand.

Salud,
Johnny

   Hughes's biographer Arnold Rampersad describes this as "a maudlin dia-
lect poem in ballad-epistle form" and says it is typical of the sort of "proletar-
ian doggerel" Hughes wrote in the 1930s and 1940s.[20] Rampersad also re-
ports, apparently echoing Hughes's account in *I Wonder as I Wander,* the

second volume of his autobiography, that some of the American soldiers objected to Hughes's use of dialect, since most of the black volunteers were educated.[21] Since the poem adopts the voice and persona of a black volunteer in the Lincoln Battalion, it is understandable that some Americans felt the use of dialect misrepresented their comrades, but it is equally easy to imagine that others among the Lincolns would have understood why Hughes put the poem in what is actually a rather mild form of dialect—not simply to appeal to common people, as Rampersad suggests, but to make a specific political point: that the common sense of oppressed people gives them an appropriate experiential basis for understanding international politics. For all their fabled ferocity, the Moors were partly there as canon fodder, expendable because they were black. The view from Alabama therefore had the potential of clarifying fascism's racist character—linking Franco's use of Moorish troops with Mussolini's conquest of Ethiopia, for example—and identifying imperialism as a form of international racism, a lesson that each generation apparently has to relearn. The universality of working-class interests, moreover, also made for a vantage point from which it was possible to understand why British industrialists and financiers supported Franco; a progressive Spain threatened not only one source of potential profit but also, by its example, many others. A fairly complex set of political relationships is thus condensed into a brief poem in ordinary language, and the ordinary language asserts more clearly than any other kind of language might that expertise in international politics need not be restricted to those in power and authority. One of the notable things about the volunteers in Spain was the diversity of their class background. Political understanding is thus not an elite, moneyed, high cultural capacity; it is in some ways the clarity that comes when some of that obfuscation is swept away. The use of dialect in the poem makes possible the material instanciation of some of those insights. When the speaker looks across to Africa, makes the appropriate connections between his Spanish experience and global racial and financial relationships, the moment of recognition makes it possible to envision the existing structures of power undone, to "seed foundations shakin'." "Seed," an improper usage quite proper to dialect, is actually a pun: it is a moment of sight and insight that is also the fertile seed of radical change. The proffered handshake is an offer of alliance politics, a simple gesture of solidarity dependent on nothing less than a different understanding of the world. Yet the difficulty of reaching such understanding, the power national cultures have to impede such knowledge, is apparent in the Moor's failure to recognize the speaker's offer.

These interrelationships are foregrounded and heightened in the republication of the poem in the January 23, 1938, issue of the *Daily Worker*.[22] There, three of Hughes's poems in the voice of the black volunteer Johnny, "Dear Folks at Home," "Love Letter from Spain," and "Dear Brother at Home," are printed as a dramatic full-page poster bordered with illustrations that blur the distinction between the Spanish peasant and the American worker. The sombrero-clad peasant plowing a field behind a horse in Spain is substantially interchangeable with an American sharecropper. The farmer taking a hoe to the land before his modest home could easily be in either the United States or Spain; the Spanish industrial strikers just below him carry signs in English. The Republican soldiers in the images clearly stand guard over their mutual interests. Grouped together this way, the poems also reinforce these connections. "Folks over here don't treat me / Like white bosses used to do," Hughes writes in the first poem, which he entitled "Postcard from Spain" in *Volunteer for Liberty;* those who might are on the other side. In "Love Letter from Spain," he elaborates: "Fascists is Jim Crow peoples, honey— / And here we shoot 'em down."

Hughes, of course, was in Spain when he wrote "Dear Brother at Home" and gave it to Edwin Rolfe in Madrid at International Brigades headquarters to publish in the *Volunteer for Liberty.*[23] Matters were somewhat different for those who remained in the United States. For many of those who remained here the vivid visual images coming out of Spain and the powerful reports from those returning were enough to put them securely on the Loyalist side but not enough to generate their most important writing. Near the end of the war, for example, Kenneth Rexroth demonstrates in two poems published in Alan Calmer's 1938 anthology *Salud! Poems, Stories and Sketches of Spain by American Writers* that his only real subject is his radical distance from the reality in Spain: "I am caught in a nightmare, the dead flesh / Mounting over half the world presses against me." In the safety of California he hears a plane overhead at night:

As the sound departs I am chilled and grow sick
With the thought that has come over me. I see Spain
Under the black windy sky, the snow stirring faintly,
Glittering and moving over the pallid upland,
And men waiting, clutched with cold and huddled together,
As an unknown plane goes over them.[24]

This passage helps make for a successful poem, because Rexroth is able to write about his own cultural positioning, a positioning that many other American readers share. That results in a politically relevant poem, one that helps readers understand and articulate their own relationship to the war. Rexroth is less effective when he writes about life in the International Brigades, which he does not know about directly and cannot yet learn about from the detailed accounts that began to be published in 1939. The cliché that one had to be there to write productively about the war is thus only partly warranted; being there made a difference, often a critical one, but it did not constitute the only reality worth articulating.

In a sensitive analysis of Rexroth's "Requiem for the Spanish Dead," Richard Gray tracks the poem's argument:

> It begins, as so many of his poems do, with a vision of the stars and the High Sierras. . . . For Rexroth, the Western landscape dwarfs human beings. . . . Yet it also makes their occasions of contact and community all the more precious. . . . The feeling of continuity begins to emerge in the second stanza of "Requiem," after Rexroth has described the colossal landscape of mountains and sky, and observed a distant plane passing overhead. He thinks of another mountainous landscape where "an unknown plane" may be passing over: in Spain where, at that time, there is Civil War. He imagines "men waiting" in those other, Spanish mountains, "clutched with cold and huddled together," tensing with fear as the plane "flies southeast / Into the haze above the lines of the enemy," relaxing when it passes and then growing "tense again as their own thoughts return to them." He considers "The unpainted pictures, the interrupted lives . . . / . . . / . . . the quick grey brains broken and clotted with blood." Then suddenly, under the impact of these thoughts, he is "caught in the nightmare." "Alone on a hilltop in San Francisco," he feels "the dead flesh / Mounting over half the world" pressing against him. . . . Originating in personal vision, the poem has moved into interpersonal communication: an act of imaginative identification, between the poet who has certain beliefs and the many men and women suffering and dying for those beliefs in other parts of the world—in particular, the Spanish Republicans.[25]

Rexroth is, of course, not merely telling his own story; he is offering to all of us a model of how to perceive, politicize, and internationalize our own natural worlds. He is also suggesting the most pertinent use now for our human sympathies and possibilities for empathy. He is telling each of us that the starched blue sky above us, to invoke another writer's metaphor, should evoke the skies above Spanish cities and battlefields. "Requiem" is Rexroth's answer to the critical question of how to be here and there at the same time.

Even being in Spain, however, where experiential claims might seem most straightforward, could make for more complex arguments than some critics have recognized. When Rolfe in "City of Anguish" recites his catalogue of war's immediacies—"No man knows war / who never has crouched in his foxhole, hearing / the bullets an inch from his head, nor the zoom of / planes like a Ferris wheel strafing the trenches"—he is not quite reporting his own experiences but rather is honoring his comrades at the front. When Rolfe wrote the poem, reprinted in this volume, he was editing *Volunteer for Liberty* in Madrid, and while he regularly visited the Lincolns, he is not likely to have been strafed in the trenches. As much as anything else, it is his troubled separation from the front that drives that part of the poem. It testifies not, as one critic has erroneously assumed,[26] to a wartime belief in unmediated experience but at one anguished remove, and thus the poem points to the impossibility of direct testimony at the same time it demands it. The image of the Ferris wheel, more a retrospective visual analogue than a figure that would have been ready at hand in the trenches themselves, suggests the inevitability of literary mediation. Yet Rolfe also wants to emphasize that those who have been in battle do have unique experiences the rest of cannot quite share. You can imagine what it is like to see the man next to you die, to be surrounded by enemy troops, or to be under fire in the open, but a difference will remain between your best empathic efforts and the experience itself.

   The more historically specific problems noncombatant writers faced were, however, not experiential but social and political. The first problem was to reveal the specific social and political understanding Spain required. Hughes's success at that is one reason why Rampersad's willingness to collapse "Letter from Spain" into a nonexistent universal 1930s poem is so inadequate and unfair. The second problem was one of commitment, the demand that Spain and all it stood for placed on people everywhere. Something of that problem is evoked in "How Much for Spain?" a short but very striking poem that Mike Quin published in the August 8, 1937, issue of the *Daily Worker:*

The long collection speech is done
        And now the felt hat goes
From hand to hand its solemn way
        Along the restless rows.
In purse and pocket, fingers feel
        And count the coins by touch.
Minds ponder what they can afford
        And hesitate . . . how much?
In that brief, jostled moment when
        The battered hat arrives,
Try, brother, to remember that
        Some men put in their lives.

There were, of course, frequent collections of funds for Spanish relief. Early on, the Nationalist forces had captured major food production areas, and basic necessities were in short supply everywhere in Loyalist Spain. Quin's poem is partly a fund-raising device, a reminder of just how much (and how much more than money) some had already given to the cause. But Quin's poem also reminds us implicitly of how unqualifiedly justice was on the side of the Republic. The narrow self-interest involved in secretly counting coins invokes all the hesitation built into deciding how much to give to Spain. The counting of coins is not only personal but also political and institutional; it mimics the calculations Western business was making about which victor would be a better ideological ally. Nonetheless, on the left, for a while, it was possible to argue that seeing Spain clearly meant being willing to give every-thing. Holding back suggested more than cowardice or small-mindedness; it suggested a kind of social, political, and moral blindness. Quin's poem made its way to Spain, as did many others. One American volunteer in the field, Frances Feingersh (later Frank Lister), copied "How Much for Spain?" onto two postcards and sent it to his mother in the United States. The poem thus trav-eled back and forth across the Atlantic because it was a fitting vehicle for both self-expression and political commitment. When Feingersh wrote it out in holograph in the fall of 1937, it became a somewhat different poem than it was when Quin wrote it in the safety of the United States; wounded at Bru-nete, Feingersh had taken the risk of putting in his life. To send it back in his own hand was to make it partly his own poem or at least to put it in his own voice, as he had already embodied its message, and thus simultaneously to comment on his own commitment and to give Quin's question to noncomba-tant Americans singular moral and political urgency.

The problem for a poet, then, was not so much whether to volunteer for service. For one thing, not every poet was young enough or healthy enough to serve. Moreover, getting to Spain to fight was far from easy, since U.S. pass-ports were invalid for Spanish travel except for correspondents. The chal-lenge, or at least one challenge, was to discover how to give everything *in a poem*. How does a poet, in other words, put in his or her life? Spain demand-ed that a poet put everything at risk, wager everything on the poem that was yet to be written. Those who could not do that—and few could—in some ways failed. Others succeeded because they understood the special character of Spanish Civil War writing—its collective antifascist and international identity. It was a distinctive historical necessity that set the Spanish Civil War apart and made its poetry potentially different from other war poetry. The historical forces bearing on the decision to write about Spain were considerable: in the brief moment when the battered hat—symbol of Spain's arrival in your life—appears, remember that some have already given everything to a cause wor-thy of nothing less. Now, with all that in mind, with all that is at stake in the politics of the occasion, write.

For poets outside Spain, moreover, the war arrived already significantly spoken for—in the dozens, eventually thousands, of poems Spanish nation-als wrote during the course of the conflict. Just how quickly poetry took a significant place in the war remains startling even today. The rebellion began on July 18, 1936. On August 27, the first issue of *El mono azul* appeared with a two-page, poster-sized spread of poems with a large illustration under the heading "Romancero de la guerra civil." By the next issue, there were several smaller illustrations, but the same double-page format held, with the poems dedicated to a specific subject or a particular person.[27] The format would be maintained for eleven issues (see figure 4), after which the journal adopted a larger page with a poem under the masthead. By October copies of the journal were arriving in the United States. The poems generally followed the traditional form of the Spanish romance—epic narratives restricted to an eight syllable line (employing assonance instead of full rhyme in every second line) that was well suited to oral delivery and memorization. Many of *El mono azul*'s poems were read aloud in the trenches around Madrid before being published, and some were written there. American translations of some of these poems were read to groups in East Coast cities in 1937. A separate collection devoted entirely to poems by soldier poets appeared in Madrid under the title *Poesia en las trincheras.*[28] The poems built solidarity and morale, celebrated new heroes, and gave combatants a sense of their historical mission. Moving all these issues so rapidly into poetry also lent the war an aura of epic scale—not only its larger outcomes but also its daily progress. The poems gave soldiers and civilians alike a common mode of recitation, remembrance, and recognition. Like the songs sung everywhere on the Loyalist side, the poems were a shared language, a communal speech, a social text strengthened in every reading and recitation. They were rapidly gathered into books, translated into other languages, and distributed around the world. The collection *Romancero de la guerra civil* was issued in Madrid by the Ministry of Public Instruction in November of 1936 and included thirty-five poems from *El mono azul.* The Communist Fifth Regiment's cultural wing issued *Poesias de guerra* near the end of the year, using poems from *El mono azul* and other sources. *Poetas en la España leal* appeared in July of 1937, drawing most heavily on poems previously published in the journal *Hora de España;* a number of copies of the book were sent to people in the United States. As visitor and volunteer poets arriving in Spain and poets in other countries began to write about the war, they did so against the background of these accessible and rapidly disseminated texts. The American poets Hughes and Rolfe, among others, read the Spanish romances when they were in Spain and spent a good deal of time with the editors of *El mono azul.* To a significant degree, then, the wartime poetry written by American and British poets took its first inspiration from the work of Spanish poets. Poets from other countries adopted forms, themes, and metaphors from their frontline Spanish compatriots. The International Brigades published *Romancero de los voluntarios de la libertad* in October of 1937; it included poems by foreign volunteers in Spanish, French, Polish, and English, and it was regularly

Figure 4. Illustrated two-page spread of poems in El mono azul (1936).
University of Illinois Library.

mailed to countries in both hemispheres. Suddenly, modern poetry had a distinctly international configuration. Its first subject was the heroic defense of the city of Madrid.

From 1936 to 1939 there erupted something like a chorus of voices calling back and forth to each other about the besieged capital of Spain. In poem after poem, in country after country, the name Madrid is used as a rallying cry and an incantation, sometimes with and sometimes without an exclamation mark. The poems echo one another across time and space and national or political difference, ring changes on the suffering and courage of the Madrileños, and establish in print, in voice, and in dream and nightmare the point of articulation of an antifascist politics for its time.

This international poetic dialogue began, as it happens, not with a poem but with a series of proclamations and slogans that captured people's imaginations immediately after the war began. "Madrid is the heart of our Republic, of our country," declared La Pasionaria (Dolores Ibarruri, the Spanish Communist party's spiritual leader during the war) in the pages of *Mundo obrero* on September 25, 1936, two months into the war.[29] Soon that claim was supplemented with a special rallying cry—"Madrid will be the tomb of fascism"—and with a proclamation on Madrid radio. On the night of November 8, with Madrid under assault by fascist troops, Fernando Valera, a Republican deputy, read this statement over the air: "Here in Madrid is the universal frontier that separates Liberty and slavery. It is here in Madrid that two incompatible civilizations undertake their great struggle: love against hate, peace against war, the fraternity of Christ against the tyranny of the Church. . . . This is Madrid. It is fighting for Spain, for humanity, for justice, and, with the mantle of its blood, it shelters all human beings! Madrid! Madrid!"[30]

By then numerous poems had already been published, and more followed. Norman Rosten inserted a slogan between each stanza of "The March" and ended the poem with the words "Madrid—*Madrid*—MADRID!"[31] In Spain Francis Fuentes wrote "Revolutionary Madrid"; Manuel Altolaguirre wrote "Madrid"; and José Moreno Villa wrote "Madrid Front."[32] The October 29, 1936, issue of *El mono azul* had included Rafael Alberti's "Defensa de Madrid," Manuel Bolin's "Alerta los madrileños," Luis Perez Infante's "A Madrid," and Manuel Altolaguirre's "Arenga," which declared the city the capital of Europe. The Catalan anthology *Poesias de guerra* included Ernest Mateu's "Als defensors de Madrid" and Adriá Jori's "Record de Madrid."[33] In France Jacques Roumain answered with "Madrid," Paul Eluard with "November 1936."[34] In Britain Richard Church answered with "The Madrid Defenders," Elisabeth Cluer with "Analogy in Madrid."[35] In Ecuador E. Gil Gilbert published "Buenas Dias, Madrid!" and G. Humberto Mata wrote "Madrid."[36] Among Americans Joy Davidman wrote "Snow in Madrid"; Langston Hughes wrote "Madrid—1937"; Ben Maddow in "The Defenses" cried out, "Madrid, Madrid! [. . .] your great trenches hold / Death back from love"; Norman Rosten hailed "Madrid! / Burning in the night [. . .] but still standing" and turned the famous slogan into a command: "Make Madrid the tomb of Fascism!"; Sol Funaroff wrote in "The Bull in the Olive Field" that "Madrid awoke, / toreador in overalls: / [. . .] people poured like rain / upon the face of the streets."[37] Such poems continued to appear through 1939.

Part of what is notable about the poetry focused on Madrid is its uncanny mixture of sloganeering and invention. "Greetings, Madrid, heart of the country," wrote Luis de Tapia in "Salud"; Rafael Alberti called the city "heart of Spain, / heart of earth"; "Madrid is the heart," W. H. Auden wrote in "Spain," echoing La Pasionaria.[38] "Pasionaria speaks," wrote Rosten in "Spanish Sequence," "and the silence / is greater than the soaring of birds"; he included this stanza:

Spain, the body,
and in its center
calmly beating
the great heart, Madrid.[39]

Stanley Richardson addressed Madrid as "Life's glorious capital."[40] George Barker, in contrast, said the city was "like a live eye in the Iberian mask," while José Moreno Villa described the besieged city in winter as "an island tomb, / Alone, in an asphalt sky," and Paul Eluard said it was a "city as if at the base of the ocean made of only one saved drop of water."[41] Like the more broadly revolutionary poetry of the 1930s, this poetry is partly echolalic, with poet after poet deploying some of the same images and phrases in a choral literary project of political commitment. In a 1935 essay in *Partisan Review* Edwin Rolfe simultaneously expressed his doubts about the place of slogans in poetry and defended their potential in certain contexts, an argument that is as much anticipatory as it is pertinent to the revolutionary poetry that preceded the Spanish Civil War.[42] Years later, no longer able to place himself within the culture of the Left, the American poet and critic Malcolm Cowley would recall Rolfe's point from a conversation and note with incredulity the willingness to use slogans in poetry.[43] The sloganeering in the poetry of 1928–36 was often more implicit than explicit, with thematic and imagistic repetition, reinforcement, and counterpointing far more common than the repetition of full sentences or explicit slogans. There were, to be sure, instances of recurring slogans, such as the line "All Power to the Soviets!" in Sol Funaroff's poem "What the Thunder Said: A Fire Sermon" that also appears in Richard Wright's poem "I Am a Red Slogan."[44] It is a slogan with a complex history in the USSR—evoking both local workers' councils (soviets) and the USSR as a whole—and one that appears in other American documents as well. But for the most part the explicit reoccurrence of full slogans is uncommon in American poetry of the early years of the depression.

The rhetorical differences between the poetry of the first half of the decade and that of the second half have their roots in political and historical realities. In the first half of the 1930s the poetics of revolution had sufficient support to achieve a degree of autonomy, an autonomy in turn that gave its utopian vision some considerable intertextual force. But there were always competing political positions and competing poetries on the national scene. A commitment to the broadly revolutionary intertext was not quite the same as the specific Communist commitment implied in the use of the slogan "All Power to the Soviets!" Poets could commit themselves to the Red revolution and still feel their politics to be flexibly revolutionary; after all, the red flag had been raised by American socialists, the Industrial Workers of the World, and other partly homegrown groups as well as the Communist party. There was a revolutionary intertext that overcame these political differences, but it had shared subjects, images, convictions, developmental structures, and aspirations, rather than fixed slogans, at its disposal. Spain was another matter.

With the advent of the Spanish Civil War, the range of pertinent literary topics did not dramatically narrow, but a limited number of topics did gain a special international authenticity; outside Spain, the awareness of contesting political positions on the left and the significance of contesting poetries temporarily receded into the background as well. The Comintern had begun to support broadly democratic antifascist alliances in 1935, and by July 1936 and the opening of the Spanish Civil War these views had become widely shared among progressive constituencies. With Madrid under assault an antifascist alliance politics had its historical imperatives and its universal slogans, and the slogans rapidly made their way into the poetry of the war.

Patently sloganeering discourse—at least in the form of explicit quotation or adaptation of familiar, preexisting slogans—does not make up a major portion of many Republican poems. Yet there are hortatory poems urging action and solidarity that effectively invent slogans of their own, and the quoted slogan is a notable part of many poems otherwise devoted to lyrical and rhetorical invention of the sort we expect from poetic language. Moreover, even though many Spanish Civil War poems do not have explicit hortatory moments—overt calls to arms, slogans, calls for commitment—enough of them do so that the will to international political solidarity is part of the implied context of any poem about the war. The most inward-looking and reflective Spanish Civil War poems, then, cannot be wholly separated from the most straightforwardly militant. *The Penguin Book of Spanish Civil War Verse* and *The Wound and the Dream* include examples of both. The poems written at the front and the poems written behind the lines are part of the same discursive field. In reading one poem you read others by implication. So we need to ask whether the slogans that are the most striking points of similarity between these poems are central or peripheral. Are they a fatal flaw that undermines the rest of the text? An aberration forgivable in the context of the historical pressures these poets faced? Or are they pivot points for Spanish Civil War poems, providing at once a grounding in material politics and the links in a chain of verbal correspondences that connect poem to poem and poet to poet and poet to soldier across the world? I think the last explanation brings us closest to the historical reality in which the poems were forged. One Spanish scholar, Serge Salaün, suggests it is necessary to understand all the Spanish Civil War romances written on behalf of the Republic—more than ten thousand of them, many of them anonymous—as one vast poem, a huge intertext.[45] But the full text of this final 1930s metapoem is not Spanish alone. It is also American, British, Canadian, French, German, Italian, and Russian. Into its journey from defiance to lamentation are integrated texts from throughout Europe and all of the Americas. At that point we have left behind any mode of understanding typical of national literary studies as we know it.

With the outbreak of the war the significance of slogans in poetry changes. There is now a more constrained—or at least more focused—semiosis at work in these repetitions and verbal clusters than there was in the revolutionary poetry of the early 1930s. The constraint, of course, is fascism's threat and Spain's peril, which gave wartime writers and readers the precise political pressure they felt. The revolutionary intertext of the early 1930s reflected wide social dislocation and diverse aspirations for change. But victory for worldwide socialism was a far more abstract and hypothetical goal than the defeat of fascism. The Popular Front poetry about Spain confronted a specific enemy on confined terrain. In that context the *highest calling for a single voice* was to choose to echo the slogan signifying solidarity with the defenders of Madrid, to step forward and speak the words that kept the signifying chain alive, that carried it forward in time and sustained its spread across the globe. The use of slogans in this poetry has yet an added dimension, for the slogans circulate from street and newspaper into poems and back to the street again. There is thus a transit through poetry for critical pieces of universal public rhetoric. In the process, the slogans are infused with all the values poetry itself has historically acquired, and the slogans become not merely instrumental but also literary, lyrical signposts of an ongoing history already eternal and monumentalized. Their deployment in the street thereafter has the feel of poetry at work in public life.

The war produced a small number of highly focused topics—the defense of Madrid, the murder of the poet Federico García Lorca, the role of the internationals who came to fight for the Republic—that were unlike anything in the poetry of the first half of the decade. No single depression setting had the real and symbolic force of Madrid under siege. Poverty in London was readily understandable from the vantage point of poverty in New York, but few could confidently have proclaimed either city the "heart of the world." For a few years, that is exactly how people did describe Madrid. Indeed, that figure reflected the beliefs of a broad international constituency. From Paris to Edinburgh to Boston to Mexico City every person sympathetic to the Left held Madrid in special honor. It was the focus of a Manichaean conflict that might shape not only Spain's destiny but also that of the entire West.

As the fascist troops worked to encircle the city and Hitler's planes bombed civilian neighborhoods, it seemed increasingly likely Madrid would fall. Embassies closed, newspaper headlines proclaimed the city's imminent loss, and even the Spanish government abandoned its capital and moved to Valencia. Then, against every reasonable assessment, the people recruited their own militias, built barricades, raided military depots, and—with the dramatic and inspiring entrance of the International Brigades—held their city by the power of their collective will. The presence of the International Brigades, in which ordinary British and French citizens stood with their Spanish comrades—in battalions whose names honored their national origins—made the conflict one with which almost every nation could easily identify. It gave people across the world symbolic agency in the battle. When the American volunteer Ben Leider took his plane aloft to battle Hitler's air force, he was every progressive American's agent in the clouds.

In this context so central and productive were the slogans of the war that we hear them echoed and embroidered even when they are not explicitly quoted. On July 19, the day after the rebellion started, La Pasionaria gave her first speech on Madrid radio, calling on Spaniards to resist the generals. "No pasaran!" she declared, echoing the rallying cry at Verdun, they shall not pass. The phrase would be repeated again and again over the next months. La Pasionaria adapted it herself in a speech delivered before 100,000 people at Mestal Stadium in Valencia and published in *Mundo obrero* in August. The fascists will not pass, she cried out, "whenever they pass they sow death and desolation." "No Pasaran!" appeared on banners stretched across Madrid streets; soon audiences would call out the slogan together in response to La Pasionaria's speeches. In September another of her slogans was set to work: "Better die standing, than live kneeling!" "Better to die on your feet than to submit on your knees" was another version.[46] "Much worse to be alive and bend / a slave's knee in the living," wrote the Cuban poet Nicolás Guillén in his poem sequence *España,* first published in Madrid.[47] Miguel Hernández in "The Winds of the People," repeatedly published in Spain and issued in Britain and the United States in a variety of translations, put the slogan in his own words: "If I must die may I / with my head held high at least."[48] When José Herrera Petere closes "El dia que no vendra" with his promise that the day shall never dawn on that night when the fascist dream of taking Madrid is realized, we hear it as a version of the slogan "No Pasaran!"[49] In every anthology that includes poems with one or more of these slogans, the phrase ripples empathically through every poem in the book.

But the slogan also occurs unchanged or in fresh contexts. Félix V. Ramos titled one of his poems in *Poesias de guerra* "No pasaran!"[50] Apel·les Mestres, a Catalan poet who died on the day of the generals' revolt, had an earlier poem given new meaning when "No passareu!" was reissued in *Poesias de guerra* in the midst of the war; the poem was also published as an illustrated braodside (see figure 5).[51] "We, the men of the fields," writes Francis Fuentes, "shout out like a word of command / our slogan: They shall not pass!"[52] George Barker, answering from England, imagines blood soaked "stones that rise and call / tall as any man, 'No pasaran!'"[53] A. S. Knowland ends his poem "Guernica" with the cry *"They shall not pass to ruin Spain!"* and Jack Lindsay recalls "the voice that cried out over Spain: / They shall not pass!"[54]

In the decades since World War II American academics have taken the use of slogans in poetry as the surest sign of the disavowal of poetry's essential character. The use of slogans is invoked as self-evident proof that poetry has given way to politics, that the aims of self-expression and linguistic invention have both been subverted by prefabricated rhetoric. But for a moment in the

Figure 5. A broadside version of "No passareu!" published in Barcelona during the first year of the Spanish Civil War. Author's collection.

1930s verbal creativity and political slogans were considered poetic partners. As the war proceeded, the slogans chanted in poem after poem were trumpet calls and calls to arms. Like bricks in the barricades constructed in Madrid streets in the summer of 1936, the poems mounted serially to build consensus and solidarity across the world.

Whatever the intricacies of diction, whatever the metaphoric invention, nothing takes us away from the poetry's representational and agitational aims. The most striking metaphors invade representation to heighten and reshape it, to make what we see, what we believe must be done, more vivid and compelling. Whatever their aesthetic aims, these are poems of political action. Though the political and the aesthetic are relational forces here, they are not in stark conflict, for the commitment to Spain sweeps up many of the cultural values historically articulated to aesthetics, from transcendentalizing images of what is just to transformative images of unsettling beauty. To give one's will, one's desire, one's fear and hope and anger to Spain and antifascism is now the beautiful thing that must be done.

In echoing and counterpointing one another—even when the poets themselves are not aware of all existing parallel passages—and in accumulating a field of potential correspondences for future poems, the poems of the Spanish Civil War do more than just contribute to a growing international intertext. They hail one another—and their writers and readers—with extraordinary directness and intensity. To be hailed in that way is to be positioned as an international political subject—and to experience that cultural positioning with pathos, anguish, pride, and anger. The effects of varied lines on similar subjects, then, are not simply additive, complicating our view, say, of how civilians suffered under fascist bombing or how Madrid withstood fascist assault. A sense of strong linkage, of shared necessity, of centripetal focus on the heart of Spain coalesces in each of the metaphors, phrases, and topics that recur in the worldwide poems about the war.

When Auden writes in "Epitaph on a Tyrant" that "when he cried, the little children died in the streets," we see the pictures of dead children that were widely distributed after Franco's air attacks on civilian populations, an element of modern war first experienced on a large scale in Spain.[55] The British poet George Barker had one of those photographs—a powerful image of a young girl killed in a Barcelona bombing raid—printed carefully on coated paper and tipped in like an art photograph across from the opening stanza of his April 1939 *Elegy on Spain*:

O ecstatic is this head of five-year-joy—
Captured its butterfly rapture on a paper:
And not the rupture of the right eye may
Make any less this prettier than a picture.
O now, my minor moon, dead as meat
Slapped on a negative plate, I hold
The crime of the bloody time in my hand.[56]

We are forced by this device to take the description both literally and figuratively, for we hold the girl's image in our hands as we read. Barker's stanza, meanwhile, anticipates Jacques Roumain's comparable image: "On the torn and bloodied face of that child / A smile; like a pomegranate crushed under the tramp of a heel."[57] Both poems echo the opening lines of Herbert Read's "Bombing Casualties in Spain": "Doll's faces are rosier but these were children / their eyes not glass but gleaming gristle."[58] "Spanish suns at Badajoz," writes Somhairle Macalastair, "are bleaching baby bones."[59] "A hundred children in one street, / Their little hands and guts and feet," reports the *Left Review* editor Edgell Rickword, are "scattered where they'd been playing ball."[60]

Each new metaphor, each comparable passage, some strikingly graphic, reanimates and reinforces the same space of political recognition. Each metaphor that evokes memories of lines in other poems casts out a net to gather together the experience of Spain. The repetition and variation of slogans is thus only the first instance of the pervasive political and rhetorical unity of these poems. As others have noted, the poems are linked by their anger and hope, by their explicit antifascism, by the places and events they cite repeatedly, and by the blood that soaks so many passages worldwide. In the poetry of the Spanish Civil War the red dawn of revolution that was so frequently a binding element in the Left's poetry of the early 1930s is mostly exchanged for the blood of victims or for the red rags tied around wounds, emblems of violence that unify these poems rather differently.[61] Even such patterns as the recurrent references to the olive trees of Spain help bind the poems to a common enterprise. Finally, as poet after poet comes forward to list Spain's cities and provinces that are sites of battle, heroism, and terror, the lists at once overlay one another and make up a continuing intertextual recitation spread out in time and space. The lists, in effect, are at once deeply additive and simultaneous. The one difference that matters most here is the stark moral difference between a just cause and an unjust one, between democracy and the gathering forces of evil.

This is, of course, partly a collective emotion, a mass emotion if you will, and such impulses were widely demonized after World War II. In reflecting on the 1930s, many liberal intellectuals were effectively able to collapse the radical Left into the radical Right and thus equate all recent collective claims on our ideals. Collective action of all kinds seemed unseemly, corrosive, and antithetical to any notion of individual identity. When the British poet Richard Church wrote in "The Madrid Defenders" that "our love is another; / much greater than one / For husband, for mother," declaring his own and his compatriots' love for "the People, the One," he was in one way citing a familiar 1930s conviction—that the individual self should find its realization in the common good.[62] Before the war the notion of "the people" was sometimes an abstraction. In Spain, however, sustained worldwide attention was focused on the imperiled defenders of Madrid—from its already legendary leaders to the masses of ordinary men, women, and children facing daily bombardment. One of the cultural legacies of the poetry of the Spanish Civil War—in the wake of a full century when English and American poetry was repeatedly linked with lyrical self-expression—is a record of how lyricism could be marshaled for collective aims and how subjectivity could be realized in public action. Since such impulses run counter to every dominant model in professional literary studies, recovering the cultural context of Spanish Civil war poetry amounts to acquiring a form of antidisciplinary knowledge.

Because the confrontation between democracy and fascism literally took on a global character when World War II began, the lesson of Spain retained its urgency for some years despite Franco's victory in the spring of 1939. The antifascist anthologies that appeared over the next several years—notably *War*

Poems of the United Nations (1943) and *Seven Poets in Search of an Answer* (1944) in the United States—included a substantial number of poems about the Spanish Civil War.[63] Once World War II came to an end, however, the pattern changed. The ruling emotion for those focused on the Spanish experience changed. Franco's Spanish supporters had issued a series of celebratory poetry anthologies in 1939, and the few poets elsewhere in the world who stood with fascism—most notably the South African poet Roy Campbell—could cling to their one great victory. But the poets of the Republic were dead, in prison, or in exile. Antonio Machado had died of pneumonia shortly after crossing the French border in 1939. Miguel Hernández, an Alicante goatherd as a child who later became a soldier and poet in the Fifth Regiment, had been captured trying to leave Spain and died in a Franco prison of untreated tuberculosis.

For the others who were still alive, scattered across the world—Spaniards, volunteers in the International Brigades, and international sympathizers alike—a new category of experience took over their work. Surprisingly, Rukeyser anticipated the focus early on in "Mediterranean." Reflecting on the way memory seemed so quickly to magnify and clarify the experience of the war after she left Spain abruptly, she grasped what would be a hallmark of Republican experience for decades—exile. As Susan Schweik astutely realizes, it is exile straining for agency:

> Rukeyser was part of the American contingent to the anti-Fascist games, and although she had passionately wanted to stay and fight with the Loyalists, she was compelled to evacuate the country, as were all foreign women without nursing experience. The scene of compulsory banishment from Spain recurs again and again in the next decade of Rukeyser's work; her poetic treatise *The Life of Poetry* (1949) begins with a version of it, as if it somehow contains the origin and summation of all her writing:
>
> > I think now of a boat on which I sailed away from the beginning of a war. . . . This was the first moment of stillness in days of fighting. We had seen the primitive beginnings of the open warfare of this period: men running through the silvery groves, the sniper whose gun would speak, as the bullet broke the wall beside you; a child staring upward at a single plane. More would come; in the city, the cars burned and blood streamed over the walls of houses and the horses shrieked; armies formed and marched out; the gypsies, the priests, in their purity and violence fought. Word from abroad was coming in as they asked us to meet in the summer leafy Square, and told us that they knew. They had seen how, as foreigners, we were deprived; how we were kept from, and wanted, above all things one: our responsibility.
> >
> > This was a stroke of insight: it was true. "Now you have your responsibility," the voice said, deep, prophetic, direct, "go home: tell your peoples what you have seen."

Most striking about this scene is its rapid transformation of deprivation and exclusion—the situation of the American woman who is excluded categorically from eligibility for the Lincoln Brigade—into compensatory power, a singular ability to memorialize and prophesy. Something similar happens in "Mediterranean." . . . Each appearance of the ship in Rukeyser's wartime work effects a similar transmutation of the woman's shipboard look; what starts as spectatorship transforms itself into witness.[64]

In the aftermath of the war, as exile, elegy, and loss took over Spanish Civil War discourse and as these impulses coalesced into the distinctive contextualized form of *exiled witness,* a different kind of choral pattern emerged from poetry written throughout the Americas and Europe. Edna St. Vincent Millay's "Say That We Saw Spain Die" would prove one of the signature poems of this new mood in the United States. As dust settled on blasted stone, as blood soaked into the land, the parallel metaphors in different poems acquired a mutual transparency, a palimpsestic quality of shared and layered memory. Poet after poet remained haunted by Spain, and that haunting was less personal than historical and generational. It was a shared experience, and those who gave witness to it in their poetry constituted a far-flung chorus amidst the ruins of memory. Those modern poets of the Left who survived the modern period took with them this experience of international solidarity and subsequent disaster. It haunted their work far more powerfully than did the memory of the purported giants of modern poetry. "What was left to be done?" one critic, in effect, reports a series of postmodern poets asking, looking back on the achievements of Pound, Eliot, and Yeats.[65] "What more was to be done?" others sometimes asked—among them Rolfe and Rukeyser in the United States, Neruda in Chile, Hugh MacDiarmid in Scotland, Altolaguirre in exile in Mexico—"now that we have lost Spain?"

What was to be done was to keep the memory alive, to maintain witness through the years. That did not require abandoning all the central topics of the war itself. The militant *romanceros* written during the defense of Madrid were now unwritable, but the image of the city itself still held its power. "Madrid   Madrid   Madrid   Madrid," Rolfe wrote in "Elegia" in 1948, "I call your name endlessly, savor it like a lover." "Ten irretrievable years have exploded," he reports, "since last I slept / in your arms of tenderness and wounded granite." In the last phrase we can hear an echo of Rolfe's own wartime observation about people strolling in the paseo in Madrid: "In the candle-light their faces were granite," along with echoes of Neruda's wartime image of the city's "eyes still wounded by dream, / with carbine and stone, freshly wounded Madrid," as well as his celebration of the internationals' "ardent brigade of stone."[66] In the fall of 1937 Charles Donnelly, an Irish volunteer who was killed in Spain, had called out to Spain, "Your flag is public over granite."[67] Alvah Bessie, of course, would write of Spain in his prison poem "November 7, 1950," which first invokes the Russian Revolution and then recalls the defense of the Spanish capital "fourteen long and painful years ago":

The other date concerns a Spanish city,
jewel of the Castilian plain,
naked to the white and blinding sun,
blazing like a diamond, coveted
by thieves and pimps and cut-throats who
marched in open columns down the hills
of Guadarama to the gates—
then stopped and never moved another inch.
They had been met—by men,
by men who came without the benefit of exhortation,
speaking many tongues but cherishing
in common, first, a simple, shining word:

Freedom!

and then a phrase, in common:

Death to fascism![68]

Spain, its lost cause unresolved, haunted Bessie, but it also strengthened him for the present battle. If a history of support for the Spanish Republic was a near-fatal error in the political economy of the American inquisition, it was also, paradoxically, in a very real sense a tremendous resource, a force apparent in Sherry Mangan's poem as well. As Bessie's unpublished poems repeatedly make clear, an American brand of fascism was now lose in the land. Those who stood against Franco could now try to stand against J. Edgar Hoover or Joseph McCarthy. The commitment to Spain made real—embodied in "wounded granite"—those values now under assault in the United States.

Hence the undying power of the heroic defense of the Spanish capital. The city held throughout the war, despite the massed fascist troops a subway ride away at its western suburbs. It opened its gates to Franco only when the war was clearly over. Now the fallen city could still be a talisman for the city that never fell and for the cause it represented and the alliances it galvanized. Its slogans could be scribbled on walls, whispered in secret. The moment of its defense defined a generation and sustained them in the years of physical and political exile. Now, in the 1950s that generation was losing Spain yet again; those in power were stigmatizing and red-baiting the cause that first bound together the international Left in one body. The memory of the city that was once the heart of the world—Madrid under assault defended by its people—would be torn out of the world's body. But some of the city's children would do it proper honor, and its whispered name seemed almost to draw its scattered, surviving defenders into a secret society in opposition to those in love with death.

One other more specific topic held its power through the years as well, partly because it fused loss and aspiration, betrayal and solidarity, death and longing from the outset—the murder of Federico García Lorca. The poetic memorial service for García Lorca started almost immediately after his death in August 1936 at the outset of the Spanish Civil War, continued heavily for more than a decade, and sustained itself for the rest of the century. *El mono azul* dedicated its September 17, 1936, two-page spread of poems to García Lorca and opened with Emilio Prados's elegy. The League of Revolutionary Writers and Artists in Mexico published a selection of García Lorca's poems in November 1936, within months of his death, under the title *Breve antología,* accompanied by an astonishing preface of revolutionary solidarity by Juan Marinello. The anthology was issued on the occasion of a November 14 evening at Mexico City's Palace of Fine Arts celebrating García Lorca's life and work. The following September a comparable event was staged at the Spanish Pavilion at the International Exposition in Paris; this time the performers included the French actor Jean-Louis Barrault. The programs for these two events (see figures 6 and 7), among others, reach out to each other to create a performative alliance, a time and space of simultaneous solidarity and mourning. These mementos of events join with all the worldwide publications honoring García Lorca. In Argentina the People's Theater performed his play *Bodas de sangre* (Blood wedding) in November 1936, three months after his death, and published the play along with a poem to him, "El cantor de los gitanos" (The singer of the gypsies) by the theater's director, Eugenio Navas. *Madre España: Homenaje de los poetas chilenos a Federico García Lorca* was issued in Santiago in 1937, and *Hommage à F. García Lorca* was published in Brussels in 1938. Emilio Prados's anthology *Romancero general de la guerra de España* is dedicated to García Lorca, and the July 1937 anthology *Poetas en la España leal* opens with Antonio Machado's poem about García Lorca. That same year Emilio Prados edited a 200-page collection of elegies for García Lorca, *Homenaje al poeta García Lorca: Contra su muerta.* By the time *Poems for Spain* was published in England in 1939, elegies for García Lorca were among the central and inescapable categories used to construct the war's intelligibility and its continuing power in the experience and memory of the Left. The Spender and Lehman anthology is divided into six thematic categories—"Action," "Death," "The Map," "Satire," "Romances," and finally, bringing the text full circle back to the war's opening months and to its core poetics of anguish, "Lorca." García Lorca is thus there at the beginning and the end of the war; his death prefigures the defeat of the Republic and the necessity of continuing witness to its values. Among the poems devoted to him in books, magazines, and broadsides are Rafael Alberti's "Elegía a un

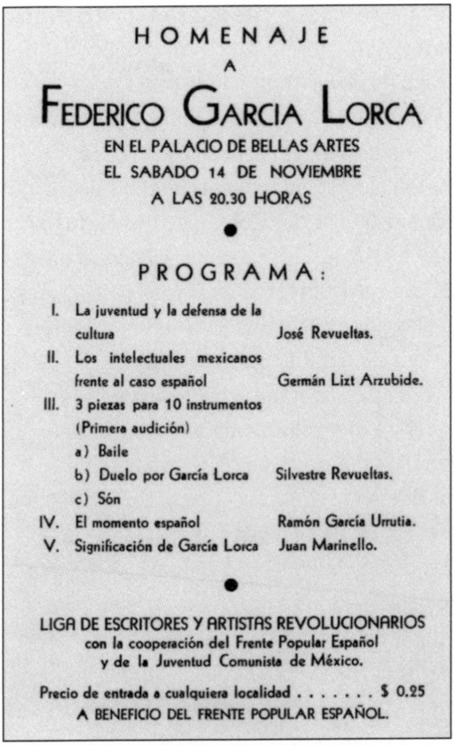

HOMENAJE

A

FEDERICO GARCIA LORCA

EN EL PALACIO DE BELLAS ARTES
EL SABADO 14 DE NOVIEMBRE
A LAS 20.30 HORAS

●

PROGRAMA:

I. La juventud y la defensa de la
cultura — José Revueltas.

II. Los intelectuales mexicanos
frente al caso español — Germán Lizt Arzubide.

III. 3 piezas para 10 instrumentos
(Primera audición)
a) Baile
b) Duelo por García Lorca — Silvestre Revueltas.
c) Són

IV. El momento español — Ramón García Urrutia.

V. Significación de García Lorca — Juan Marinello.

●

LIGA DE ESCRITORES Y ARTISTAS REVOLUCIONARIOS
con la cooperación del Frente Popular Español
y de la Juventud Comunista de México.

Precio de entrada a cualquiera localidad . . . . . . $ 0.25
A BENEFICIO DEL FRENTE POPULAR ESPAÑOL.

Figure 6. The program for "Homenaje a Federico García Lorca," held in Mexico City on November 14, 1936. Author's collection.

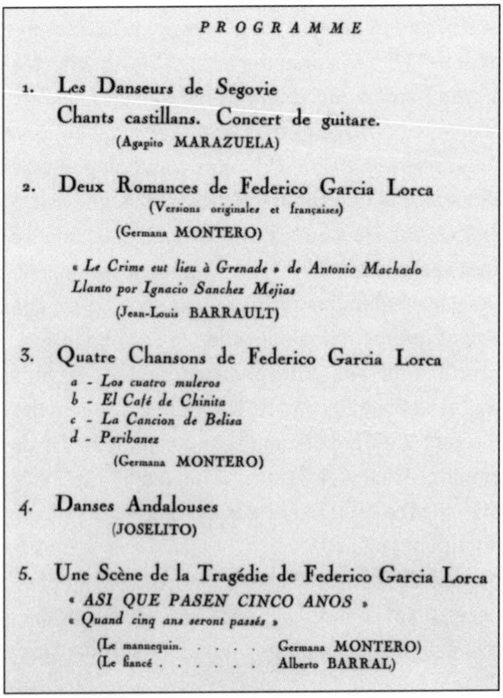

Figure 7. The program for "Hommage à Federico García Lorca: Poète fusillé à Grenade," held at the Spanish Pavilion at the 1937 World's Fair in Paris on September 23, 1937. Author's collection.

PROGRAMME

1. Les Danseurs de Segovie
Chants castillans. Concert de guitare.
(Agapito MARAZUELA)

2. Deux Romances de Federico Garcia Lorca
(Versions originales et françaises)
(Germana MONTERO)

« Le Crime eut lieu à Grenade » de Antonio Machado
Llanto por Ignacio Sanchez Mejias
(Jean-Louis BARRAULT)

3. Quatre Chansons de Federico Garcia Lorca
a - Los cuatro muleros
b - El Café de Chinita
c - La Cancion de Belisa
d - Peribanez
(Germana MONTERO)

4. Danses Andalouses
(JOSELITO)

5. Une Scène de la Tragédie de Federico Garcia Lorca
« ASI QUE PASEN CINCO ANOS »
« Quand cinq ans seront passés »
(Le mannequin. . . . . Germana MONTERO)
(Le fiancé . . . . . . Alberto BARRAL)

poeta que no tuvo muerte," Manuel Altolaguirre's "Elegía a nuestro poeta," Antonio Aparicio's "A Federico García Lorca," Jacob Bronowski's "The Death of García Lorca," Luis Cardoza y Aragon's "Ballad of Federico García Lorca," Alejandro Carrion's "Pascua serena de tu muerte," Oscar Castro Z's "Responso a García Lorca," Louis Cernuda's "Elegía a un poeta muerto," Joy Davidman's "Elegy for García Lorca," Sol Funaroff's "To Federico García Lorca," Eldon Grier's "In Memory of García Lorca," Jorge I. Guerrero's "Holocausto gitano," Miguel Hernández's "Elegía primera," Aaron Kramer's "García Lorca," Juan Gil Albert's "A Federico García Lorca," Pedro Garfias's "A Federico García Lorca," Raúl Gonzalez Tuñón's "Muerta del poeta," Jorge Guillén's "Federico García Lorca," Nicolás Guillén's "Anguish Number Four: Federico," Pedro Jorge Vera's "Muerte y vida de Federico García Lorca," Claudia Lars's "Romance de romancero gitano," Pedro García de Lorca's "Romance a Federico," Leopoldo de Luis's "Romancero a la muerte de Federico García Lorca," Hugh MacDiarmid's "In Memoriam García Lorca," Antonio Machado's "The Crime Took Place in Granada: To Federico García Lorca," Ricardo Madas's "Poema a Federico," Martha Millet's "Song for Federico García Lorca," Rodrigo Miró's "Lamento por Federico García Lorca," Vincius de Moraes's "La muerte de madrugada," Leopoldo Panero's "España hasta los huesos," Geoffrey Parsons's "Lorca," Emilio Prados's "Estancia en la muerte con Federico García Lorca," Pablo Neruda's "Ode to Federico García Lorca," Emilio Prados's "The Arrival," Alfonso Reyes's "Cantata en la tumba de Federico García Lorca," Edwin Rolfe's "A Federico García Lorca," Norman Rosten's "To Federico García Lorca," Héctor Suanes's "Romance de los cuatro gitanos," Leopoldo Urrutia's "Romancero a la muerta de Federico García Lorca," Edmond Vandercammen's "Ode à Federico García Lorca," and Lorenzo Varela's "Copla sencilla." Prose tributes came from, among others, Vicente Aleixandre, José Bergamin, José Moreno Villa, Pablo Neruda, Arturo Serrano Plaja, and William Carlos Williams. Of these, Cardoza y Aragon was Guatemalan, Mados and González Tuñón were Argentinean, Miró was Panamanian, Lars was Salvadoran, Moraes was Brazilian, Reyes was Mexican, Nicolás Guillén was Cuban, MacDiarmid was Scottish, and Carrion, Castro Z., Guerrero, Jorge Vera, Neruda, and Suanes were Chilean, though only nominally so in this context. Vandercammen was Belgian; Grier and Parsons were British. Bronowski was a Polish-born British émigré. Davidman, Funaroff, Kramer, Millet, Rolfe, Rosten, and Williams were Americans, though in this context, again, only nominally so.

The poems, prose poems, and statements that make up this unique and extended international wake are almost impossible to think about only as discrete texts, for they make up a kind of reflexive García Lorca cantata whose music is the sound of love amidst war and lamentation. Among the distinctive and sometimes uncanny continuities in these elegies to García Lorca are the number of times poets address him directly by his first name and the affectionate, plaintive, and often rather childlike calls to him many poets issued. He is repeatedly "Federico," friend, brother, comrade, lover, and lost child. Nothing else in the modern elegy has quite this haunting tone or this elaborately international sixty-year history. Vicente Aleixandre simply titles his prose memoir "Federico," and the name ever after echoes with loss. American poets sometimes address Walt Whitman by his first name, as Hart Crane did, but there the effort is to link hands with a poet whose whole rich career invites fraternity, not to commemorate the impossibility of contact with a poet whose life and career were brutally curtailed. Largely unrecognized in literary histories, even in histories of the modern elegy, the elegies to García Lorca are nonetheless one of the hallmarks of twentieth-century poetry.[69] As they echo common concerns and forms of address, drawing on recurrent tropes in García Lorca's own poetry, they soon form a choral response that helps define the war and haunts the century's collective memory:

The Crime Took Place in Granada (Machado)

You watched the monster, Federico,
That Yeats saw stirring in the desert. (Rexroth)

from the choked south, from your buried city (Rolfe)

They killed Federico
when first light appeared. (Machado)

He did not die like a gypsy:
he was not stabbed to death.
Five rifles went searching,
by five roads, for his soul (Castro Z.)

And he stopped and turned and faced them, standing still;
He stared at their aiming eyes, his imminent murder;
He was one with the people of Spain and he stood as they
          stand. (Parsons)

and they split wide his heart
the same as a pomegranate,
and the fountain of his blood
shot up to stain the stars! (Castro Z.)

[. . .] the way you died, with surprise in your eyes,
          as you recognized your assassins (Rolfe)

Why is Federico not here?
I have wonderful news for Federico!—
news for his private ear [. . .]
Federico! Federico! Too soon! [. . .]
Federico, wait for me! Wait!
I must talk with you! Look! [. . .]
I have so much to tell you, Federico! (Prados)

I cry in pain, "Oh, Federico! Federico!" [. . .]
where does a gypsy go to die?
Where do his eyes change to silver frost? [. . .]
Where will Federico be,
where will he be that he won't be back? (Guillén)

Ay, Federico García,
How swiftly death, dagger in hand, draws nigh! [. . .]
Ay, Federico García,
Death is here, is here! (Urrutia)

O this is your end, your end, your end [. . .]
You joked with the dead: did you not hear
their voices lower year by year? (Bronowski)

We used to see him walk alone with her,
Unfearful of her sickle [. . .]
And Federico, in his courteous way,
Would talk with Death and she would listen (Machado)

Were there stars in the sky, Federico,
when the ignorant rifles struck you down
[. . . . .]
Call down the stars to blind them
for their rifles are raised, Federico! (Rosten)

Federico, do you remember
under the ground,
do you remember my house with balconies where
June light smothered flowers in your mouth? (Neruda)

Women on the balconies,
and naiads and tritons
sang songs of mother-of-pearl

to the poet of Granada:
"Come this way, Federico:
make the oranges fragrant,
and the pineapples and the custard-apples." (Cardoza y Aragon)

When he burst into song
the whole of Spain sang with him. (Castro Z.)

where now there is only silence and no
darkness we can say is his, Federico's. (Philip Levine)

They shot him and made a bonfire of his books (MacDiarmid)

They heard his poem rising up, and spreading over Spain. (Kramer)

          carve a monument
out of dream stone
for the poet in the Alhambra,
over a fountain where the grieving water
shall say forever
The crime was in Granada, his Granada. (Machado)

Lorca, you who were the morning song of Spain,
the song is on the lips of the people! (Funaroff).[70]

More powerfully than in any single poem, this collective elegy makes García
Lorca a figure for the Republic as a utopian return to a prelapsarian cultural
moment. It would be a moment when difference—so often fatal in Spain and
throughout the modern world—was merely polymorphous diversity, when
every impulse and desire were purified of worldly corruption. García Lorca's
verbal resources become after his death the poetic equivalent of the Spanish
harvest, a literary version of the earth's bounty. In some fundamental way,
then, García Lorca's death demonstrated that it was at once innocence and
poetry itself the fascists sought to kill. García Lorca was not primarily a politi-
cal writer in the conventional sense of addressing current events; nor did he
join a political party, though he was visibly active in support of the Popular
Front. The day before the February 16, 1936, national elections in Spain, the
major Communist newspaper *Mundo obrero* published a manifesto entitled
"The Intellectuals and the Popular Front" with three hundred signatures; at
the top of the list was Federico García Lorca. That spring, with rumors of a
right-wing coup in the air, García Lorca read before a mass meeting at the
Madrid Workers' Club his poem "Ballad of the Spanish Civil Guard," an in-

tense attack on the widely hated paramilitary police force, the Guardia Civil.[71] Even if his support for the Left had not been widely publicized, which it was, his lines attacking the Guardia Civil and the church were not neutral and were unlikely to prove harmless in the fatal world of Spanish politics.[72] Moreover, he was to a remarkable degree a people's poet. As Leslie Stainton puts it in a 1999 biography, García Lorca "viewed poetry as 'something that walks along the streets,' that exists everywhere: in men, in women, in the 'unpredictable path of a dog.'"[73] His consistent stands against social and sexual repression carried political implications in Spain. That class positioning of his work made it a rallying point for the people's aspirations. His work was known to many working people; his books were everywhere; his poems could be quot-ed throughout the country. García Lorca's death was thus a figure for the will to kill the people's soul. It was, moreover, as if all progressive poets felt themselves (and every value they held dear) under a murderous gaze, under a potential death sentence to be carried out immediately if Franco, Hitler, and Mussolini had their way.

The special poignancy of poets' relationships to García Lorca—both real and imaginary—was underlined during and after the Spanish Civil War. In 1938, when the Duchess of Atholl was to be presented with a portfolio of texts and paintings in appreciation for her help for the Republic, Bernardo Clariana's prose tribute to García Lorca was copied out in holograph on parchment and hand illuminated as part of the gift.[74] When Manuel Altolaguirre reached Cuba shortly after the civil war, one of the first things he did was issue a miniature anthology of García Lorca's poems. He had published a small volume of García Lorca's poems a few years earlier in Spain, *Primeras canciones* (First songs), and now he wished both symbolically and materially to renew the commitment and bring it full circle. *Primeras canciones* had been issued in January 1936, only half a year, as it turned out, before García Lorca was mur-dered. *Poemas escogidos de Federico García Lorca* would not only show that García Lorca's voice would survive in the new world but also make Havana a symbolic outpost of the undefeatable spirit of the Republic. Both commit-ments would be the work of Altolaguirre's own hands; they were intimate loy-alties. "This gathering of poems does not," he pointed out in the Spanish in-troduction to the 1939 selection, "emphasize his best verses, something I do not like to calculate, but those I heard frequently from his own lips."[75]

That sense of a startlingly intimate relationship with García Lorca's po-ems—poems not merely read but spoken into one's ear—is thereby partly transferred to the reader. The poems are shared almost in the manner of a lover's caress, and this aura of sensual ripeness permeates much of the cul-tural force his image retains. At the same time the sense of loss permeates the withdrawal of his presence and the unresolvable agony of his unmarked grave. "Under what crossless Calvary lie your lost bones, García Lorca?" asks

Thomas Merton. "Where are his bones now? Where's his blood?" asks Martha Millet. "Somewhere, / Buried, / Is a silver skull," answers Eldon Grier.[76]

The questions and the need poets feel to mark that invisible grave site persist through the years. Alberti reissued García Lorca's *Romancero gitano* in 1943 in Argentina, framed by a prose introduction and by his own elegy to him. That same year the Argentinean dramatist Eugenio Navas adapted the title of Antonio Machado's elegy for his play *Federico García Lorca: "El crimen fué en Granada"* (see figure 8). Philip Levine, the contemporary American poet who has matched Edwin Rolfe and Muriel Rukeyser of the 1930s generation in doing sustained work about the war, opens and closes his 1994 volume *The Simple Truth* with poems about García Lorca and European fascism. "On the Meeting of García Lorca and Hart Crane" is the book's first poem, while "My Mother with Purse the Summer They Murdered the Spanish Poet" and "My Father with Cigarette Twelve Years before the Nazis Could Break His Heart" are the book's concluding poems. In one passage Levine, like so many

Figure 8. The cover of Eugenio Navas's three-act play about García Lorca's last days and death, produced in Buenos Aires in 1943. Author's collection.

poets before him, travels back to the moment of García Lorca's death among "the shale hills / above Granada where all time stopped":

[. . .] Wide-eyed he sees nothing. White shirt
worn open, dark trousers with no belt, the olive skin appalled.
When the same wind he loved and sang to touches his cheek
he tries to rub it away. There are others, too, walking over
the flat, gray stones to where a line of men smokes and waits.[77]

For Levine, as for so many poets, García Lorca's image would not cease haunting him. In *The Mercy* (1999) Levine returns again to the Granada hillside and writes yet another elegy, "The Search for Lorca's Shadow."[78]

For other writers, García Lorca would remain a touchstone for everything poetry aimed to achieve and for all the forces poetry sought to resist. Lawrence Ferlinghetti registered both senses of the García Lorca legacy in several poems of the 1960s and 1970s. Bob Kaufman returned to García Lorca repeatedly to sustain himself amidst adversity. "The night that Lorca comes," he wrote in a prayer for deliverance, "shall be the time when negroes leave the / South / forever." Every poet who "protests the / death he sees around / him," he declared in a manifesto laced with lamentation, "dies like Lorca did." They reach meanwhile for that "Federico García Lorca sky, immaculate scoured sky, equaling only itself" yet containing "all the distances."[79]

For Spanish writers in exile and for foreign writers who fought in Spain or visited it during the war, the symbolism of García Lorca's life and death and the memory of the war as a whole were especially intense. For these writers at least, I suspect, as well as for their audiences, all Spanish Civil War elegies echo one another. All such elegies lament at once a person, a state, and a state of mind. All Spanish Civil War elegies are thus García Lorca elegies whether or not they refer to the murdered poet. The experience of exile touched all of these writers, not just the Spanish nationals. Nor does the work of mourning carried out in these poems follow the normal trajectory of seeking to move beyond the moment of anguish, for only the continually deferred victory over fascism can compensate for Federico's loss. Notably, then, Eduardo Castro published his *Muerte en Granada: La tragedia de Federico García Lorca* in Madrid in 1975, the year of Franco's death; it includes his new poem "Muerto, pero no se murió solo," which links García Lorca with Christ and with the possible birth of a new Spain.[80]

In the United States, however, the Left underwent an internal exile and the memory of Spain acquired a special inflection, for supporting the Spanish Republic became a hallmark of politically unacceptable beliefs and commitments. Genevieve Taggard wrote and published a poem in 1941, "To the Veterans of the Abraham Lincoln Brigade," that captured the gathering demonizing of Spain and all it stood for; it was published on the front page of the *Volunteer for Liberty*:

Say of them
They knew no Spanish
At first, and nothing of the arts of war
At first,
            how to shoot, how to attack, how to retreat
How to kill, how to meet killing
At first.
Say they kept the air blue
Grousing and griping,
Arid words and harsh faces. Say
They were young;
The haggard in a trench, the dead on the olive slope
All young. And the thin, the ill and the shattered,
Sightless, in hospitals, all young.

Say of them they were young, there was much they did not know,
They were human. Say it all; it is true. Now say
When the eminent, the great, the easy, the old,
And the men on the make
Were busy bickering and selling,
Betraying, conniving, transacting, splitting hairs,
Writing bad articles, signing bad papers,
Passing bad bills,
Bribing, blackmailing,
Whimpering, meaching, garroting,—they
Knew and acted
Understood and died.

Or if they did not die came home to peace
That is not peace.
            Say of them
They are no longer young, they never learned
The arts, the stealth of peace, this peace, the tricks of fear;
And what they knew, they know.
And what they dared, they dare.[81]

Two years later Don Gordon published "Spain."[82] Already, with the surviving veterans still in their prime, the legacy of Spain is cast in terms of present responsibility. We cannot merely honor them; that would be too easy. We must ask ourselves what it would mean to be their children, to inherit not only their memories but also their weapons. What would it mean to carry on the struggle, to act in their name?

By the time Taggard wrote her poem, one that reaches powerfully for the complex human reality of the volunteers, Lincoln Battalion veterans had already been through their first round of testimony before the House Committee on Un-American Activities. There their loyalty was questioned, and they defended themselves aggressively, as they would have to again throughout the 1950s. Under remission during World War II, antipathy toward the Spanish Republic rose again during the postwar inquisition. By then, it was no longer necessary to have fought in Spain to be marked as subversive. Merely having signed a petition or having contributed funds was enough to get you fired and blacklisted. During those dark years, the commitment to Spain remained a kind of beacon with which to read the betrayals of the decades to follow. Thus many of those who suffered because of their devotion to Spanish democracy also found the memory a powerful resource amidst oppression.

In the United States, a number of poets on the left who had worked through the radical 1930s and made a commitment to Spain never quite outlived that period of unique intensity. Those who held to their beliefs through the long postwar inquisition of the 1940s and 1950s—the widespread purge of the Left from both public and private employment that culminated in the McCarthy period—could hardly forget that earlier moment of alliance politics when the Left at least seemed able to mount an organized resistance to fascism. When Edwin Rolfe, a veteran of the Lincoln Battalion in Spain, turned to write of García Lorca one last time in 1948 in "A Federico García Lorca," he was, in effect, recalling not only the martyred poet but also the whole imperiled coalition that stood with the Spanish Republic:

Ten years have passed since I found in a book shop in Albacete,
The paper-bound case of jewels which I treasure still, the book *Romancero*
    Gitano,
And turned to the first poem, the "Romance de la Luna, Luna,"
And read and found fabulous peace in the midst of the war.

Later, in Madrid, the lads of the guerrilleros
Crossed the midnight lines from madness to the light of the Casa de Alianza.
And told us (Langston was there, and Rafael, and María Teresa)
That they came from the choked south, from your buried city, Granada.

And they told how they met in the streets the people who told them in
    whispers

Of the way you died, with surprise in your eyes, as you recognized your
    assassins,
The men with the patent-leather hats and souls of patent-leather.

In the last lines of the poem Rolfe imagines the moment of García Lorca's
death and in so doing cements its relation to the moment of the poem's com-
position. The men with the souls of patent leather, first named in García Lor-
ca's "Ballad of the Spanish Civil Guard," were abroad in the land again, this
time in the United States as well as Spain. Rolfe kept with him a newspaper
clipping of Langston Hughes's translation of "Ballad of the Civil Guard," a
translation that helped cement the connection between political oppression
in Spain and the United States. In Rolfe's poem García Lorca *recognizes* his
assassins, a recognition that is preeminently political but also—because of
the force of the verb—unstably personal and familial as well. The Guardia
Civil represents members of the lethal family of Spanish politics. They are
among the agents tearing apart Spain's body politic. So, too, are the agents
of the American inquisition at once neighbors and representatives of recog-
nizable political institutions. That is also why Alvah Bessie, whose poem "For
My Dead Brother" I quoted at the outset, turned to write of Spain as well
when he was in federal prison for asserting his First Amendment rights. In
Bessie's poem there is a strong suggestion that no less than everything is at
stake, for the plains and seas that the International Brigades took, despite
losing the war, are terrains of principle and witness, ranges of value, cities of
history. It is a geography of honor and things done, not simply a geography of
contested lands. Consider, for example, the list of cities in Archibald Mac-
Leish's "The Spanish Lie," Olga Cabral's "To Spain," or Walter Snow's
"Spain—The Modern Phoenix."[83] Over a thousand Americans lost their lives
in Spain, a country that was not their own but whose cause they made indi-
vidual decisions to support. Though as a larger culture we have largely forgot-
ten that commitment, it has echoed through the Left and through American
poetry ever since.

Yet the story of when and how some of these poems were published is a
complex and troubled one. The case that sets the standard for the postwar
experience, arguably, occurred near the end of the Spanish Civil War. Manuel
Altolaguirre had set up a printing press on the eastern front in an old monas-
tery and set about printing Neruda's *España en el corazón*. Neruda tells the
story himself in his *Memoirs*:

The soldiers at the front learned to set type. But there was no paper.
They found an old mill and decided to make it there. A strange mixture
was concocted, between one falling bomb and the next, in the middle of
the fighting. They threw everything they could get their hands on into the

mill, from an enemy flag to a Moorish soldier's bloodstained tunic. . . .
My book had just been printed and bound when the Republic's defeat
was suddenly upon us. . . . Among those lines of people going into exile
were the survivors of the eastern front, and with them Manuel Altola-
guirre and the soldiers who had made the paper and printed *España en
el corazón.* My book was the pride of these men who had worked to bring
out my poetry in the face of death. . . . many carried copies of the book
in their sacks, instead of their own food and clothing. . . . The endless
column walking to exile was bombed hundreds of times. Soldiers fell
and the books were spilled on the highway. . . . The last copies of this
impassioned book that was born and perished in the midst of fierce
fighting were immolated in a bonfire.[84]

Neruda, of course, saw his book reprinted and translated numerous times.
Rolfe, however, could find no one to publish his 1948 poem "Elegia" until
Altolaguirre issued a Spanish translation in Mexico City, and Rolfe died in
1954 without publishing his poem to García Lorca; Jefferson Hendricks and I
published it thirty-nine years later.[85]

The German poet Erich Weinert, in exile from his homeland after Hitler
came to power, moved from Switzerland to France and then to the Soviet
Union. From there he traveled to Spain and joined the International Brigades,
where he was assigned to cultural work both at the front and behind the
lines. Toward the end of the war he had hoped to publish *Camaradas,* a col-
lection of his Spanish Civil War poems and prose. He had a publisher lined
up in Barcelona, but it was not to be. Instead, as the war ended he joined the
columns of refugees headed toward France. At the entrance to the coastal
concentration camp at St. Cyprien, the suitcase with his manuscript was
dumped on the ground, slit open with bayonets, and its contents scattered
over the sand. Guards watched as the northern wind, the Mistral, blew his
poems to oblivion. A few years later he was in the trenches at Stalingrad, op-
posing Germany again as he had in Spain. After World War II he returned to
East Germany. There he gathered together those few of his poems that sur-
vived—those few he had carried into St. Cyprien in the small pack he had un-
der his arm or those he had published in newspapers or journals during the
Spanish Civil War—and published an abbreviated *Camaradas,* issued in
Berlin by Verlag Volk und Welt in 1951. Langston Hughes's notable poem
"Madrid," first issued in the obscure International Brigades magazine *Our
Fight* in July 1938, would wait thirty-five years to be published more visibly.
Hughes sent the manuscript to Arthur Spingarn during the war, and it ended
up in Spingarn's papers at Howard University. Faith Berry found the poem
there and included it in *Good Morning Revolution,* her collection of Hughes's
social protest writings published by Lawrence Hill in 1973.

Walter Snow, a friend of Rolfe in the 1930s who helped publish Jack Conroy's radical magazine *Anvil,* turned against the Left in the 1950s. A decade later, he had second thoughts, sought out those of his friends on the left who were still alive, and gave thought to publishing his long poem on Spain, completed during the war but abandoned in his papers. Finally, he wrote a prologue to it, briefly suggesting why young readers today might still care about a war over for decades, along with a brief conclusion, and issued it shortly before his death in his self-published book of poems, *The Glory and the Shame* (1973).[86] The original opening of the poem, now section two, was a long tribute to the International Brigades. Here is its first stanza:

They came with the four great winds in their leaf-green youth.
They were students with quicksilver minds, more footloose,
more sensitive to the barometer of history than
tenured teachers. They were the disillusioned
unemployed, frayed victims
of the Great Depression, deciding it was time to act.
They were the young colts of the prairies, the dreamers who still read poetry
instead of doping Daily Doubles and Three-Horse Parlays;
the tailors from sweatshops who still bled at the prick of needles;
belt-line assembly robots from Detroit who rebelled
at obsolescence planned in chrome-plated coffins.
They were miners long accustomed to coughing out their lungs and
    protesting
but willing to be jolted now in cattleboats five thousand miles
to set off dynamite blasts for a better world.

Whether Snow meant these Whitmanesque lines that way, they may also stand for many of the young poets, some of them volunteers as well, who began to write of Spain in 1936 or 1937 and continued doing so through the modern era and as far into the century as their lives reached. Aaron Kramer wrote "Smiles and Blood," reprinted here, when he was sixteen years old. He visited Spain after Franco died and published "Barcelona: the Last Night" in 1991 at age seventy. His life was—in the deepest political and cultural sense—framed and illumined by Spain. Rukeyser wrote of the Spanish Civil War in *U.S.1* (1938), *A Turning Wind* (1939), *Beast in View* (1944), and *The Speed of Darkness* (1968), and in "Neruda, the Wine" in her last book, *The Gates* (1976), she called Spain "that core of all our lives, / The long defeat that brings us what we know." Rukeyser's lines effect an intertextual alliance politics, an elegiac politics at once personal, historical, generational, and literary. "Neruda, the Wine" testifies to shared memories and shared commitments, just as it honors the Neruda of "How Spain Was" in the third installment of his *Residence on Earth:*

How, with my soul and my tears,
I have cherished your obstinate soil, your destitute bread
and your peoples; how, in the deepest
recess of my being, the flower of your villages,
furrowed, immobile in time, lives for me, lost,
with your flinty savannas[87]

Those lines might as well have been written by Rolfe or by any number of
other writers on the left. Norman Rosten's ambitious epic *The Fourth Decade
and Other Poems* (1943) includes an unmarked, untitled sequence of poems
about Spain, at least thirteen poems in length (depending on how many one
assigns to the group). He immediately began tinkering with the sequence,
uncertain what should be said and unsaid, what should stay and what should
go. At that point, in 1943, with the Soviet Union still very much our ally, he felt
the sequence could sustain a poem in tribute to the Russian ship *Komsomol*
unloading grain and guns in Barcelona's harbor. Indeed, the book as a whole
is framed by poems devoted to the World War II American struggle for Bataan
in the Pacific and the siege of the Russian city of Sevastopol. But the follow-
ing year he cut the sequence to only five poems for the anthology *Seven Po-
ets in Search of an Answer,* meanwhile giving each poem a title for the first
time: "Invocation," "To Federico García Lorca," "Pastorale," "The Internation-
al Brigades," and "Shadow of Our Years." Eight years later the sequence gets
an overall title for the first time, and it is expanded to seven poems when it
appears in the 1952 anthology *Heart of Spain.* In his 1979 *Selected Poems* it is
seven poems again, but only three of the poems are from the 1952 version;
the other four are from *The Fourth Decade.* Most significant, however, he
adds the haunting new poem "Journey to Madrid," an elegy to his own youth
and to its defining devotion to the cause of Spain. Both *The Fourth Decade*
and the *Selected Poems* also include a verse play about the duplicitous Non-
Intervention Committee, which denied arms to Spain but sat by passively
while Hitler and Mussolini armed Franco. At one point García Lorca returns,
while British and French politicians are on stage:

Lorca's corpse is dragged on, blindfolded,
the bullet-holes showing like sores.
He is propped up, against the back wall.
Chamberlain rises, adjusts his tie,
"What is the meaning of this outrage?
And has there been a fair trial?
Besides, this is no place for executions."
Franco, gentle and pious, "This man, sir,
you forget is dangerous, representing
the full flower of the bolshevist menace.

Europe must above all be kept sanitary.
I regret I shall have to kill him again,
for the photographers."
                              Daladier perspires,
"There must be no atrocities, gentlemen!
I will not tolerate atrocities in any form!
Please remember I was once a socialist."
They smile. Daladier is the man for humor.

Leon Blum receives a momentary spotlight
(he insisted on a soliloquy in tights).
He sits in his theoretical room,
meditating aloud on good and evil.
The courier enters with news of murder.
He rises, hand at the antique dagger.
This is the scene he always wanted to play!
"Now might I do it pat, now he is praying;
and now I'll do't; and so he goes to heaven:
and so I am revenged."
                              and so and so and so
Angels on the proscenium turn their eyes
at the sight of rifles. "Fire!" shouts Franco.
Lorca slides to the floor.[88]

The "we" of Rukeyser's poem that feels these events so deeply is very
much the generation that came of age in the crucible of the 1930s. For them
Spain was the fulcrum event of the decade; it crystallized at once aspiration
and anxiety. When Spain fell and fascism spread across the rest of Europe,
their fears were not merely confirmed but amplified. Spain's lesson was both
wound and dream, but the dream persists, as in the last lines of Randall Jar-
rell's 1942 "A Poem for Someone Killed in Spain," even after the wounds
seemed fatal: "To think that their friend is dying, and their whispers / Are not
patient but breathless, are passionate / With the songs of the world where no
one dies."[89]

Why did a number of these American poets continue to write about the
Spanish Civil War for decade after decade? There were, to be sure, innumera-
ble British poets writing about Spain from 1936 to 1939, but few kept writing
about Spain thereafter. MacDiarmid is one British poet who did, and Jeremy
Reed published a beautiful limited edition of his poem *Lorca's Death* in 1990.
Yet two groups of poets above all others returned to the topic throughout
their lives—Spanish exiles and Americans. One can easily enough gauge the
nature of the exile commitment. As Juan Rejano writes in his untitled poem in

the pamphlet *Steve Nelson,* a 1953 tribute to the Lincoln Battalion's embat-
tled political commissar, "I pace the land of Mexico, uprooted / from my sor-
rowing, captive country, / and yet I live each minute in Spain."[90] And so Al-
berti would be editing anthologies of Spanish Civil War poetry in Argentina
well into the 1940s; his 1941 anthology *Para un Castillo de Penas,* issued in
Buenos Aires, opens with Machado's elegy to García Lorca. The difference for
the Americans, I believe, was the long inquisition that culminated in the Mc-
Carthy era, the 1947–60 period that cast Spain and its defining ideals out of
the social contract. It marked these American poets—speaking for thousands
of others—as exiles in their own land.

To the extent that the "we" of Rukeyser's "Neruda, the Wine" encompasses
those who came of age in later generations as well, it does so most notably
only if by choice or upbringing they absorb that history and make it their own.
There is a cost, as Barbara Guest writes decisively:

To make an Elegy of Spain
is to make a song of the abyss.

It is to cut a gorge into one's soul
which is suddenly no longer private.[91]

For those Americans who cannot imagine a public space within the soul,
Spain signals more what they do not know, what they and their fellow Ameri-
cans have willfully forgotten. Levine and many other American poets have
chosen to remember. But as the decades passed, the nature of the memory
for some begins to change. The International Brigades continue to be hon-
ored with powerful poems of testimony. Martín Espada's "The Carpenter
Swam to Spain" (1999), first published in the *Volunteer for Liberty,* is the
most recent example, but other poets, including Ai in "They Shall Not Pass"
(1986), have felt the need to register a betrayal of innocence in the bloody
cauldron of Spanish and world politics. "I have to remind myself," Ai's speak-
er remarks, "why I'm dying here in Madrid."[92] To some degree that impulse
was already present in Robinson Jeffers's 1937 poem "Sinverguenza," which
is essentially a protest against the murderous politics of nation states: "They
snarl over Spain like cur-dogs over a bone."[93] But a more specific lesson is
built into such poems as Robert Hass's 1989 "Rusia en 1931," which registers
Soviet communism's failure to live up to its ideals.[94] Levine's memorials to
the Spanish anarchists also implicitly attack the Communist party's suppres-
sion of revolutionary Marxism in Spain in May of 1937. Antifascism, in con-
strast, remains an area of solidarity that helps turn these poems—from those
of Edwin Rolfe, Langston Hughes, and Aaron Kramer ("Smiles and Blood,"
1937) through James Wright ("Eisenhower's Visit to Franco, 1959," 1959) and

Lawrence Ferlinghetti ("Into Darkness, in Granada," 1961) to Carolyn Kizer ("The Valley of the Fallen" and "Ingathering," 1986)[95]—into a coherent sixty-five-year tradition, a tradition mostly unrecognized heretofore but confirmed in *The Wound and the Dream*.

From 1936 to 1938 "No Pasaran!" was a newspaper headline, the lettering on a banner stretched across a street, a rallying cry from a charismatic speaker and a choral response from a crowd, the caption on posters and leaflets to be found in nearly every free city on earth. One particularly famous photograph of a Madrid street leading up to the wide Plaza Major, the "No Pasaran!" banner hung high above, was published throughout the world. Yet some graphic artists wanted more than just the original image. They wanted to feel the words enacted in the sinews of their drawing hand, so they redrew the photograph in a variety of styles, illustrating books or articles. Once the site of the Inquisition's autos-da-fé and the place where Spanish kings were crowned, the Plaza Major was now a bulwark against majesty and religious oppression.

"No Pasaran!" was also the title of a song sung on behalf of the Spanish Republic and the closing line in letter after letter sent home by American volunteers on battlefields in Spain. It was the title of a novel by Upton Sinclair and a memoir by Ilya Ehrenburg. It was a title for poems, the substance of stanzas, and a line renewed in poem after poem wherever poets were world citizens. It figured in a dance called a poem, and it was the sound of a mass chant. As a result, banners became poems, poems became posters, and poetic speech became the people's common cry. For a moment a certain dream of possible poetries had taken form before mounting terror. Poetry was the language of history and the story of ordinary lives. It was one of the indisputable terms in which history burnt its name into the living flesh of its time. Then night came, and it was over. But no one who had been part of it would ever forget.

Notes

The introduction is a revised and expanded version of an essay first published in my *Revolutionary Memory: Recovering the Poetry of the American Left* (Routledge, 2001). The illustrations appear here for the first time. The epigraphs are from Thomas O'Brien, "International Brigade Dead," in *Poesía anglo-norteamericana de la Guerra Civil española,* ed. Román Alvarez Rodríguez and Ramón López Ortega (Salamanca: Junta de Castilla y León, Consejería de Educación y Cultura, 1986), 184; Muriel Rukeyser, "Otherworld," in *The Collected Poems of Muriel Rukeyser* (New York: McGraw-Hill, 1978), 167; Ewart Milne, "Sierran Vigil," in *The Penguin Book of Spanish Civil War Verse,* ed. Valentine Cunningham (Harmondsworth, England: Penguin, 1980), 339–40; Byron Vazakas, "Lorca," in his *Transfigured Night* (New York: Macmillan, 1946), reprinted herein. Cunningham's anthology is the best collection of British Spanish Civil War poetry. Milne was an Irish volunteer who served with a medical unit.

1. Fifteen years later, Alvah Bessie, as reported in his *Inquisition in Eden* (New York: Macmillan, 1965), could view the incident with some humor:

    I received a copy of a new translation of *Don Quixote* from my wife, prior to her arrival with my daughter for their scheduled visit. The control room told me the book was there—and that they had no intention of giving it to me.
    "Why not?" I asked.
    "This *Don Quicks-oat*," said the captain. "Never heard of it. Books gotta be passed by the supervisor."
    "It's one of the world's great classics," I said. "You'll find it in every library in the world."
    "All new books gotta be read and approved."
    "It's not new. It was written in the first decade of the seventeenth century," I protested.
    "You don't think I'm gonna *read* it, do you? It's over a thousand pages long!"
    So I did not get it until the educational supervisor returned and assured the control room that it was perfectly all right for me to have it. (149)

2. Alvah Bessie, "Technicality," in "The *Free* World and Other Captive Verse," 1952 manuscript, photocopy of entire manuscript in author's possession.
3. Alvah Bessie, preface to "The *Free* World and Other Captive Verse."
4. Alvah Bessie, "Buried Alive," in ibid.
5. Alvah Bessie, "September 23, 1950," in ibid.
6. Alvah Bessie, "And Then There Were Nine," in ibid.; Edwin Rolfe, "Political Prisoner 123456789," in his *Permit Me Refuge* (Los Angeles: California Quarterly, 1955), reprinted in *Collected Poems,* ed. Cary Nelson and Jefferson Hendricks (Urbana: University of Illinois Press, 1993), 233; Alvah Bessie, "Memory of Battle," in "The *Free* World and Other Captive Verse," and "For My Dead Brother," herein.
7. There are a number of interesting critical books on the international literature of the Spanish Civil War, including several that devote space to British and American poetry. See, for example, Hugh D. Ford, *A Poets' War: British Poets and the Spanish Civil War* (Philadelphia: University of Pennsylvania Press, 1965); John M. Muste, *Say That We Saw Spain Die: Literary Consequences of the Spanish Civil War* (Seattle: University of Washington Press, 1966); Marilyn Rosenthal, *Poetry of the Spanish Civil War* (New York: New York University Press, 1975); and Stanley Weintraub, *The Last Great Cause: The Intellectuals and the Spanish Civil War* (New York: Weybright and Talley, 1968). All these books are heavily influenced by American New Critical assumptions and thus concentrate on evaluating the achievements of individual poets who wrote about the Spanish Civil War. Given when the books were written, that bias was inevitable. Nonetheless, it slights the collective and interactive nature of the literature and, in many cases, misses possibilities for valuing particular poems in that light.
8. Stephen Hart, "Some Notes on the Conventions of Spanish Civil War Poetry: The *Romance*," in *Leeds Papers on Lorca and Spanish Civil War Verse,* ed. Margaret A. Rees (Leeds: Trinity and All Saints College, 1988), 109–27.
9. Kenneth Rexroth, *Between Two Wars* (Athens, Ohio: Labyrinth Editions, 1982), n.p.; Kenneth Rexroth, "Requiem for the Spanish Dead" and "Autumn in California," in his *The Collected Shorter Poems* (New York: New Directions, 1967), reprinted herein.
10. For the "Faustian bargain" interpretation, see Mark Naison, "Remaking America:

Communists and Liberals in the Popular Front," in *New Studies in the Politics and Culture of U.S. Communism,* ed. Michael E. Brown (New York: Monthly Review Press, 1993), 45–73.

11. Manuel Altolaguirre, *Las islas invitadas,* Nueva Edición Aumentada (Madrid: Manuel Altolaguirre, July 1936).

12. For an interesting and detailed reading, see Jorg Thunecke, "Jack Lindsay's Mass Declamation *On Guard for Spain* (1937) and the Speech Chorus tradition of the Workers' Theatre Movement (1926–1936)," in *German and International Perspectives on the Spanish Civil War: The Aesthetics of Partisanship,* ed. Luis Costa, Richard Critchfield, Richard Golsan, and Wulf Koepke (Columbia, S.C.: Camden House, 1992), 199–222.

13. The unpublished manuscript of the shortened manuscript of "On Guard for Spain!" is in the author's collection.

14. Jack Lindsay, letter to Valentine Cunningham, quoted in *The Penguin Book of Spanish Civil War Verse,* ed. Cunningham, 45. "On Guard for Spain!" was published in a separate pamphlet and in *New Left Review* in March 1937. Cunningham's notes (478–79) include an additional unpublished passage added for some performances, though not in the typed version in my possession.

15. R. Vernon Beste, "On Mass Declamations," *Our Time* 11 (May 1943), quoted in *The Penguin Book of Spanish Civil War Verse,* ed. Cunningham, 45–46.

16. For Lutz's complete letter, see Cary Nelson and Jefferson Hendricks, ed., *Madrid 1937: Letters of the Abraham Lincoln Brigade from the Spanish Civil War* (New York: Routledge, 1996), 116–17. The original is at the Rare Books and Special Collections Library of the University of Illinois Library.

17. M. J. Benardete and Rolfe Humphries, eds., *And Spain Sings: Fifty Loyalist Ballads Adapted by American Poets* (New York: Vanguard, 1937); Stephen Spender and John Lehman, eds., *Poems for Spain* (London: Hogarth, 1939).

18. Peter Monteath, *Writing the Good Fight: Political Commitment in the International Literature of the Spanish Civil War* (Westport, Conn.: Greenwood, 1994), 78.

19. "Mediterranean," reprinted herein, was published in *New Masses* in 1937 and first collected in Rukeyser's *U.S. 1* (New York: Covici, Friede, 1938).

20. Arnold Rampersad, *The Life of Langston Hughes,* vol. 1, *1902–1941—I, Too, Sing America* (New York: Oxford University Press, 1986), 351.

21. As Hughes makes clear in *I Wonder as I Wander* (1956; reprint, New York: Hill and Wang, 1993), it was actually *white* American volunteers who wondered whether the use of dialect "might mistakenly be aiding in perpetuating a stereotype" (378). Hughes defended the poem during the war and stood by it twenty years later. It was one of the few poems he reprinted in *I Wonder as I Wander* (353–54).

22. Langston Hughes, "Addressed to Alabama," *Daily Worker,* January 23, 1938, sec. 2:8.

23. For information on Hughes's interactions with Rolfe in Spain, see Cary Nelson and Jefferson Hendricks, eds., *Edwin Rolfe: A Biographical Essay and Guide to the Rolfe Archive at the University of Illinois at Urbana-Champaign* (Urbana: University of Illinois Press, 1990).

24. Kenneth Rexroth, "Two Poems," in *Salud! Poems, Stories and Sketches of Spain by American Writers,* ed. Alan Calmer (New York: International Publishers, 1938), 28–29. Rexroth's poems are untitled in this version. One of them, from which the quotes are drawn, is reprinted herein as "Requiem for the Spanish Dead." The other, also reprinted herein, is "Autumn in California."

25. Richard Gray, *American Poetry of the Twentieth Century* (New York: Longman, 1990), 170–71.

26. See Alan Filreis's comments on "City of Anguish" in his *Modernism from Right to Left: Wallace Stevens, the Thirties, and Literary Radicalism* (New York: Cambridge University Press, 1994), 42.

27. *El mono azul* was reprinted in 1975 by Kraus, which also reprinted *Hora de España* as part of a series.

28. *Poesia en las trincheras* (Madrid: Publicaciones del Subcomisariado de Agitación, Prensa y Propaganda del Comisariado General de Guerra, 1937). Sixty-three pages long, the paperbound book included an introduction and thirty-three poems.

29. Dolores Ibarruri, *Speeches and Articles: 1936–1938* (Sydney: Modern, 1938), 31.

30. Quoted in Hugh Thomas, *The Spanish Civil War,* rev. and enlg. ed. (New York: Harper, 1977), 475, 481. Valera, a Republican deputy, was undersecretary of communications. He was one of only two undersecretaries left in Madrid. The government as a whole had decided to evacuate on November 6.

31. Norman Rosten, "The March," in *Salud!* ed. Calmer, 31, reprinted herein.

32. Francis Fuentes, "Revolutionary Madrid," trans. Sylvia Townsend Warner, in *The Penguin Book of Spanish Civil War Verse,* ed. Cunningham, 279–80; Manuel Altolaguirre, "Madrid," trans. Stephen Spender, in *New Statesman,* July 9, 1938, 73; José Moreno Villa, "Madrid Front," trans. Stanley Richardson, *New Writing* 1, new series (Autumn 1938): 34–35, reprinted in *The Penguin Book of Spanish Civil War Verse,* ed. Cunningham, 297–99. In citing Spanish wartime romances, I have placed some titles in English to signal poems that were available in English translation during the war. Some American poets, however, also read the poems in Spanish. The titles I mention are only a tiny fraction of the Spanish romances written about Madrid. *Romancero de la defensa de Madrid,* ed. Serge Salaün (Barcelona: Ibérico, 1982), includes 143 poems, and it is far from comprehensive. English translations include Carlos Bauer, *Cries from a Wounded Madrid: Poetry of the Spanish Civil War* (Athens, Ohio: Swallow, 1984); and Michael Rossman, *Winds of the People: The Poetry of the Spanish Civil War* (Berkeley: privately published, 1986).

33. Ernest Mateu, "Als defensors de Madrid," and Adriá Jori, "Record de Madrid," in *Poesias de guerra* (Madrid: Ediciones 5 Regimento, 1937), 91–92, 62–64.

34. Jacques Roumain, "Madrid," trans. Nancy Cunard, *Left Review* 3 (April 1938): 909–10, reprinted in *The Penguin Book of Spanish Civil War Verse,* ed. Cunningham, 164–65; Paul Eluard, "November 1936," first collected in his *Cours naturel* (Paris: Gallimard, 1938), was translated into English in Rosenthal, *Poetry of the Spanish Civil War,* 303–4.

35. Richard Church, "The Madrid Defenders," *New Statesman,* December 5, 1936, 886, reprinted in *The Penguin Book of Spanish Civil War Verse,* ed. Cunningham, 232–33; Elisabeth Cluer, "Analogy in Madrid," *New Statesman,* April 8, 1939, 536, reprinted in *The Penguin Book of Spanish Civil War Verse,* ed. Cunningham, 382.

36. E. Gil Gilbert, "Buenas Dias, Madrid!" and G. Humberto Mata, "Madrid," in *Nuestra España: Homenaje de los poetas y artistas ecuatorianas* (Quito, Ecuador: Editorial Atahuallpa, 1938), 5–9, 26–29.

37. Joy Davidman, "Snow in Madrid," in *Letter to a Comrade* (New Haven, Conn.: Yale University Press, 1938), 40; Langston Hughes, "Madrid—1937," in *Good Morning Revolution: Uncollected Social Protest Writings by Langston Hughes,* ed. Faith Berry (Westport, Conn.: Lawrence Hill, 1973), 104–6; David Wolff (Ben Maddow), "The

Defenses," in *Salud!* ed. Calmer, 14–15, reprinted herein; Norman Rosten, "Invocation," in *Seven Poets in Search of an Answer,* ed. Thomas Yoseloff (New York: Bernard Ackerman, 1944), 100–101; Sol Funaroff, "The Bull in the Olive Field," in his *Exile from a Future Time* (New York: Dynamo, 1943), reprinted herein.

38. Luis de Tapia, "Salud," trans. Isidor Schneider, *International Literature,* no. 10–11 (1937): 191; Rafael Alberti, "Defense of Madrid," trans. Millen Brand, in *And Spain Sings,* ed. Benardete and Humphries, 22–23; W. H. Auden's "Spain" was first published as a pamphlet in 1937.

39. Norman Rosten, "Spanish Sequence," in his *The Fourth Decade and Other Poems* (New York: Farrar and Rinehart, 1943), reprinted herein.

40. Stanley Richardson, "To a Certain Priest," *Spain at War,* no. 3 (June 1938): 112.

41. George Barker, *Elegy on Spain,* section 3 (Manchester, England: Contemporary Bookshop, April 1939), 9; Villa, "Madrid Front," 299; Eluard, "November 1936," 303.

42. Edwin Rolfe, "Poetry," *Partisan Review* 2 (April–May 1935): 32–42.

43. Malcolm Cowley, "While They Waited for Lefty," *Saturday Review,* June 6, 1964, 16–19, 61; Malcolm Cowley, "A Remembrance of the Red Romance," two-part essay, *Esquire,* March 1964, 124, 126–31, and April 1964, 78–81.

44. Sol Funaroff, "What the Thunder Said: A Fire Sermon," in his *The Spider and the Clock* (New York: International Publishers, 1938), 25–32; Richard Wright, "I Am a Red Slogan," in *The World of Richard Wright,* by Michel Fabre (Jackson: University Press of Mississippi, 1985), appendix B.

45. Serge Salaün, "L'expression poétique pendant la guerre d'Espagne," in *Les écrivains et la guerre d'Espagne,* ed. Marc Hanrez (Paris: Pantheon, 1975), 105–13.

46. Ibarruri, *Speeches and Articles,* 7–21.

47. Nicolás Guillén, "Spain," trans. Lloyd Mallan, in *The Heart of Spain,* ed. Alvah Bessie (New York: Veterans of the Abraham Lincoln Brigade, 1952), 148.

48. Miguel Hernández, "Winds of the People," trans. A. L. Lloyd, in *Poems for Spain,* ed. Spender and Lehman, 39.

49. José Herrera Petere, "El dia que no vendre," trans. Sylvia Townsend Warner, in *The Penguin Book of Spanish Civil War Verse,* ed. Cunningham, 291–92.

50. Felix V. Ramos, "No pasaran!" in *Poesias de guerra,* 24.

51. Apelles Mestres, "No passareu!" in ibid., 150–51.

52. Fuentes, "Revolutionary Madrid," 279–80.

53. Barker, *Elegy on Spain,* section 1, 3.

54. A. S. Knowland, "Guernica," *Spain at War,* no. 8 (November 1938): 307; Jack Lindsay, "On Guard for Spain!" *Left Review,* 3 (March 1937): 79–86.

55. W. H. Auden, "Epitaph on a Tyrant," *New Statesman,* January 21, 1939, 81.

56. Barker, *Elegy on Spain,* opening stanza, 1.

57. Roumain, "Madrid," 164.

58. Herbert Read, "Bombing Casualties in Spain," in *Poems for Spain,* ed. Spender and Lehman, 41.

59. Somhairle Macalastair, "Ballyseedy Befriends Badajoz," *Left Review* 2 (December 1936): 817.

60. Edgell Rickword, "To the Wife of Any Non-Intervention Statesman," *Left Review* 3 (March 1938): 835.

61. Valentine Cunningham's *British Writers of the Thirties* (New York: Oxford University Press, 1989) gathers a broad sample of blood images in Spanish Civil War poetry. See his last two chapters, "Spanish Front" and "Too Innocent a Voyage," for his

often challenging comments on the literature and politics of commitment. The discussion of blood imagery is on 425–27.

62. Church, "The Madrid Defenders," 233.
63. Joy Davidman, ed. *War Poems of the United Nations* (New York: Dial, 1943); Yoseloff, ed., *Seven Poets in Search of an Answer*.
64. Susan Schweik, *A Gulf So Deeply Cut: American Women Poets and the Second World War* (Madison: University of Wisconsin Press, 1991), 151–52.
65. See James E. B. Breslin's summary of the belatedness of the contemporary in the opening chapter of his *From Modern to Contemporary: American Poetry, 1945–1965* (Chicago: University of Chicago Press, 1984).
66. Edwin Rolfe, "Elegia," in his *Collected Poems,* ed. Nelson and Hendricks, reprinted herein; Edwin Rolfe, "City of Anguish," in ibid., reprinted herein; Pablo Neruda, "Spain within My Heart," trans. Lloyd Mallan, in *War Poems of the United Nations,* ed. Davidman, 240; Pablo Neruda, "Arrival in Madrid of the International Brigade," in *Poetry of the Spanish Civil War,* by Rosenthal, 297.
67. Charles Donnelly, "Poem," *Ireland Today* 2 (January 1937): 48–49.
68. Alvah Bessie, "November 7, 1950," in "The *Free* World and Other Captive Verse."
69. There is an excellent bibliography of elegies to García Lorca in Francesca Colecchia, ed., *García Lorca: A Selectively Annotated Bibliography of Criticism* (New York: Garland, 1979).
70. Antonio Machado, "The Crime Took Place at Granada," trans. Rolfe Humphries, in *And Spain Sings,* ed. Benardete and Humphries, 62–63; Kenneth Rexroth, "Blood and Sand," in his *The Collected Shorter Poems* (New York: New Directions, 1967), reprinted herein; Edwin Rolfe, "A Federico García Lorca," in his *Collected Poems,* ed. Nelson and Hendricks, reprinted herein; Machado, "The Crime Took Place at Granada," 62; Castro Z, "Responsory for García Lorca," in *Anthology of Contemporary Latin-American Poetry,* ed. Dudley Fitts (Norfolk, Conn.: New Directions, 1942), 527; Geoffry Parsons, "Lorca," in *The Penguin Book of Spanish Civil War Verse,* ed. Cunningham, 207; Castro Z, "Responsory for Garcia Lorca," 527; Rolfe, "A Federico García Lorca"; Emilio Prados, "The Arrival (To Federico García Lorca)," trans. Edna St. Vincent Millay, in *And Spain Sings,* ed. Benardete and Humphries, 61; Nicolás Guillén, "Spain (A Poem in Four Anguishes and One Hope)," trans. Lloyd Mallan, in *War Poems of the United Nations,* ed. Davidman, 254–55; Leopoldo Urrutia, "Lorca," trans. Sylvia Townsend Warner, in *Poems for Spain,* ed. Spender and Lehman, 107–8; Jacob Bronowski "The Death of García Lorca," in *Poems for Spain,* ed. Spender and Lehman, 105; Machado, "The Crime Took Place at Granada," 62; Norman Rosten, "To Federico García Lorca," in *Seven Poets in Search of an Answer,* ed. Yoseloff, 101, 102; Pablo Neruda, "I Explain a Few Things," in his *Residence on Earth,* trans. Donald D. Walsh (New York: New Directions, 1973), 257; Luis Cardoza y Aragon, "Ballad of Federico García Lorca," in *Anthology of Contemporary Latin-American Poetry,* ed. Fitts, 531; Castro Z, "Responsory for Garcia Lorca," 527; Philip Levine, "The Search for Lorca's Shadow," in his *The Mercy: Poems* (New York: Alfred A. Knopf, 1999), reprinted herein; Hugh MacDiarmid, "Lorca," in his *Collected Poems* (New York: Macmillan, 1962), 182; Aaron Kramer, "García Lorca," in his *'Til the Grass Is Ripe for Dancing* (New York: Harbinger House, 1943), reprinted herein; Machado, "The Crime Took Place at Granada," 63; Sol Funaroff, "To Federico García Lorca," in his *Exile from a Future Time,* 46.
71. Ian Gibson, *Federico García Lorca: A Life* (New York: Pantheon Books, 1989), 428–34.

72. One undated edition of García Lorca's *Romancero gitano* makes the connection explicit. Issued by Editorial Patria, the jacket copy may be translated as follows: "In 1936, the distinguished Andalusian poet Federico García Lorca was felled by rifle fire. The cause? His *romances* about the Civil Guard—which form part of *Romancero Gitano*—were not to the liking of certain enemies of culture, and the order was given. . . ."

73. Leslie Stainton, *Lorca: A Dream of Life* (New York: Farrar, Straus and Giroux, 1999), 459.

74. Two or three copies of the portfolio of paintings and illuminated holograph manuscripts were made in Spain during the war. One was given to the Duchess of Atholl, whose work included the widely read pro-Republican *Searchlight on Spain*. One copy is now in the Rare Books and Special Collections Library at the University of Illinois at Urbana-Champaign.

75. Translated from Manuel Altolaguirre's one-page introduction to *Poemas escogidos de Federico García Lorca* (Havana, 1939). It is a miniature book sixty pages in length, the second in a series of such volumes Altolaguirre published in Havana from 1939 through the early 1940s: José Marti, *Versos sencilios;* García Lorca's *Poemas escogidos;* Jorge Manrique, *Coplas;* Miguel Hernández, *Sino sangriento y otros poemas;* Manuel Altolaguirre, *Nube temporal;* Antonio Machado, *La tierra de Alvar González;* José de Espronceda, *Canto a Teresa;* José Marti, *Versos libres;* Concha Méndez, *Lluvias enlazadas;* and Alejandro Pushkin, *"El convidado de Piedra," y Festin durante la peste.*

76. Thomas Merton, "In Memory of the Spanish Poet Federico García Lorca," in *The Collected Poems of Thomas Merton* (New York: New Dimensions, 1977), reprinted herein; Martha Millet, "Song for Federico García Lorca," in *Seven Poets in Search of an Answer,* ed. Yoseloff, 87; Eldon Grier, "In Memory of García Lorca," in *Poesía anglo-norteamericana de la Guerra Civil española,* ed. Alvarez Rodríguez and López Ortega, 92.

77. Philip Levine, "My Mother with Purse the Summer They Murdered the Spanish Poet," in his *The Simple Truth* (New York: Alfred A. Knopf, 1994), reprinted herein.

78. Levine, "The Search for Lorca's Shadow," reprinted herein.

79. Bob Kaufman, "The Night That Lorca Comes," in his *Cranial Guitar: Selected Poems* (Minneapolis: Coffee House Press, 1996), 128; "The Poet," in ibid., 129; "The Ancient Rain," in ibid., 133. These three poems were first collected in Kaufman's *The Ancient Rain* (New York: New Directions, 1981).

80. Eduardo Castro, "Muerto, pero no se murió solo," in his *Muerte en Granada: La tragedia de Federico García Lorca* (Madrid: Akal, 1975), 40–41.

81. Genevieve Taggard, "To the Veterans of the Abraham Lincoln Brigade," *Volunteer for Liberty,* February 1941, reprinted herein.

82. Don Gordon, "Spain," in *Heart of Spain,* ed. Bessie, reprinted herein.

83. All in this volume.

84. Pablo Neruda, *Memoirs,* trans. Hardie St. Martin (New York: Farrar, Straus and Giroux, 1977), 125–26.

85. Rolfe, "A Federico García Lorca," in *Collected Poems,* ed. Nelson and Hendricks, 50–51.

86. Walter Snow, "Spain—The Modern Phoenix," in his *The Glory and the Shame* (Coventry, Conn.: Pequot, 1973), reprinted herein.

87. Muriel Rukeyser, "Neruda, the Wine," in her *The Gates* (New York: McGraw-Hill, 1976), reprinted herein; Aaron Kramer, "Smiles and Blood," in his *The Alarm Clock*

(New York: Young Communist League, 1938), reprinted herein; Aaron Kramer, "Barcelona: The Last Night," in his *Indigo and Other Poems* (New York: Cornwall Books, 1991), reprinted herein; Pablo Neruda, "How Spain Was," in *Selected Poems of Pablo Neruda,* trans. Ben Belitt (New York: Grove, 1961), 115. In Rukeyser's "Neruda, the Wine" it is Neruda "in the hall of students / Speaking at last of Spain," who occasions Rukeyser's characterization of the war's lasting impact, but she is clearly speaking not only for both of them but also for this "link deep in our peoples."

88. Norman Rosten, "A Scenario for Peace in Three Acts," in his *The Fourth Decade and Other Poems* (New York: Farrar and Rinehart, 1943), reprinted in Norman Rosten, *Selected Poems* (New York: George Braziller, 1979), 60–61.

89. Randall Jarrell, "A Poem for Someone Killed in Spain," in his *The Complete Poems* (New York: Farrar, Straus, and Giroux, 1969), reprinted herein.

90. Juan Rejano, [untitled], in *Steve Nelson: A Tribute* (New York: Provisional Committee to Free Steve Nelson, 1953), 11.

91. Barbara Guest, "All Elegies Are Black and White," in her *Poems: The Location of Things* (Garden City, N.Y.: Doubleday, 1962), reprinted herein.

92. Martín Espada, "The Carpenter Swam to Spain," *Volunteer for Liberty,* October 1999, reprinted herein; Ai, "They Shall Not Pass," in her *Sin* (New York: Houghton Mifflin, 1986), reprinted herein.

93. Robinson Jeffers, "Sinverguenza," in *The Collected Poetry of Robinson Jeffers,* vol. 3, ed. Tim Hunt (Stanford, Calif.: Stanford University Press, 2000), reprinted herein.

94. Robert Hass, "Rusia en 1931," in his *Human Wishes* (New York: Ecco, 1989), reprinted herein.

95. Kramer, "Smiles and Blood," herein; James Wright, "Eisenhower's Visit to Franco, 1959," in his *Above the River: The Complete Poems* (Middleton, Conn.: University Press of New England, 1990), reprinted herein; Lawrence Ferlinghetti, "Into Darkness, in Granada," in his *Landscapes of Living and Dying* (New York: New Directions, 1979), reprinted herein; Carolyn Kizer, "The Valley of the Fallen" and "Ingathering," in her *Harping On: Poems, 1985–1995* (Port Townsend, Wash.: Copper Canyon, 1996), reprinted herein.

Women of Spain

Have you seen on the barricades the women of Spain?
They shoulder rifles, shoot with their men,
Calculate distance, take aim, report,
Trigger fingers untrembling and alert.

From sacks of sand, sticks of chairs,
Chunks of wood, posts of beds, iron scraps
They erect barricades, packed close and firm;
Stones torn from mother grip of cobbled streets
To fortify the blast—stones hard and smooth
That have known the passionless tread of foot—
Now they shall know impassioned days.

The structures fall, brick crashes, walls collapse.
The sky goes black, smoke pours and dims the sun.
Empty stand the kitchens.
The women of Spain speak from the front lines.

Their guns for the cause of the people
Drive bullets, scatter foe,
Fire volleys of mass anger into the black heart of reaction.

They are fighting for their homes
And the free stride of their men
And the bright future of their laughing children.

Empty are the kitchens.
The women of Spain are on the barricades.

¡Salud!

O peasant-Cids with sickles for your swords!—
Davids with hand-grenades for smooth round stones!
You now once more against invading hordes
undam your blood, heap bulwarks of your bones!
Kin to conquistadors who sadly gave
a new world, wrested from the tropic main,
to church and king, today you fight to save
a greater world, O valiant folk of Spain!

Stern Christs in overalls!—the Bourbon white
of leprosy, the Jesuits' gangrened black,
still rule the temples where the stake and rack
long served as altars to the Golden Lords
of crown and cope. Futile the whip of cords—
only avails the scourge of dynamite!

Autumn 1936

The Men That Are Falling

God and all angels sing the world to sleep,
Now that the moon is rising in the heat

And crickets are loud again in the grass. The moon
Burns in the mind on lost remembrances.

He lies down and the night wind blows upon him here.
The bells grow longer. This is not sleep. This is desire.

Ah! Yes, desire . . . this leaning on his bed,
This leaning on his elbows on his bed,

Staring, at midnight, at the pillow that is black
In the catastrophic room . . . beyond despair,

Like an intenser instinct. What is it he desires?
But this he cannot know, the man that thinks,

Yet life itself, the fulfillment of desire
In the grinding ric-rac, staring steadily

At a head upon the pillow in the dark,
More than sudarium, speaking the speech

Of absolutes, bodiless, a head
Thick-lipped from riot and rebellious cries,

The head of one of the men that are falling, placed
Upon the pillow to repose and speak,

Speak and say the immaculate syllables
That he spoke only by doing what he did.

God and all angels, this was his desire,
Whose head lies blurring here, for this he died.

Taste of the blood upon his martyred lips.
O pensioners, O demagogues and pay-men!

This death was his belief though death is a stone.
This man loved earth, not heaven, enough to die.

The night wind blows upon the dreamer, bent
Over words that are life's voluble utterance.

Mediterranean

On the evening of July 25, 1936, five days after the outbreak of
the Spanish Civil War, Americans with the Anti-Fascist Olympic
Games were evacuated from Barcelona at the order of the
Catalonian Government. In a small Spanish boat, the Ciudad di
Ibiza, *which the Belgians had chartered, they and a group of five*
hundred, including the Hungarian and Belgian teams as well as
the American, sailed overnight to Sète, the first port in France.
The only men who remained were those who had volunteered in
the Loyalist forces: the core of the future International Column.

I

At the end of July, exile. We watched the gangplank go
cutting the boat away, indicating: sea.
Barcelona, the sun, the fire-bright harbor, war.
Five days.
      Here at the rail, foreign and refugee,
we saw the city, remembered that zero of attack,
alarm in the groves, snares through the olive hills,
rebel defeat: leaders, two regiments,
broadcasts of victory, tango, surrender.
The truckride to the city, barricades,
bricks pried at corners, rifle-shot in street,
car-burning, bombs, blank warnings, fists up, guns
busy sniping, the town walls, towers of smoke.
And order making, committees taking charge,
foreigners commanded out by boat.

I saw the city, sunwhite flew on glass,
trucewhite from window, the personal lighting found
eyes on the dock, sunset-lit faces of singers,
eyes, goodbye into exile. Saw where Columbus rides
black-pillared : discovery, turn back, explore
a new found Spain, coast-province, city-harbor.
Saw our parades ended, the last marchers on board listed by nation.

I saw first of the faces going home into war
the brave man Otto Boch, the German exile, knowing
he quieted tourists during machine gun battle,
he kept his life straight as a single issue—
left at that dock we left, his gazing Breughel face,
square forehead and eyes, strong square breast fading,
the narrow runner's hips diminishing dark.
I see this man, dock, war, a latent image.
The boat *Ciudad di Ibiza,* built for 200,
loaded with 500, manned by loyal sailors,
chartered by Belgians when consulates were helpless,
through a garden of gunboats, margin of the port,
entered: Mediterranean.

II

Frontier of Europe, the tideless sea, a field of power
touching desirable coasts, rocking in time conquests,
fertile, the moving water maintains its boundaries
layer on layer, Troy—seven civilized worlds:
Egypt, Greece, Rome, jewel Jerusalem,
giant feudal Spain, giant England, this last war.

The boat pulled into evening, underglaze blue
flared instant fire, blackened towards Africa.
Over the city alternate lights occurred;
                                        and pale.
in the pale sky emerging stars.
No city now, a besieged line of lights
masking the darkness where the country lay.
But we knew guns
bright through mimosa
singe of powder
and reconnoitering plane
flying anonymous
scanning the Pyrenees
black now above the Catalonian Sea.
Boat of escape, dark on the water, hastening, safe,
holding non-combatants, the athlete, the child,
the printer, the boy from Antwerp, the black boxer,
lawyer and communist.

The Games had not been held.
A week of Games, theatre and festival;
world anti-fascist week. Pistol starts race.
Machine gun marks the war. Answered unarmed,
charged the Embarcadero, met those guns.
And charging through the province, joined that army.
Boys from the hills, the unmatched guns,
the clumsy armored cars.
Drilled in the bullring. Radio cries:
To Saragossa! And this boat.

Escape, dark on the water, an overloaded ship.
Crowded the deck. Spoke little. Down to dinner.
Quiet on the sea: no guns.
The printer said, In Paris there is time,
but where's its place now; where is poetry?

This is the sea of war; the first frontier
blank on the maps, blank sea; Minoan boats
maybe achieved this shore;
mountains whose slope divides
one race, old insurrections, Narbo, now
moves at the colored beach
destroyer wardog. "Do not burn the church,
compañeros, it is beautiful. Besides,
it brings tourists." They smashed only the image
madness and persecution.
Exterminating wish; they forced the door,
lifted the rifle, broke the garden window,
removed only the drawings : cross and wrath.
Whenever we think of these, the poem is,
that week, the beginning, exile
remembered in continual poetry.

Voyage and exile, a midnight cold return,
dark to our left mountains begin the sky.
There, pointed the Belgian, I heard a pulse of war,
sharp guns while I ate grapes in the Pyrenees.
Alone, walking to Spain, the five o'clock of war.
In those cliffs run the sashed and sandalled men,
capture the car, arrest the priest, kill captain,
fight our war.

The poem is the fact, memory fails
under and seething lifts and will not pass.

Here is home-country, who fights our war.
Street-meeting speaker to us:
                          ". . . came for Games,
            you stay for victory; foreign? your job is:
            go tell your countries what you saw in Spain."
The dark unguarded army left all night.
M. de Paîche said, "We can learn from Spain."
The face on the dock that turned to find the war.

III

Seething, and falling back, a sea of stars,
Black marked with virile silver. Peace all night,
over that land, planes
death-lists   a frantic bandage
the rubber tires burning   monuments
sandbag, overturned wagon, barricade
girl's hand with gun   food failing, water failing
the epidemic threat
the date in a diary   a blank page opposite
no entry—
however, met
the visible enemy heroes: madness, infatuation
the cache in the crypt, the breadline shelled,
the yachtclub arsenal, the foreign cheque.
History racing from an assumed name, peace,
a time used to perfect weapons.

If we had not seen fighting,
if we had not looked there
            the plane flew low
            the plastic ripped by shots
            the peasant's house
if we had stayed in our world
between the table and the desk
between the town and the suburb
slowly disintegration
male and female

If we had lived in our city
sixty years might not prove
    the power this week
    the overthrown past
    tourist and refugee
Emeric in the bow speaking his life
and the night on this ship
the night over Spain
quick recognition
male and female

And the war in peace, the war in war, the peace,
the faces on the dock
the faces in those hills.

IV

Near the end now, morning. Sleepers cover the decks,
cabins full, corridors full of sleep. But the light
vitreous, crosses water; analyzed darkness,
crosshatched in silver, passes up the shore,
touching limestone massif, deserted tableland,
bends with the down-warp of the coastal plain.

The colored sun stands on the route to Spain,
builds on the waves a series of mirrors
and on the scorched land rises hot.
Coasts change their names as the boat goes to
France, Costa Brava softens to Côte Vermeil,
Spain's a horizon ghost behind the shapeless sea.

Blue praising black, a wind above the waves
moves pursuing a jewel, this hieroglyph
boat passing under the sun to lose it on the
attractive sea, habitable and kind.
A barber sun, razing three races, met
from the north with a neurotic eagerness.

They rush to solar attraction; local daybreak finds
them on the red earth of the colored cliffs; the little islands
tempt worshippers, gulf-purple, pointed bay.
We crowd the deck,
welcome the islands with a sense of loss.

V

The wheel in the water, green, behind my head.
Turns with its light-spokes. Deep. And the drowning eyes
find under the water figures near
in their true picture, moving true,
the picture of that war enlarging clarified
as the boat perseveres away, always enlarging,
becoming clear.

Boat of escape, your water-photograph.
I see this man, dock, war, a latent image.
And at my back speaking the black boxer,
telling his education : porter, fighter, no school,
no travel but this, trade-union sent a team.
I saw Europe break apart
and artifice or martyr's will
cannot anneal this war, nor make
the loud triumphant future start
shouting from its tragic heart.

Deep in the water Spanish shadows turn,
assume their brightness past a cruel lens,
quick vision of loss. The pastoral lighting takes
the boat, deck, passengers, the pumice cliffs,
the winedark sweatshirt at my shoulder.
Cover away the fighting cities
but still your death-afflicted eyes
must hold the print of flowering guns,
bombs whose insanity craves size,
the lethal breath, the iron prize.

The clouds upon the water-barrier pass,
the boat may turn to land; the shapes endure,
rise up into our eyes, to bind
us back; an accident of time
set it upon us, exile burns it in.
Once the fanatic image shown,
enemy to enemy,
past and historic peace wear thin;
we see Europe break like stone,
hypocrite sovereignties go down
before this war the age must win.

VI

The sea produced that town : Sète, which the boat turns to,
at peace. Its breakwater, casino, vermouth factory, beach.
They searched us for weapons. No currency went out.
The sign of war had been search for cameras,
pesetas and photographs go back to Spain,
the money for the army. Otto is fighting now, the lawyer said.
No highlight hero. Love's not a trick of light.

But. The town lay outside, peace, France.
And in the harbor the Russian boat *Schachter;*
sharp paint-smell, the bruise-colored shadow swung,
sailors with fists up, greeting us, asking news,
making the harbor real.
                              Barcelona.
Slow-motion splash. Anchor. Small from the beach
the boy paddles to meet us, legs hidden in canoe,
curve of his blade that drips.
Now gangplank falls to deck.
          Barcelona
everywhere, Spain everywhere, the cry of Planes for Spain.
The picture at our eyes, past memory, poem,
to carry and spread and daily justify.
The single issue, the live man standing tall,
on the hill, the dock, the city, all the war.
Exile and refugee, we land, we take
nothing negotiable out of the new world;
we believe, we remember, we saw.
Mediterranean gave
image and peace, tideless for memory.

For that beginning
make of us each
a continent and inner sea
Atlantis buried outside
to be won.

Death by Water

On May 30, 1937, the small Spanish coastal steamship Ciudad
de Barcelona *was torpedoed and sunk off the coast of Malgrat
by a submarine which the Non-Intervention Committee preferred
to designate as "of unknown nationality." More than a hundred
volunteers, twelve of them Americans, perished.*

Nearing land, we heard the cry of gulls and
saw their shadows in sunlight on the topmost deck,
or coasting unconcerned on each wavecrest, they rested
after their scavenging, scudding the ship's length.

And we thought of the albatross—an old man going crazy,
his world an immenseness of water, none of it to drink;
and the vultures descending on an Ethiopian plain:
all of us were the living corpse, powerless, bleeding.

And suddenly the shock. We felt the boat shiver.
I turned to Oliver, saw his eyes widen,
stare past the high rails, waiting, waiting . . .
Others stumbled past us. And suddenly the explosion.

Men in twenty languages cried out to comrades
as the blast tore the ship, and the water, like lava,
plunged through the hull, crushing metal and flesh before it,
splintering cabins, the sleepers caught unconscious.

Belted, we searched for companions but lost them
in turmoil of faces; swept toward the lifeboats
and saw it was useless. Too many were crowding them.
Oliver dived. I followed him, praying.

In the water the sea-swell hid for a moment
Oliver swimming, strongly, away from me.
Then his voice, calmly: "Here, keep his head above."
We helped save a drowning man, kept him afloat until

dories approached. Looking backward, we saw
the prow high in air, and Carlos, unconcerned,
throwing fresh belts to the tiring swimmers.
Steam, flame crept toward him, but he remained absorbed . . .

2

On shore, later, a hundred of us gone,
we are too weak to weep for them, to listen to
consoling words. We are too tired
to return the grave smiles of the rescuing people.
Too drained. Sorrow can never be the word.

But beyond the numbness the vivid faces
of comrades burn in our brains: their songs
in quiet French villages, their American laughter
tug at responding muscles in our lips,
shout against ears that have heard their voices living.

Fingers, convulsive, form fists. Teeth
grate now, audibly. We stifle curses,
thought but unuttered. While many grieve,
their hands reach outward, fingers extended—
the image automatic—ready for rifles

until night brings us sleep, and dreams
of violent death by drowning, dreams
of journey, slow advances through vineyards,
seeking cover in wheatfields, finding always
the fascist face behind the olive tree.

August 1937
Madrid

Elegy for Our Dead

There is a place where, wisdom won, right recorded,
men move beautifully, striding across fields
whose wheat, wind-marshalled, wanders unguarded
in unprotected places; where earth, revived, folds
all growing things closely to itself: the groves
of bursting olives, the vineyards ripe and heavy with
glowing grapes, the oranges like million suns; and graves
where lie, nurturing all these fields, my friends in death.

With them, deep in coolness, are memories of France and
the exact fields of Belgium, midnight marches in snows—
the single-file caravan high in the Pyrenees: the land
of Spain unfolded before them, dazzling the young Balboas.
This earth is enriched with Atlantic salt, spraying
the live, squinting eyelids, even now, of companions—
with towns of America, towers and mills, sun playing
always, in stone streets, wide fields—all men's dominions.

Honor for them in this lies: that theirs is no special
strange plot of alien earth. Men of all lands here
lie side by side, at peace now after the crucial
torture of combat, bullet and bayonet gone, fear
conquered forever. Yes, knowing it well, they were willing
despite it to clothe their vision with flesh. And their rewards,
not sought for self, live in new faces, smiling,
remembering what they did here. Deeds were their last words.

September 20, 1937
Madrid

City of Anguish

For Milton Wolff

At midnight they roused us. In the distance we heard
verberations of thunder. "To the cellar," they ordered.
"It's safest under the stairway." Pointing,
a veteran led us. The children, whimpering,
followed the silent women who would never
sing again strolling in the *Paseo* on Sunday evenings.
In the candle-light their faces were granite.

"Artillery," muttered Enrico, cursing.
Together we turned at the lowest stair.
"Come on," he said. "It's better on the rooftop.
More fireworks, better view." Slowly we ascended
past the stalled lift, felt through the roof door,
squinted in moonless darkness.

We counted the flashes, divided the horizon,
90 degrees for Enrico, 90 for me.
"Four?" "No, five!" We spotted the big guns when
the sounds came crashing, split-seconds after light.
Felt the slight earthquake tremor when shells fell
square on the Gran Via; heard high above our heads
the masculine shriek of the shell descending—
the single sharp rifle-crack, the inevitable dogs
barking, angry, roused from midsummer sleep.
The lulls grew fewer: soon talking subsided
as the cannonade quickened. Each flash in darkness
created horizon, outlined huge buildings.
Off a few blocks to the north, the *Telefónica*
reared its massive shoulders, its great symbol profile
in dignity, like the statue of Moses pointing,
agèd but ageless, to the promised Land.

2

Deafening now, the sky is aflame with
unnatural lightning. The ear—
like the scout's on patrol—gauges each explosion.
The mind—neither ear nor eye is aware of it—
calculates destruction, paints the dark pictures
of beams fallen, ribs crushed beneath them; beds
blown with their innocent sleepers to agonized
death.
            And the great gaping craters in streets
yawn, hypnotic to the terrified madman,
sane a mere hour ago.
                     The headless body
stands strangely, totters for a second, falls.
The girl speeds screaming through wreckage; her
            hair is
wilder than torture.
                     The solitary foot,
deep-arched, is perfect on the cobbles, naked,
strong, ridged with strong veins, upright, complete . . .

The city weeps. The city shudders, weeping.

The city weeps: for the moment is silent—
the pause in the idiot's symphony, prolonged
beyond the awaited crashing of cymbals, but
the hands are in mid-air, the instruments gleaming:
the swastika'd baton falls! and the clatter of
thunder begins again.
                     Enrico beckons me.
Fires there. Where? Toward the *Casa de Campo.*
And closer. There. The *Puerta del Sol* exudes
submarine glow in the darkness, alive with
strange twisting shapes, skyfish of stars,
fireworks of death, mangled lives, silent lips.
In thousands of beds now the muscles of men are
aroused, flexed for springing, quivering, tense,
that moments ago were relaxed, asleep.

3

It is too late for sleep now.
Few hours are left before dawn. We wait for

the sun's coming . . . And it rises, sulphurous
through smoke. It is too late for sleep.

The city weeps. The city wakens, weeping.

And the Madrileños rise from wreckage, emerge
from shattered doorways . . .
                            But always the wanderer,
the old woman searching, digging among debris.
In the morning light her crazed face is granite.

And the beggar sings among the ruins:

>   All night, all night
>   flared in my city the bright
>   cruel explosion of bombs.
>   All night, all night,
>   there, where the soil and stone
>   spilled like brains from the sandbag's head,
>   the bodiless head lay staring;
>   while the anti-aircraft barked,
>   barked at the droning plane,
>   and the dogs of war, awakened,
>   howled at the hidden moon.
>   And a star fell, omen of ill,
>   and a man fell, lifeless,
>   and my wife fell, childless,
>   and, friendless, my friend.
>   And I stumbled away from them, crying
>   from eyeless lids, blinded.
>   Trees became torches
>   lighting the avenues
>   where lovers huddled in terror
>   who would be lovers no longer.
>
>   All night, all night
>   flared in my city the bright
>   cruel explosion of hope—
>   all night
>   all night . . .

4

Come for a joyride in Madrid: the August morning
is cleared of smoke and cloud now; the journalists
dip their hard bread in the *Florida* coffee,
no longer distasteful after sour waking.
Listen to Ryan, fresh from the lines, talking
>   (Behind you the memory of bombs beats
>   the blood in the brain's vessels—the dream broken,
>   sleep pounded to bits by the unending roar of
>   shells in air, the silvery bombs descending,
>   rabid spit of machine guns and the carnival flare
>   of fire in the sky):
>   "Why is it, why?
when I'm here in the trenches, half-sunk in mud,
blanket drenched, hungry, I dream of Dublin,
of home, of the girls? But give me a safe spot,
clean linen, bed and all, sleep becomes nightmare
of shrapnel hurtling, bombs falling, the screaming of bullets,
their thud on the brain's parapet. Why? Why?"

Exit the hotel. The morning constitutional.
Stroll down the avenues. Did Alfonso's car
detour past barricades? Did broken mains splatter him?
Here's the bellyless building; four walls, no guts.
But the biggest disaster's the wrecking of power:
thirty-six hours and no power: electric
sources are severed. The printer is frantic:
how print the leaflet, the poster, or set the type for the bulletin?
>   After his food
a soldier needs cigarettes, something to read,
something to think about: words to pull
the war-weary brain back to life from forgetfulness:
spirited words, the gestures of Dolores,
majestic Pasionaria speaking—
mother to men, mother of revolutions,
winner of battles, comforter of defenders;
her figure magnificent as any monument
constructed for heroes; her voice a symphony,
consoling, urging, declaiming in prophecy,
her forehead the wide plateaus of her country,
her eyes constant witness of her words' truth.

5

Needless to catalogue heroes. No man
weighted with rifle, digging with nails in earth,
quickens at the name. Hero's a word for
peacetime. Battle
knows only three realities: enemy, rifle, life.

No man knows war or its meaning who has not
stumbled from tree to tree, desperate for cover,
or dug his face deep in earth, felt the ground pulse with
the ear-breaking fall of death. No man knows war
who never has crouched in his foxhole, hearing
the bullets an inch from his head, nor the zoom of
planes like a Ferris wheel strafing the trenches . . .

War is your comrade struck dead beside you,
his shared cigarette still alive in your lips.

Madrid 1937

Song of Spain

Come now, all you who are singers,
And sing me the song of Spain.
Sing it very simply that I might understand.

What is the song of Spain?

Flamenco is the song of Spain:
Gypsies, guitars, dancing
Death and love and heartbreak
To a heel tap and a swirl of fingers
On three strings.
Flamenco is the song of Spain.

I do not understand.

Toros are the song of Spain:
The bellowing bull, the red cape,
A sword thrust, a horn tip,
The torn suit of satin and gold,
Blood on the sand
Is the song of Spain.

I do not understand.

Pintura is the song of Spain:
Goya, Velasquez, Murillo,
Splash of color on canvass,
Whirl of cherub-faces.
La Maja Desnuda's
The song of Spain.

What's that?

Don Quixote! España!
Aquel rincon de la Mancha de

Cuyo nombre no quiero acordarme. . . .
That's the song of Spain.
You wouldn't kid me, would you?
A bombing plane's
The song of Spain.
Bullets like rain's
The song of Spain.
Poison gas is Spain.
A knife in the back
And its terror and pain is Spain.

Toros, flamenco, paintings, books—Not Spain.
The people are Spain:
The people beneath that bombing plane
With its wings of gold for which I pay—
I, a worker, letting my labor pile
Up millions for bombs to kill a child—
I bought those bombs for Spain!
Workers made those bombs for a Fascist Spain!
Will I make them again, and yet again?
      Storm clouds move fast,
      Our sky is gray.
      The white devils of the terror
      Await their day
When bombs'll fall not only on Spain—
      But on me and you!
      Workers, make no bombs again!
      Workers, mine no gold again!
      Workers, lift no hand again
      To build up profits for the rape of Spain!
      Workers, see yourselves as Spain!
      Workers, know that we too can cry.
      Lift arms in vain, run, hide, die:
        Too late!
        The bombing plane!
      Workers, make no bombs again
      Except that they be made for us
        To hold and guard
      Lest some Franco steal into our backyard
Under the guise of a patriot
Waving a flag and mouthing rot
And dropping bombs from a Christian steeple
      On the people.

I made those bombs for Spain.
I must not do it again.
I made those bombing planes.
I must not do it again.

I made rich the grandees and lords
Who hire Franco to lead his gang-hordes
Against Spain.

I must never do that again.

I must drive the bombers out of Spain!
I must drive the bombers out of the world!
I must take the world for my own again—

A workers' world
Is the song of Spain.

Letter from Spain

Addressed to Alabama
Lincoln Battalion,
International Brigades,
November Something, 1937.

Dear Brother at home:

We captured a wounded Moor today.
He was just as dark as me.
I said, Boy, what you been doin' here
Fightin' against the free?

He answered something in a language
I couldn't understand.
But somebody told me he was sayin'
They nabbed him in his land

And made him join the fascist army
And come across to Spain.
And he said he had a feelin'
He'd never get back home again.

He said he had a feelin'
This whole thing wasn't right.
He said he didn't know
The folks he had to fight.

And as he lay there dying
In a village we had taken,
I looked across to Africa
And seed foundations shakin'.

Cause if a free Spain wins this war,
The colonies, too, are free—

Then something wonderful'll happen
To them Moors as dark as me.

I said, I guess that's why old England
And I reckon Italy, too,
Is afraid to let a workers' Spain
Be too good to me and you—

Cause they got slaves in Africa—
And they don't want 'em to be free.
Listen, Moorish prisoner, hell!
Here, shake hands with me!

I knelt down there beside him,
And I took his hand—
But the wounded Moor was dyin'
And he didn't understand.

Salud,
Johnny

Hero—International Brigade

Blood,
Or a flag,
Or a flame
Or life itself
Are they the same:
Our dream?
        I came.
An ocean in-between
And half a continent.
Frontiers,
And mountains skyline tall,
And governments that told me NO,
YOU CANNOT GO!
        I came.
On tomorrow's bright frontiers
I placed the strength and wisdom
Of my years.
Not much,
For I am young.
(*Was* young,
Perhaps it's better said—
For now I'm dead.)

But had I lived four score and ten
Life could not've had
A better end.
I've given what I wished
And what I had to give
That others live.
And when the bullets
Cut my heart away,
And the blood
Gushed to my throat
I wondered if it were blood
Gushing there.

Or a red flame?
Or just my death
Turned into life?
They're all the same:
Our dream!
   My death!
   Your life!
   Our blood!
   One flame!
They're all the same!

How Much for Spain?

The long collection speech is done
      And now the felt hat goes
From hand to hand its solemn way
      Along the restless rows.
In purse and pocket, fingers feel
      And count the coins by touch.
Minds ponder what they can afford
      And hesitate . . . how much?
In that brief, jostled moment when
      The battered hat arrives,
Try, brother, to remember that
      Some men put in their lives.

Requiem for the Spanish Dead

The great geometrical winter constellations
Lift up over the Sierra Nevada,
I walk under the stars, my feet on the known round earth.
My eyes following the lights of an airplane,
Red and green, growling deep into the Hyades.
The note of the engine rises, shrill, faint,
Finally inaudible, and the lights go out
In the southeast haze beneath the feet of Orion.

As the sound departs I am chilled and grow sick
With the thought that has come over me. I see Spain
Under the black windy sky, the snow stirring faintly,
Glittering and moving over the pallid upland,
And men waiting, clutched with cold and huddled together,
As an unknown plane goes over them. It flies southeast
Into the haze above the lines of the enemy,
Sparks appear near the horizon under it.
After they have gone out the earth quivers
And the sound comes faintly. The men relax for a moment
And grow tense again as their own thoughts return to them.

I see the unwritten books, the unrecorded experiments,
The unpainted pictures, the interrupted lives,
Lowered into the graves with the red flags over them.
I see the quick gray brains broken and clotted with blood,
Lowered each in its own darkness, useless in the earth.
Alone on a hilltop in San Francisco suddenly
I am caught in a nightmare, the dead flesh
Mounting over half the world presses against me.

Then quietly at first and then rich and full-bodied,
I hear the voice of a young woman singing.
The emigrants on the corner are holding
A wake for their oldest child, a driverless truck

Broke away on the steep hill and killed him,
Voice after voice adds itself to the singing.
Orion moves westward across the meridian,
Rigel, Bellatrix, Betelgeuse, marching in order.
The great nebula glimmering in his loins.

Elegy for the Spanish Dead

JULY, 1936
Life takes its final meaning
From chosen death; this stirrup-cup
History, the ancient, greedy bitch
Pours for her lovers; lacking this
The trapped fox is better, the squashed beetle; lacking this
We'd not have had you, Europe; lacking this
No play, no plot, no palaces, churches, treasures,
Science, art; no greatness, no history. Between cup and lip
In that moment, only, of noble freedom
Men have lived, bred new worlds, then the old bitch swallowed them.

Such greatness was theirs, the unlettered, unknown
Thousands on thousands, whose bare hands broke
Incredibly, in the fierce July days, the spitting guns
Of the Guard. . . . By that unreckoned gift of blood
We live; what thrust less pure could wake
Old Europe's tired womb and make
Again the miracle?

JULY, 1937
Life takes its final meaning
From chosen death; the simple men who drank
That cup, now twice-betrayed and doubly slain—
How shall we mourn, how share their pain?

They will go on, in the dark earth striving.
They will go on, nor any word or deed
Impugn that simple majesty.
They will go on, the olive and the vine
Are theirs in fee immutable; not any cold assassin's hand can reach
The hearts victorious beating underground.
They will go on, their pity and their truth will hush
Our feeble grief, and pour,

Scorn on the lying lips. . . . For they are joined
With powers implacable and just, and they will rise,
A wind within the wind that whirls
Europe to its doom, the new world to its birth.

Smiles and Blood

(To a Poet who writes only of pleasant things)

Smile at me again,
And tell me how unpleasant is the bloody War in Spain . . .
Say that all is night,
And nothing there is worth the poem I will write.
Shudder in your plea,
And say how far from poetry the Civil War must be.

> And smile again.
> —Forget the men
> That die each day
> And are reborn—
> Oh, smile away!
> A heart is torn
> In sunny Spain—
> A land gone grey.
> A million mourn,
> And your sweet smile:
> —A mocking thorn!
> So deadly, vile. . . .

They're writing a wonderful poem in Spain,
And you would not hear it.
The grandest endeavor—a portrait in pain;
An epic of courage, of deathless men slain . . .
And, smiling, you fear it!

> Oh, hear it!
> Oh, bear it!

A blood-stain has come on the earth—I must smear it.
  I cannot erase it;
    You mustn't replace it
With smiles that will not hide the fact that you fear it.
      I'll spread it—
        I'll wed it
To bravery—till all the world knows of the monster that shed it,
— —And all the world knows of the "poet" who fled it.

Smile at me again,
And tell me how unpleasant is the bloody War in Spain. . . .
Say that all is night,
And nothing there is worth the poem I will write.
Shudder in your plea,
And say how far from poetry the Civil War must be.
— — —I'll smile, too, as you rave,
And think how great the poem is: the spilt blood of the brave.

June 12, 1937

Sinverguenza

They snarl over Spain like cur-dogs over a bone, then look at each other and
    shamelessly
Lie out of the sides of their mouths.
Brag, threat and lie, these are diplomacy; wolf-fierce, cobra-deadly and
    monkey-shameless,
These are the masters of powerful nations.
I wonder is it any satisfaction to Spaniards to see that their blood is only
The first drops of a forming rain-storm.

The March

After the first mile snow fell: down the tall valley
of Wall Street   softly on our faces like children's tears
fell the snow
　　　　remember the young died   remember the sudden bomb
　　　　remember the hurt nerve   how it tortured before death
　　　　O remember from what hired gun

UNITE AGAINST WAR!

(capital letters against the sky!: take it, wind,
over continents! Make it electric at night, a big sign!)

MAKE MADRID THE TOMB OF FASCISM!

While a girl sprints from the line, solicits from traffic smiling
"Come on, mister, it's for yourself," clinking the donation box;
and in a passing car a man raises his hand from the wheel
the fist says   Give it to them between the eyes
so they can feel it!

MADRID!—TOMB!—FASCISM!—

that's how they hear us twenty floors above the town:
voice goes that high   see the burst of paper come down!
Volume in huge sound like waves   fades   returns
superbly in sheets of wind   destroys distance: fades and
echoes back like thunder passed over but still strong . . .
　　　　　　　Madrid—*Madrid*—MADRID!

To Federico García Lorca

Guitarist, singer of folk-songs,
strolling player who in the wilderness
strayed where the black pigs bred,
beasts in the ruins of a castle,
wild boars in the towers, grunting
the lord's prayer in the minarets,—
rooting in the stubble of moorish arches,
roman columns, armor of knights
and broken lances in moats;
and on the battlements
mangled limbs of the greek heroes;
swine grazing in the weeds of romances,
snouts in the leaves of the classics.
Devoured, the poems bled; yours the blood:
spilled by the shrewd bargainer,
March, the merchant, illiterate dealer in swine,
gun-runner who sought to still your voice
with gun-fire: the cries of a huckster
trading a nation.

Lorca, you who were the morning song of Spain,
the song is on the lips of the people!

The Defenses

White sky, and moonlight famous in our eyes;
locked by the tree, self-turning, kissed,
lost in our fierce imaginative love.

Then in morning heavenly the moon goes calm and transparent;
then we walk to our work, speaking subtly or smiling,

Writing in freedom, the thought moving among the papers
like a familiar bird; or looking, or asking;
the faces of everyone lighted almost with motives of love.

And then:—but the cheerful radio ends in music,
the wrist-watch continues its simple seconds, and our hands
drop in the midst of lunch:—what was it?—
and feel the sick thrill of disaster.

Reading aloud in a room in the city and there came
extras at midnight like a violent heart-beat:
we too, some time, must, must

Set guns on the marble sills of the university;
our friends dead; the fascists controlling the insane asylum;

The pale eyes of our people; the bitter retreat;
defending the square of burned grass in the park;

And that night the open faces, the bandages black with wounds,
the alive going slowly back, entrenching by stones, by brook,
cursing the fatal moonlight that brings bombardment.

Yes by this tree we kissed, for which the shells are searching
minute by minute, may find and may destroy.

O cities across an ocean, Yenan, Chungking, with dark steel
guard yourselves! And you, capital of our world,
Madrid, Madrid!—since your great trenches hold

Death back from love; and if they hold, keep safe
our trees, our harbors, and our happiness.

Snow in Madrid

Softly, so casual,
Lovely, so light, so light,
The cruel sky lets fall
Something one does not fight.

How tenderly to crown
The brutal year
The clouds send something down
That one need not fear.

Men before perishing
See with unwounded eye
For once a gentle thing
Fall from the sky.

Near Catalonia

We have the sweet noise of the sea at our back
and before us the bitter shouting of the gun;
and the brass wing of aeroplanes and the sun
that walks above us burning. Here we wound
our feet on metal fragments of the bomb,
the sword unburied and the poisoned ground.
Here we stand; here we lie; here we must see
what we can find potent and good to set
between the Fascist and the deep blue sea.

If we had bricks that could make a wall we would use them,
but bricks will break under a cannonball;
if we had iron we would make a wall,
but iron rings and splinters at the bomb
and wings go across the sky and over a wall,
and if we made a barrier with our earth
they would murder the earth with Fascist poison,
and no one will give us iron for the wall.
We have only the bodies of men to put together,
the wincing flesh, the peeled white forking stick,
easily broken, easily made sick,
frightened of pain and spoiled by evil weather;
we have only the most brittle of all things the man
and the heart the most iron admirable thing of all,
and putting these together we make a wall.

Noncombatants

(For the Spanish)

The poet's face is white like the moon.
The little children lie sleeping.
The poet looks at the children.
Like the moon he visits their faces.
Looks long, his white face travels
Past each and on each he shines.

Cloud-dark he lies in a ditch.
The bombs fall closer tonight.
He waits, and wishes to die.

1938

Silence in Mallorca

I

Our stony island, Spain's laconic child
Quiet. Nada. Cover the glowing spark.
Hush all the hótas and hush hush the wild

Arabian cries. Now in Europe's dark
Whisper weep secretly plot but never sing.
On cliffs against the sky moves the new mark

Shape of the plane, the loathed imperial thing
The hawk from Italy, the spy of black.
Ground where we labor darkens with its wing.

A few shot first. Then nothing. Then the attack.
Terror of the invader. Puff of shells,
And Juan our best man ambushed in the back.

Hide hide in the caves; listen in the dry wells. . . .
Clang—the obedient treachery of church bells.

II

They shot the mayor of Inca. They jailed
The poor the free the poor the free the brave.
Out of the puerto when the felucca sailed

Planes roared and swooped and shot them on the wave.
Our people serve the invader and his gun.
Our people, Spain. Slow tempo of the slave.

We are cut off. Africa's blazing sun
Knew these same hawks that now around us prey.
And Barcelona suffers. Is there no one

To save us but ourselves? From far away
After victorious battle. . . . Cry, we cry
Brothers, Comrades help us. Where are they?

Our island lying open to the sky.
Mallorca, the first to fall, the last to die.

III

O wild west wind. . . . Liberty's open roar,
Blow on this island, blow the ocean clean,
Drown out tormentors, blow equinox, blow war

Away from the world. Drive to us the unseen
Battalions, clouds of planes by workers flown,
Give us our land again, quiet and green,

Our children singing and our land, our own
Ways, our wives, our delegates. Blow here.
The indifferent sea washes the beach of stone,

And Mediterranean silence, primitive fear
Steps in the foot of Tomàs, the new slave.
Moves in the hovering hawk, spiraling near.

We bend, we work,—this island inferno and grave.
Come with the wind of your wings. And save.

The Program

ACT ONE, Madrid-Barcelona,
ACT TWO, Paris in springtime, during the siege,
ACT THREE, London, Bank Holiday, after an air raid,
ACT FOUR, a short time later in the U.S.A.

EAT ZEPHYR CHOCOLATES
(Do not run for the exits in case of fire;
The Rome-Berlin theater has no exits)
SUZANNE BRASSIERES FOR PERFECT FORM

CAST, IN THE ORDER OF DISAPPEARANCE:
Infants.
Women and children,
Soldiers, sailors, miscellaneous crowds—

With 2,000 wounded and 1,000 dead,
10,000 wounded and 5,000 dead,
100,000 wounded and 50,000 dead,
10,000,000 wounded and 5,000,000 dead

(Scenes by the British ruling caste,
Costumes, Bonnet, Laval, et al.,
Spanish embargo by the U.S. Congress,
Music and lighting by Pius XI)

SMOKE EL DEMOCRACIES,
TRY THE NEW GOLGOTHA FOR COCKTAILS AFTER THE SHOW.

Puigcerdà

Let us find a suitable ditch, for the siren has sounded
and the air already aches with the humming of wings.
They are coming, the beasts that swim on the brink of our vision:
there will be ash and blood over familiar things.

Over the hearth and the field there will be weeping
when they have spun to their Pyrenean nest
to count with diligent glee the estate of their cargo,
joke at our terror, feed and lie down to rest.

They are here. Lie flat to the earth that bore you.
You may be part of it soon enough again.
Lie close, listen and tremble, tremble:
this is the thundering charge of the pirate men.

But the swan there,
the swan upon the water—
the swan's enchantment over the silver water—
moves still,
pure and proud,
disdains the shrapnel,
scorns the thunder.

The swan in beauty floats upon the lake,
serene before the choice that death must make.

Epitaph

For Arnold Reid
D. July 27, 1938
at Villalba de los Arcos

Deep in this earth,
deeper than grave was dug
ever, or body of man ever lowered,
runs my friend's blood,
spilled here. We buried him
here where he fell,
here where the sniper's eye
pinned him, and everything
in a simple moment's
quick explosion of pain was over.

Seven feet by three
measured the trench we dug,
ample for body of man ever murdered.
Now in this earth his blood
spreads through far crevices,
limitless, nourishing vineyards for miles around,
olive groves slanted on hillocks, trees
green with young almonds, purple with ripe figs,
and fields no enemy's boots
can ever desecrate.

This is no grave,
no, nor a resting place.
This is the plot where the self-growing seed
sends its fresh fingers to turn soil aside,
over and under earth ceaselessly growing,
over and under earth endlessly growing.

July 30, 1938
Villalba de los Arcos

For a Young Poet Dead in Spain

Music has saluted you,
And those assembled few
Felicities they bring the hero dead:
The praised imperfect flowers
Found on foreign moors,
Broken a little when the children fled
That monster with his wings across
The sudden Spanish wilderness.

Journals have recorded
What the music said.
The quick black print has named the circumstance,
The date not incorrect,
Not any outward fact
Impaled in paragraphs but does convince.
Impoverished of days, I know
Now ramparts that we stumbled to:

That genius of our thought,
(That sandalled runner) caught
Tall instants on the flood of some shared poem
Who, vision-weighted, slipped
Our vulnerable grip
And spread himself in shadows through the room.
Now he is yours, my dear, and far
Beyond the mirroring of fear.

O, Youth, who hesitated,
Precarious, April-hearted,
On the wide incommunicable plain,
Until our new world tracks
That headsman with his axe,
Immune our eyes to any land but Spain's;
In such communion to inspire
Glad squadrons from the hemispheres.

When new Spanish skies
In moon on moon of peace
Look down, un-swastikaed, on peoples' hills;
When earth, resurgent, springs
With prouder offerings,
Forsworn with love in their great common halls,
Men will re-name those passionately kept
In freedom's necessary crypt.

Harvest: June 1938

For Donald Henry (Dodge City, pre-medic, University of Kansas),
first-aid man, mortally wounded, Belchite, Sept. 2, 1937; Ray
Jackson, Jr. (Syracuse), missing, Gandesa, Apr. 1 1938; also:
James Cleveland Hill (ex-U.S. soldier; Ness City oilworker),
lieutenant, killed in action, Corbera, Sept. 9, 1938; Kenneth
Graeber (Lawrence, student of journalism, University of Kansas),
ambulance-driver, honorably discharged; Paul O'Dell (Wichita,
worker and student), infantry and engineers, honorably
discharged; for all Jayhawkers of the Lincoln-Washington
Battalion, in the body or out of the body.

Half-waking in the day-coach east from Denver
an elevator named the town. A month
before my low-keyed mind might momently
have drifted down associative pathways:
". . . Sicilian city, Athens' great misfortune. . . .
town in New York where once I spent a month
slapping the dust from documents century-old. . . ."
as well, of course, as: ". . . western Kansas village—
home of the Negro who answered instructor's compliments
on his Spanish accent by reference to the doubly
fortunate presence in town of a Mexican barber. . . ."
A month ago. . . .
But now
Syracuse is a name:
Ray Jackson. . . .

The wheatfields were a heliograph. The porter
passed through the car with his warning: ". . . twenty-five minutes. . . ."
Till the zero-hour? No, time allowed for breakfast.
What did I think of, leaving the train a year
ago? Boot Hill and Wyatt Earp. . . .
the heaps of buffalo-hides in the 1870's—
bones in the decade after. . . .
a college-girl who named this town as hers. . . .

But now
forever
Dodge City is
Don Henry. . . .

O prairie-village,
your houses hiding among the wheatfields—
prairie-chickens in bunch-grass—
only your grain-elevator against the sky,
a giant metallic gopher;
O prairie-towns
insulated by ocean and 2,000 miles of complacency—
blubber of wood-pulp, of celluloid-reels, and of air-waves—
against the fierce currents of death that are crackling through Europe,
what voice pierced deliberate static and ear-plugs to call
your sons from these plains to the fight on the Spanish *meseta?*

Young men, with their minds sharpened pitchforks, tore through the foul
    tangle
of lies, sheathing bales of hearstpapers heaved off at the stations,
as threshers strip off the tough mildew from wheatstacks to come
at the last to the good central grain of the truth.

These men were Americans—blood of America's heart—
their names say "America":
1776
the long Decherd rifle
Donald Henry
Ray Jackson
They were Kansans
their schoolbooks had not yet forgotten
John Brown
They were men from the wheatfields
Spain was a furious sun which drew them along paths of light
as the water ascends from the trickle through sand, from the buffalo-wallow,
to swoop like a billion bright *chatos* which speed to relief
of the drought-besieged fields.
Theirs too was a lean and stubborn land.
For five years it had known
the dictatorship of the drought, the blackshirted dust-storm. . . .
the dust still swirls in a gas-cloud,

heads have fallen. . . .
but the lines hold . . .
irrigation-canals have brought up reinforcements. . . .
No pasaran!

Life which lay seemingly buried has broken the darkness
(the stones of their prisons shall split) and the germs which today
still hide underground shall next season leap forth with a shout—
or, dying, enrich with their spirit the soil for their comrades. . . .
Pasaremos!

Cedillo is in Bight, and Chamberlain
teeters goutily, the spirit of
Ziska's flail-wielding peasants in armored farm-wagons
patrols the Czech frontiers,
about Addis Ababa the Ethiopians
cut roads, lie in the brush, and wait for the rains
to ground the Fascist planes,
trucks in continuous caravan are rushing
the new combines to the fields of the west, and wheat
pours into Dodge City and Syracuse bins (but O where
are the bullets, the guns, and the planes for the wheatfields of Spain?);
at Valencia the comrades
feet on the earth are shouldering the sky. . . .

If a Spanish trench gashes a ripened wheatfield with gigantic and sterile
        furrow
there are men who are rubbing the heads between powder-black palms.
men who winnow the kernels with battle-hot breath, and who wonder
about the Three A's, the FU, and about yields per acre,
weight per bushel, and protein-content—above all, the price—
of wheat at the Dodge City co-ops. . . .

John Brown of Kansas still goes marching on—
his tread is on the plains of Aragon!

Autumn in California

Autumn in California is a mild
And anonymous season, hills and valleys
Are colorless then, only the sooty green
Eucalyptus, the conifers and oaks sink deep
Into the haze; the fields are plowed, bare, waiting;
The steep pastures are tracked deep by the cattle;
There are no flowers, the herbage is brittle.
All night along the coast and the mountain crests
Birds go by, murmurous, high in the warm air.
Only in the mountain meadows the aspens
Glitter like goldfish moving up swift water;
Only in the desert villages the leaves
Of the cottonwoods descend in smoky air.

       Once more I wander in the warm evening
Calling the heart to order and the stiff brain
To passion. I should be thinking of dreaming, loving, dying,
Beauty wasting through time like draining blood,
And me alone in all the world with pictures
Of pretty women and the constellations.
But I hear the clocks in Barcelona strike at dawn
And the whistles blowing for noon in Nanking.
I hear the drone, the snapping high in the air
Of planes fighting, the deep reverberant
Grunts of bombardment, the hasty clamor
Of anti-aircraft.

       In Nanking at the first bomb,
A moon-faced, willowy young girl runs into the street,
Leaves her rice bowl spilled and her children crying,
And stands stiff, cursing quietly, her face raised to the sky.
Suddenly she bursts like a bag of water,
And then as the blossom of smoke and dust diffuses,
The walls topple slowly over her.

       I hear the voices
Young, fatigued and excited, of two comrades
In a closed room in Madrid. They have been up

All night, talking of trout in the Pyrenees,
Spinoza, old nights full of riot and sherry,
Women they might have had or almost had,
Picasso, Velasquez, relativity.
The candlelight reddens, blue bars appear
In the cracks of the shutters, the bombardment
Begins again as though it had never stopped,
The morning wind is cold and dusty,
Their furloughs are over. They are shock troopers,
They may not meet again. The dead light holds
In impersonal focus the patched uniforms,
The dog-eared copy of Lenin's Imperialism,
The heavy cartridge belt, holster and black revolver butt.
        The moon rises late over Mt. Diablo,
Huge, gibbous, warm; the wind goes out,
Brown fog spreads over the bay from the marshes
And overhead the cry of birds is suddenly
Loud, wiry, and tremulous.

Madrid

Damaged by shells, many of the clocks on the public buildings
in Madrid have stopped. At night, the streets are pitch black.
—News Item

Put out the lights and stop the clocks.
Let time stand still,
Again man mocks himself
And all his human will to build and grow.
     Madrid!
The fact and symbol of man's woe.
     Madrid!
Time's end and throw-back,
Birth of darkness,
Years of light reduced:
The ever minus of the brute,
The nothingness of barren land
And stone and metal,
Emptiness of gold,
The dullness of a bill of sale:
BOUGHT AND PAID FOR! SOLD!
Stupidity of hours that do not move
Because all clocks are stopped.
Blackness of nights that do not see
Because all lights are out.
     Madrid!
Beneath the bullets!
     Madrid!
Beneath the bombing planes!
     Madrid!
In the fearful dark!

Oh, mind of man!
So long to make a light
Of fire,
     of oil,
     of gas,

And now electric rays,
So long to make a clock
Of sun-dial,
       sand-dial,
       figures,
And now two hands that mark the hours.
Oh, mind of man!
So long to struggle upward out of darkness
To a measurement of time—
And now:
These guns,
These brainless killers in the Guadarrama hills
Trained on Madrid
To stop the clocks in the towers
And shatter all their faces
Into a million bits of nothingness
In the city
That will not bow its head
To darkness and to greed again:
That dares to dream a cleaner dream!
Oh, mind of man
Molded into a metal shell—
Left-overs of the past
That rain dull hell and misery
On the world again—
Have your way
And stop the clocks!
Bomb out the lights!
And mock yourself!
Mock all the rights of those
Who live like decent folk.
Let guns alone salute
The wisdom of our age
With dusty powder marks
On yet another page of history.
Let there be no sense of time,
Nor measurement of light and dark,
In fact, no light at all!
Let mankind fall
Into the deepest pit that ignorance can dig
For us all!
Descent is quick.

To rise again is slow.
In the darkness of her broken clocks
Madrid cries NO!
In the timeless midnight of the Fascist guns,
Madrid cries NO!
To all the killers of man's dreams,
Madrid cries NO!

     To break that NO apart
     Will be to break the human heart.

Madrid, September 24, 1937

Postcard from Spain

Addressed to Alabama
Lincoln-Washington Battalion,
April, 1938

Dear Folks at home:

I went out this mornin'
Old shells was a-fallin'
Whistlin' and a-fallin'
When I went out this mornin'.

I'm way over here
A long ways from home,
Over here in Spanish country
But I don't feel alone.

Folks over here don't treat me
Like white bosses used to do.
When I was home they treated me
Just like they treatin' you.

I don't think things'll ever
Be like that again:
I done met up with folks
Who'll fight for me now
Like I'm fightin' now for Spain.

Salud,
Johnny

    Tell me,
    Is there peace
    Behind your high stone walls—
    Peace

Where no worldly duty calls—
Or does some strange
Insistence beckon
With a challenge
That appalls?

Air Raid: Barcelona

Black smoke of sound,
Curls against the midnight sky.

Deeper than a whistle,
Louder than a cry,
Worse than a scream
Tangled in the wail
Of a nightmare dream,
      The siren
Of the air raid sounds.

Flames and bombs and
Death in the ear!
The siren announces
Planes drawing near.
Down from bedrooms
Stumble women in gowns.
Men, half-dressed,
Carrying children rush down.
Up in the sky-lanes
Against the stars
A flock of death birds
Whose wings are steel bars
Fill the sky with a low dull roar
Of a plane,
      two planes,
        three planes,
          five planes,
            or more.
The anti-aircraft guns bark into space.
The searchlights make wounds
On the night's dark face.
The siren's wild cry
Like a hollow scream

Echoes out of hell in a nightmare dream.
        Then the BOMBS fall!
All other noises are nothing at all
        When the first BOMBS fall.
All other noises are suddenly still
        When the BOMBS fall.
All other noises are deathly still
As blood spatters the wall
And the whirling sound
Of the iron star of death
Comes hurtling down.
No other noises can be heard
As a child's life goes up
In the night like a bird.
Swift pursuit planes
Dart over the town,
Steel bullets fly
Slitting the starry silk
        Of the sky:

A bomber's brought down
In flames orange and blue,
And the night's all red
Like blood, too.
        The last BOMB falls.

The death birds wheel East
To their lairs again
Leaving iron eggs
In the streets of Spain.
With wings like black cubes
Against the far dawn,

The stench of their passage
Remains when they're gone.
In what was a courtyard
A child weeps alone.

Men uncover bodies
From ruins of stone.

Lines Written for the Occasion
of a Sale of Manuscripts

Think what went into these—
        Seclusion, craft, and toil:
What fever brought to book
        These pages time will soil!

That, soiled or fading, grow
        Or fade in price with time:
Corrections made by hand,
        Erasures, altered rhyme,—

All these are here for sale,
        Though not for this designed,
The ordering of thought,
        The profit of the mind.

Lucky, to buy and sell
        While men in Spain are dead
Who battle for a world
        Where books may still be read.

Acquire these residues
For more than single use.

      League of American Writers
      New York, March 1938

Give Us This Day

mejor morir a pie que vivir en rodillas.
—Pasionaria

Deep in the olive groves at sunset
    longer than the memory of police chiefs
        grow the shadows of headstone olive trees
Deadmen's shoes march on other feet
    long after laces and soles are gone:
        rifle straps fell away and string broke
Worn by the sweat of many a comrade's back:
    fondly shells still slide into the chamber
        the breechlocks of the anti-tank batteries
Have turned to museums of fingerprints
    but their beloved muzzles will throw
        explosives so long as there is night.

how are the lines holding? where are the lines?
bring up cannon before sunrise, ammo, water

How could Spain have been rich?
    nowhere were fat Swiss landscapes
        or comfortable park-like rural scenes
No mellow pastures or dreaming spires
    the streaked shoulders of the hills
        always a proving-ground for sunsets
For mobile brigades of battle clouds,
    hands of the wind fast scene-shifters
        preparing stagelike landscapes always for tragedy:
Thorn bushes burned toward evening
    like liquid flame: what wealth was there
        but in the skies and the hard empty hands?
Where was the glamour of historians?
    were they here? what did they see?
        who was rich? where was the wealth?

Long deserts with oases of olive trees
        mirages of wheatfields and vines
            exhausted salt plains of Castile
Monotonous one-well towns of Aragon
        mud walls rising from mud ridge-strung
            like cascades of standing reddish dust

kitchens should be underground, dig schools deep
take the children to the deepest end of the refugio, dig.

The church towers were pretty
        the walls of monastery gardens strong
            churchwalls were strong as fortresses
The hermitage where the bishop
        summered was as pretty as a calendar also
            his cedars were firewood for Alcorisa
Monotonously the people cooked
        in one dish and ate from one plate
            there were stoves only in the convents
Monotonously we used the half-built
        Republican schoolhouses for hospitals
            these were the only white walls in Aragon
Where was the glamour of that
        luminescent past of gilt and gold
            silver brass and flea-ridden satins?
Of banners pennants flags as red as blood
        and yellow as gold? none but belfry saints
            had seen the past: they looked down on us
With stone eyes full of grandeur
        as we marched out of the rising sunlight
            leaving our dead but taking their guns

because of the sky there was no rearguard
no rear every nursery and fireplace a trench

They were thirsty for Madrid
        ravenous for the spinal fluid of Madrid
            howitzers chewed away at the Gran Via
What they wanted They first destroyed
        they wanted Hijar and they dropped all
            but landing gear and tailskid on Hijar

They wanted Guernica Durango
         Lerida Barbastro Caspe Alcaniz and all
               the towns villages and hamlets in Spain
But that would have taken too long
         so They destroyed only what They wanted most
               with planes for every roof and all that moved
They always told us what They
         wanted: the telling came in the crackle
               of lead whips on the hams of the earth
Whistling iron lead copper zinc
         came out of the rock hills rose from
               the desert plain arched over the valley
We wanted their infantry our gunsights
         were hungry for Their infantry but could find
               nothing but earth rock and the walls of tanks
Earthquakes belled into the solid air
         the day had legion eyes and all were guns
               hungry gunsights searched the empty horizon

brace every ceiling fortify the cellars open all doors
lie motionless in the ditches do not move never run

The country was bleeding to death
         every day from many small wounds
               every day the imported meat grinders
Chewed a fingertip an ear a town,
         old wounds flowed across the villages
               but our vitals could never be reached
Perfect in echelon Their silver planes
         came over like bloody Gods that
               owned the bloody bleeding sky blue skies
Swarming into the hide of the hills
         civilians scratched and clawed themselves
               into the earth like jiggers and skin lice
Breathing deep and loud and perfect
         trimotors came on slow as sunset
               birds wrangled in the dry poplars
Morosely a dog nosed bandages
         along the soiled frozen river bank
               grassblades and a sulphur jonquil shook

In the crevice where we lay
                earth fell on us and the air pounded
                        unhurt we ran toward the screaming
Remote against the icy afternoon
                our combat planes battled downward
                        guns and engines dove and climbed
Waterfalls of mixed smoke and fire
                poured like rain into the dry earth:
                        then the air was sweet and clean

they will come again today again tomorrow
out of the infected sunlight and the sick moon.

We asked for little: give us this day
                our bread gasoline and gunpowder
                        there was less bread and we did not eat
But the camions were ever ravenous
                guns would not kill without shells
                        our rifles ate us out of cartridges
There was no rest: we did not sleep
                but the camions would not run forever
                        gunbarrels grew too hot then too cold
There was little water: we did not drink
                but the Maxims were unceasingly thirsty
                        without bread water sleep we did not fail.
The hungry rifles grew too cold
                the tanks of the camions were empty
                        big hearts and empty hands were not enough

where are the grenades and stick-bombs?
is the road clear? where is the front?

pyres lit the roads at night
                bonfire pyramids of long unburied dead
                        fists and feet black as cattle hooves
All night long machine-gun pellets
                of snow drilled against the windshield
                        too tired to curse, three chofers
Amiably fought to sleep
                on a single stained still wet mattress
                        before morning many beds were empty

When the sun rose perfumed
          by bread and gelignite, black armies
              of shovel men sprang from the snowdrifts
Snow went into the steaming radiators
          we rolled a sick camion off the road
              ate snow off our backs: then moved on
We pushed our Diamond T-s through sheep
          that choked the village street, made
              towropes of bomb-torn telegraph lines
Sullen iron gray rollers of shrapnel
          hissed and broke on the beach-like road
              frozen mud plugged the bomb holes; we moved on
Planes stopped us: string chewing gum
          barbed wire and soap went into the engines
              chofers wiped glue from their eyes and drove off
Fast as ants we stripped the carcass
          of a slaughtered car of tires bolts wire
              and parts until only frame-bones were left
Fought off the back of roaring camions
          war wove through the mountains of Teruel
              fast as quicksilver red as flame gray as death
Leaving a trail of cigarette butts
          empty brandy bottles and the smell
              of hot oil in the deep tire tracks
With the echo of our songs rocketing
          like rifle shots inside the ice walls
              of the Sierra Gudár: we moved on and up

don't take a wrong road oil your rifle
save the water keep your head down

"The war's getting rough" Al said
          and those were his last words
              we stripped the tourniquet from his leg
"You can't fool Charlie Regan"
          not for forty years and three wars
              a 75 fooled him and these were his last words
What can be done for a belly case?
          a lung case a head case a liver
              —we can do much but they die anyway—

"The avions sprayed us all day
           with fire bullets I lay still
                 I did not move but I got it"
Ether other caffeine anestex:
           no hope left but a slap on the jaw
                 first sew him up with decent red silk
An old wound in one arm a fresh one
           in the other, Wild Bill laughed while
                 we put down his stretcher and rested
"I guess the war's about over for me"
           a rifle grenade caught him and it was
                 Bill took two stretcher bearers with him
—How are the lines? am I bleeding?
           who wants my shoes? where are the lines?
                 these were their last words,—salud! viva . . . viva. . . . —
Those summer girls with dreamy
           eyes white and clean as sleep
                 who slowly walk their big red mouths
Down the quiet streets of a city
           heartbreaking summer songs by the lake
                 where were they? had we forgotten?

throw olive limbs on the cars camouflage
the hospitals camouflage the earth, dig.

We snaked the wounded four
           miles out of the Segura mountains
                 on men when there were no mules
We pushed them through shellfire all
           day long through God's hideous sunlight
                 we got the wounded out on tanks in trucks
Caissons carts and ambulances
           we rolled them down plane-infested roads
                 slapped on tourniquets gauze and adhesives
We took the names and wrote last letters
           pumped the wounded full of morphine
                 saline anti-tetanus and gas-gangrene
Fortunately the hospital had been hit
           by nothing heavier than a ten-kilo egg
                 we soldered drilled sterilizer tins

Plastered wire splints to the stove pipe
        lit candles kerosene and olive oil lamps
            taped the openings in our wounded tents
We burned gasoline alcohol and wood
        over our wounded we filled them with
            good glucose blood adrenaline and morphine:
And then the bastards had to die on us
        and we had to bury them near and fast
            and at night: with neither lanterns nor songs

planes listen for those who speak of a new world
for culture peace progress freedom: dig!

Sleep had the smell of flowers
        in a funeral parlor there were flowers
            but no sleep: we longed for the perfume of
Woodsmoke, cooking and of home
        there were the tropical spring airs
            and nothing clean but children's eyes
We smoked dry olive leaves and straw
        go-lousies anti-tanks and pillow-slips
            we ate raw pork fat with wild onions
Pulled olives off the moonlit trees
        feasted the smearing of Moorish cavalry
            with beefsteak cut from their machine-gunned mounts
We slept in the olive groves of Quinto
        the plains of Aragon are scored with
            the foxholes our bayonets and mess tins dug
We curled into the frozen mud at Celadas
        stood sleeping against walls at Monte Rosario
            slept waist-deep in Escorial's irrigation ditches
Sucked moist mud in barrancas near Brunete
        came blinking out of the cellars of Teruel
            marched singing into sun-baked anthills at Valverde
But it was always a question of the lines:
        where were the trenches? were the men advancing?
            had we hauled the artillery closer each night?

yellow and red were Their banners: blood and gold
their program: blood and more blood silver and gold

Plucked clean as a tooth from the bomb-rotten
             village street then dumped on the road the Captain's
                 laundry was lost the laundress her father mother:
Sunset bleeds woodsmoke down the fuming streets
             fire warms engines and coffee, in a smashing
                 of icicles we move off, too sleepy to curse:
Headlights raised partridges which flew
             blind ahead of us up the road to the front
                 hungry, we carried guns fit only to kill men:
We blew up the trapped ambulances
             We lowered the bandaged nurse
                 to the cleanest part of the ditch:
There never was such an afternoon
             such keen Alpine evening air no such silence
                 but for the single rifle shot over the hills:
They want war Their stomachs can eat
             only war the droning of planes soothes Them
                 the sound of planes is morphine for Their sleep:
Armed with pawnshop rifles and a knowledge
             of why we had come, with memories that
                 went back through centuries the men advanced
Still in the clothes in which
             we had left our jobs, singing the
                 same song in many languages we advance:

are the trenches deep enough and dry and crooked?
have the bombing parties returned? where are the scouts?

In all the winterdry mountain deserts
             of Aragon there was no color but khaki:
                 not yet green but pink water-red rosegray
Quiet as sunset clouds pink as sunset snow
             the cherry orchard was the best cover
                 for artillery in all of lower Aragon
Under the cherry trees the throats
             of the Pasionaria battery coughed
                 soundless as an earthquake, leaving
A hush-hush of suction in the solid air
             petals drifted loose but many were left
                 the strongest would make the fattest fruit

Pasionaria's guns fired again
        cough of fire express-train vacuum rushed
            through the shattered blossom camouflage
Then planes came and power dove
        leveled off and opened up on the guns
            the gunners the cases of arms and the trees
Canvas slid from our anti-aircraft
        sunflash on the tumbling cartridges
            engine-roar hornet whistle of metal death
Wood hissed and the fresh earth rose
        number 3-gun sideslipped to her knees
            2-gun and 1 arched their throats fired
Their planes dove flattened and let fly
        spring cherry sap ran and fresher blood
            burned petals floated in the acid air
All afternoon the guns of the pasionaria
        battery fired all afternoon relays of planes
            dove unloaded wheeled soared and returned
Until blossoms were gone guns gone
        planes and orchard and gunners gone
            there would be no cherries no trees
No Spain no earth: in all the
        mountain deserts of Aragon there was
            no color but khaki and dust and blood.

bring up the archies! prime the tank-traps!
long live dynamite! death to war!

Like sea worms in the timbers of a ship
        four cavalrymen curled into a wall of clay
            but there were no beams in the shallow ceiling
"Only a direct hit"—there was a direct hit
        we shoveled four asphyxiated cavalrymen
            rushed them to the hospital courtyard
Before they were cold we had
        taken the blood out of them before
            the blood was cold we had run it
Into the arms of our wounded
        the blood of the four cavalrymen lives
            it will always live and always fight

Red as the flags on the trucks
        that roll over mountaintops hot as the vapor
            that burns inside the charging cylinder heads
The I. B.'s were the most ragged
        filthy hungry red eyed bastards
            that ever went under the name of troops
But they could fight and they fought
        they cursed their officers, groused and squawked
            but they held their lines and the lines held
Every man was his own general but they
        could obey; The Internationals never broke
            never was "some day comrade" said with such longing
Some day: no soldier has ever oiled
        or used or hated his rifle so well
            no troops ever loved peace like them

they wanted nothing for themselves not for themselves
every grove is a sanctuary each hilltop a shrine

Forget the bronze tablets and
        hand-illumined scrolls leave out
            medals citation bars and stripes
Some day their history will
        be carved ineradicably across
            the earth by tractor-drawn plows
Mercifully let a last kind bomb
        save the informal cemetery
            of the International Brigades
From him who could not take our trenches
        let the fist never come unclenched the
            calloused right forefingers never grow soft
Unknown soldiers? they were all
        unknown: international as sunrise
            misty etchings of their olive grove tombs
Will never hang reverently draped
        in lace and immortelles in chapel-like
            parlors of Back Bay and Park Avenue
Whitehall Arlington and Etoile
        will not pay bronze and marble to them
            every milestone is their cenotaph

Do not look for their metal names
　　　shaded by village memorial trees
　　　　　the horizon is their triumphal arch

write "paid up and in good standing"
save the helmets save the shoes

When in the evening secret service men
　　　lock vaults of cross-indexed fingerprints
　　　　　and the morgues of passport photographs
Where the faces of the Brigades
　　　fade and bleach but do not die
　　　　　longer than the memory of police chiefs
Grow the shadows of footstone olive trees
　　　deep in battlefield orchards at sunset
　　　　　thrushes the men had cursed for airplanes
Sleepily find places for the night
　　　secure among boughs grafted by peace
　　　　　to the seared and war-torn trunks
Only that the lines shall hold!
　　　nothing else matters there is no
　　　　　hardship no anguish no other pain
Dig the trenches deep and crooked
　　　send shells and tanks and planes
　　　　　fuel and the best guns to the Front
Let civilians feed wells of supply
　　　guard crossroads keep the highways healthy
　　　　　pulsing hot as the blood in our foreheads
Let the lines hold hard then advance
　　　let those camions wind over mountaintops
　　　　　let the color of the flags never fade
Hold them high as they flow above the
　　　roaring camions: let the memory of the songs
　　　　　the volunteers sang never die from our throats.

Say That We Saw Spain Die

Say that we saw Spain die. O splendid bull, how well you fought!
Lost from the first.
                        . . . the tossed, the replaced, the
                watchful *torero* with gesture elegant and spry,
Before the dark, the tiring but the unglazed eye deploying the bright cape,
Which hid for once not air, but the enemy indeed, the authentic shape,
A thousand of him, interminably into the ring released . . .
        the turning beast at length between converging colors caught.

Save for the weapons of its skull, a bull
Unarmed, considering, weighing, charging
Almost a world, itself without ally.

Say that we saw the shoulders more than the mind confused, so profusely
Bleeding from so many more than the accustomed barbs, the game gone
      vulgar, the rules abused.

Say that we saw Spain die from loss of blood, a rustic reason, in a reinforced
And proud punctilious land, no *espada*—
A hundred men unhorsed,
A hundred horses gored, and the afternoon aging, and the crowd growing
      restless (all, all so much later than planned),
And the big head heavy, sliding forward in the sand, and the tongue dry with
      sand,—no *espada*
Toward that hot neck, for the delicate and final thrust, having dared trust
      forth his hand.

Gautier Visited Spain

A hundred years ago? Really that long
Since you crossed into Spain, keen to record
Its quiet olive hillscape quickened by song

Of sun-bred people, then lulled by legend-stored
Cathedrals? That year, too, the flowers faded
As they fade today in the convent-yard.

While you watched, near Irun, the purling jade
Bidassoa hugging her velvet banks,
Hoping to be the theme of a serenade,

Your branching thoughts were rudely felled by the clanking
Of a heavy hammer. There! half hid
In reeds, a peasant, moody-eyed and lank,

Pounding bullets flat on sandstone—lead
From recent gunfire, picked up in the fields—
A hard harvest, smelling of the dead,

And planted by the alien slayers—yet yielding
A price at market! What else could he glean
From land that war had swiftly, blindly wheeled

Its engines over? Was he trying to clean
The soil of all that tore her breast apart?
Unhealed, he feared, she would not bear again,—

But soil's as sturdy as a Spaniard's heart!

Neutrality

America-Spain, 1938

To guide the knife in seeking out the heart,
To scatter oil upon a soaring flame,
To urge the artful lie, the lying art,
And cover War, the fact, with Peace, the name;
To fetter chains upon a hope confined,
And load with locks a prison double-barred,
Darken the windows of the wakening mind,
Against the encroaching future set a guard;

To lay a promise in the ear of love
That words by night shall be the deeds of day,
And then to kneel those eager eyes above
With Judas-lips to kiss the life away—
Is this your will, America? If it be,
Learn bondage then, unworthy to be free.

Philadelphia, Pa.

Lament

Lorca, who drank and drugged and loved
Whitewashing night, darkening day
With sleep, closed lids, is dead, is dead.

Marble-topped tables in Madrid,
Paris and Buenos Aires bear
The stains of drinks that once he spilled.

His blood has left no stain: the days
That he despised have washed away
The clues that still accused his wounds.

Now is he drowned in night and death,
Who loved the night and nightly teased
The bulls of death, spending his speech

And life-blood in the star-watched ring
Of darkness where we met. His voice
Speaks in the night that used his lips

To speak to men and me, in death
That he knew well before he died.
I think of war much as I think

Of death, remember Lorca when I dream
Of war and death. What unknown eye,
Not knowing me, prepares to aim

At empty space and shoot, and shoot?
What son of day and light shall see
In me dark death and, hating death,

Send me to drink with Lorca beyond day?

The Bull in the Olive Field

With the first banderillas of daybreak
the darkness lowered its head,
a drip of bloody snot in its nostrils,
and Madrid awoke,
toreador in overalls:

A storm of people poured like rain
upon the face of the streets,
thundering with firearms
across barricades:

Against the darkness bearing
dust winds from the desert,
hot blasts in the mouths of cannon,
drouth and carnage in the olive land:

Death, in his black cassock,
bull with the black hide,
hooded, gold cross at the neck,
fat and in folds like velvet;

his crotch full, a purse with coins,
rutted with the cows,
the whores of the old world,
rotted with the disease
in the rotten lands,

and unloosed the blessed bastards,
the young bulls, aristocrats, all of them,
raised in the sanctuaries of the dons,
bred in the stables of
Salamanca, Rome, Berlin.

The fields filled with bullfire
and the hatred of beasts; their breaths
scorching siroccos,
hot winds burning hatred against US:

the layers of water,
bidders for water rented for dry land,
haulers of water in jars at the village well,
blind mules turning the water mill,
circling the centuries in ciphers of debt.

The fields sickened
in the hate of dry winds:

the hate hot in the mouths of clerks,
the gatherers of taxes under
the smoking rifles of civil guards;

the hate hot in the brand of latifundia,
seal of state stamped in the arroyos,
hooves in the gullies and stone-choked soil;

the hate in the dust of documents
drifting in the hot winds
in the buzzing mouths of officials
breeding swarms of idlers
like flies on our bread.

Breeding illness of their idleness:
horrors on the path to the bullring,
beggars in the path of the bull:

trees sick with spore diseases,
tubercular, stunted,
the bark parched and peeling,
trunks gored and their wounds
swathed in bandages of lime;
Their limbs tortured, lifting up
bare branches of their poverty,
twisted in agony like christs in the grove.

1/26/39

When Barcelona fell, the darkened glass
turned on the world an immense ruinous gaze,
mirror of prophecy in a series of mirrors.
I meet it in all the faces that I see.

Decisions of history the radios reverse;
storm over continents, black rays around the chief,
finished in lightning, the little chaos raves.
I meet it in all the faces that I see.

Inverted year with one prophetic day,
high wind, forgetful cities, and the war,
the terrible time when everyone writes "hope."
I meet it in all the faces that I see.

When Barcelona fell, the cry on the roads
assembled horizons, and the circle of eyes
looked with a lifetime look upon that image,
defeat among us, and war, and prophecy,
I meet it in all the faces that I see.

Nineteen Thirty-Eight

Across the frontiers of the helpless world
The great planes swarm, the carriers of death,
Germs in the healthy body of the air,
And blast our cities where we stand in talk
       By doomed and comfortable fires.

In Asia famous tombs were opened so
And celebrated ancestors walked out
Into the carnage of the Rising Sun,
That horrible light upon a daughter cast,
       The new language in the torn streets.

There was a city where the people danced,
Simple and generous, traditional.
Suddenly the music stopped. Shooting
Began. Some of the living call the dead
       Of the Third Reich the lucky ones.

Terror accumulated in September
Until the island Dove divided up
A southern ally for the Eagle's feast.
And trembled as the Eagle fed, knowing
       The gratitude of appetite.

What was a civil war this year but strangers
Overhead, guns at sea, and foreign guns
And foreign squadrons in the plundered town?
A Spaniard learnt that any time is time
       For German or Italian doom.

Survivors, lean and daring and black men,
Lurked in the hills. The villages were gone,
The land given to rape and colonists.
They slept with hunger in the hills and told
       Wild legends of deliverance.

The winter sky is fatal wings. What voice
Will spare the aged and the dying Year?
His blood is on all thresholds, bodies found
In swollen rivers curse him as he dies:
  Criminal, to stand as warning.

The Spanish Lie

This will be answered.

The tears were not answered but this will be answered.

The tears of Madrid of Barcelona Valencia—
The tears were not answered.

The blood of Guernica, Badajoz, Almería—
The blood was not answered.

The tears are dry on the faces.

The blood is dry on the sand.

The tears were not answered: the blood was not answered.

This will be answered.

Because the men of Guernica do not speak,
Because the children of Almería are silent,
Because the women of Badajoz are dumb,
Are dumb, they have no voices, no voices,
Their throats are stopped with the sand of that place
They do not speak, they will never speak, and the children,
The children of Almería, they are still,
They do not move, they will never move, those children:
Their bodies are broken, their bones are broken, their mouths are—

Because they are dead, are dumb, because they are speechless,
Do not believe,
Do not believe the answer will not come.

Do not believe
Because the blood has not been answered
The lie will not be answered.

Do not believe
Because the tears have not been answered
The lie will not be answered.

Do not believe it.

This will be answered.
This will be answered with
Time.
            There is time.

The dead have time in those cities
In Badajoz, in Guernica, Almería.

They can wait: they have much time.

There is time.
They can wait.

A Gay People

fond of dancing and light wines
—old geography lesson

Without a shadow of a shadow of pride
Dead men and women wander on the streets
Of a grey city. They do not lift their eyes
Above the ground they used to call their own
Even to see bright articles in shops
Or peer at paper treatises on love,
Cheap and neglected in the open boxes.

No leaf on any tree. But many statues,
Bone-white and naked, writhing or sedate,
Gaze through the rain at nothing in the gardens,
At nothing at all.

A funny item in the morning paper
Says that in Washington, D.C., a dog,
A pet of the Italian embassy,
Was granted diplomatic recognition,
With all due status and immunities.
Here, Bonnet! Here, Berard! Here Daladier!
Chamberlain, Halifax! (Down, you sons of bitches!)

Trained hounds that hunt with modulated voice
In the late winter sessions.
                              Have your way.
Without a shadow of a shadow of pride.
What's honor? Air. Who hath it? He that died.

February. The Roman month of the dead.

Again the cock crew. Peace with honor, Britannicus.
Pray for us sinners. Not with a bang, but a whimper.
De mortuis nil nisi—

Quando ver venit meum?

Hearken! O brave, heart-breaking, noble sound!
Do I hear singing somewhere over the mountains?

—Arriba, victimas hambrientes!
Arriba, todos a luchar!

Paris, February 28, 1939

Brigadas Internacionales

To say *We were right* is not boastful,
nor *We saw, when all others were blind*
nor *We acted, while others ignored or uselessly wept.*

We have the right to say this
because in purest truth it is also recorded:
We died, while others in cowardice looked on.

Just as the man is false who never says *I*
nor asserts his own deeds in pride, or disclaims his wrongs,
so too would we be less than truly what we are

if we did not now, to all the embattled world,
proclaim in pride: *We saw. We acted. Fought.*
We died, while others in cowardice lived on.

November 1939

To a Young American the Day after
the Fall of Barcelona

Boy with honor in your heart,
The world is not the world you dream:
Recall the history of the Jews,
Hate screaming in the *Evening News*,
Eyes that beg, eyes that refuse,
Eyes that watch and scheme.

You, who fed on the pure stream
Of Aeschylean fire, have seen
Oedipus blinded, and the sun
Gleaming on Promethean spleen,
And learned to love the tragic day,
Burn your books and come away.

Throw away your little coin
Of childhood, boy, go down, go down
With whetted wits and treachery
And all resource of infamy
Against the enemy known.

Or cling to your bright innocence.
Reduce love to a virginal
Small passion pure beyond all use,
Or to a dream of Grecian sun,
And leave your world to be undone.

Reply To S. K.

Yes, Barcelona is three thousand miles
From where I write and I have not been there
To count the swollen dead and the jagged aisles
Cut by machine guns in the grain. Here
No motors brawl their anger overhead.
I have not seen the roof split to reveal,
For that one moment when the quick and dead
Are congruent, the bomb's bright cap of steel.

All I remember is the newspaper maps,
Boundaries estimated, casualties estimated, thunder
Of headlines fading away to lower caps—
Print, erroneous and glib. Or from under
The blue-buzzing tube the voice of the announcer,
Modulated, distant, saying: *It is done.*
Careful syllables reciting danger
In a lost land.

           At home there was sun—
Unmenaced bright high noon. The starlings fought
Small skirmishes with sparrows in the oak.
Robins bobbed on the lawn. I caught
A cardinal's whistle and spied him out in the crook
Of the lowest branch, bright red against the green.
The young nephews tumbling on the grass
Came racing out to meet me with a scream.
And beg a pick-back ride into the house.

Inside, the world went well: mother had lunch
Spread on the broad white table, in my room
The books were warm bright colors, and a bunch
Of some new-cut and fragrant unknown bloom
From mother's garden-puttering stood in water.
Letters arrived and welcome from far friends

Made diagrams of white on the desk blotter.
Inside the world went well, but there it ends.

Outside the house and off beyond that noon
Spain sent disaster smoking toward the sun
Or took disaster downward in the flown
Bombs shaped like tears that glisten as they come.
Or was it night in Spain? Or could there be
Day again on such ruin? Dared the light
To show . . . But the hyperbole is a lie:
Assuredly and indifferently there would be light.

The ingenuity of physical day
Would even contrive some beauty from the wreck:
A neat spiral of smoke, a rainbow gay
With spring, a bit of shadow work
On a ruined wall, or some one tower
Of all that would not take its bomb and fall—
A silhouette of some what-is-it power
Stones have and men?—You cannot break them all.

But O once let indifference close the will
Into the swivel chair and make the desk,
The immediate papers, the day's work, terminal
To the heart—nothing may save us from the wreck
Of stone and stake and every human wish.
Not one word on another shall survive
To teach the improbable sons what and how much
We meant of honor when we walked alive.

Beauty? What is it? By the river bank
Our younger bodies dreamed among the grass
Or by the back fence or the schoolyard oak
Of bright exorbitant perils we might pass
To win—to win—what? The romance is dead,
Childhood gone under. Time is the offense:
What work we do against the shriveling head
Of years is done in self-defense.

What are we sure of but the stated purpose,
The hope to make it real and the long fear

That time may stamp it VOID, and close
A canceled journal for our meaning here?
Will it be right? Will words count what we meant
In simple prose of sense marked black and sure
Across the scattering fact of incident
Chaotic as blown papers on the floor?

Seal windows tight and see your doors are shut—
No wind will scatter what you learned to say,
And what you dreamed and with long labor wrote
To mark the depth of night, the breadth of day.
You will be safe. But past your shaded light
The stars are deeper than you know, the sun
More violent than you dreamed, and day and night
Crossed wide with danger where the armed men run.

García Lorca

He felt a wind upon his face never again to feel,
and eighteen moonlights, thin as lace, stood in a line of steel.
Eighteen men were dumb as rock, the trees were loud with wind,
and far away, like a flock of stars, lamps in the village dimmed.
They shrank from the moon all swollen white, far from the lights of town;
beneath a tree they watched his eyes until their own turned down.
"Oh shoot me, brave young men!" he spoke, looking at every one,
"and hide my grave with stone before the night gives way to sun.
"Wake the town with drunken yell! Dance, and believe your dream
that Spain is safely under stone, and cannot lift a scream!"
"Fire!" four times the captain barked; thrice no pistol stirred;
then eighteen bullets found their mark, and not a groan was heard.

Blood and wind and moonlight cooled on García Lorca's face;
the soldiers quickly drove away, as from a haunted place.
No one dared to look behind—they drank themselves insane.
They heard his poem rising up, and spreading over Spain.

To the Veterans of the Abraham Lincoln Brigade

Say of them
They knew no Spanish
At first, and nothing of the arts of war
At first,
              how to shoot, how to attack, how to retreat
How to kill, how to meet killing
At first.
Say they kept the air blue
Grousing and griping,
Arid words and harsh faces. Say
They were young;
The haggard in a trench, the dead on the olive slope
All young. And the thin, the ill and the shattered,
Sightless, in hospitals, all young.

Say of them they were young, there was much they did not know,
They were human. Say it all; it is true. Now say
When the eminent, the great, the easy, the old,
And the men on the make
Were busy bickering and selling,
Betraying, conniving, transacting, splitting hairs,
Writing bad articles, signing bad papers,
Passing bad bills,
Bribing, blackmailing,
Whimpering, meaching, garroting,—they
Knew and acted
Understood and died.
Or if they did not die came home to peace
That is not peace.
              Say of them
They are no longer young, they never learned
The arts, the stealth of peace, this peace, the tricks of fear;
And what they knew, they know.
And what they dared, they dare.

1941

A Poem for Someone Killed in Spain

Though oars are breaking the breathless gaze
Of the summer's river, the head in the reeds
Has its own success; but time is brimming
From the locks in blood, and the finished heart

Gasps, "I am breaking with joy—" and joy
Suffuses with its blood the difficult fields
Where the dogs are baying. "I am not angry,"
Thinks the fox. Nor is death. And the leaves

Of the light summer are too new to joy
To think that their friend is dying, and their whispers
Are not patient but breathless, are passionate
With the songs of the world where no one dies.

For the Madrid Road

Stranger, the wages that we earned
For the skills you need not learn
Waste if you will; the traversed road
Is interrupted with our blood. . . .
The private guilt, the general grave
Are debts of yours; or so men say.
Believe what you will. Here where
The gunners looked, our lives ago,
Set if you like the stones that show
Here men's dooms were satisfied,
Here we and the strangers died. . . .
We perished, if you like, for you;
We died that—that you may die.
But when were lives men's own? Men die
For man's life, man; that men may miss
The unessential ills—but these
Are man's responsibilities.

Last Kilometer

Since morning over a knotted road
    The camions had jolted on.
Now in the shivering twilight
    They stopped. We got down.

It was deadly quiet under the sky
    With the night coming over.
We stared at the hills. We were too green
    To look for cover.

Then the ground stirred with a rumbling shudder
    As thunder runs
Solid and deep through upland fields—
    The sound of guns.

And down the road we saw two men
    Walk out of the coming night.
When they came close we saw their rags;
    Some of them were white.

They wandered past us in the cold.
    One stumbled and the other swore.
That sling had no room for a hand.
    We had met the war.

Es La Guerra

Of the bomb-wings that fell
In the hospital courtyard, we made candlesticks;
It was cold at night, colder
Than steel of our surgeon's instruments;
And always the smell of burning damp bandages,
Clothing and blankets polluting the sunrise:

Our hospital lived for sixteen days
Wide open to all the lead and iron
That poured out of the infected Spanish sunlight,
But on the morning of the seventeenth died,
Disembowelled into the village streets.

We had moved that night,
To a new place, just as close to the lines.

The Word Is Twilight

Also in Valencia there was an hour
　　　　which was neither night nor day
Arc lamps were lit and he spoke to her of his love
　　　　across saccharined tea and parched acorns:

While the sun punched its timeclock
　　　　and night had not yet put on overalls
When the siren-silent city was full
　　　　—no light no shadow, color or clouds:

Then Valencia listened for the sound
　　　　of motors blowing in from the sea
When disorder flamed in the swarming sky
　　　　of the rush of feet and mothers' calls:

For this was the hour when They
　　　　lovingly rode in from the sea and bombed
—As Their sniper friends stepped
　　　　to shuttered windows, waited and shot.

Before Battle

The Lincolns at Villanueva de la Cañada

Long after the sun has gone down,
      long into the clockless hours of the
         night, the new Battalion waits at the roadside.

Knowing that the end of all waiting
      is to come the men sit quietly and talk
         light the darkness of their minds with cigarettes;

This was summer this was Spain and night
      late at night out in the countryside where
         only the howl of dogs marks the presence of men.

They have left all behind them but guns
      to defend their lives guns with which
         to take lives rifles to answer other rifles;

Here at the frontier of death five hundred
      men wait for the sound of trucks and listen
         for the droning of planes never theirs.

Road and darkness are all they know
      the vein which will pump them like haemoglobin
         into the open festering moving wound of the Front.

No fire is lit but songs are sung,
      each man's heart is wrapped in the will
         he makes for himself "owning nothing but my rifle."

"Rich in bankruptcy, to the world
      I leave my heart to the Republic my gun
         to men's slow eyes my unvanishing footsteps":

No clock strikes when many trucks
> roll without lights out of the darkness:
>> no order is given but the men come to their feet

In a clashing of iron load themselves
> solid into the steel boxes of the trucks
>> many engines start and the convoy moves off.

Each minute is a passing kilometer
> how far is it to the Front how long?
>> when will the sun rise when but not where

On the horizon the lights of a town appear
> they curse the village fools who make targets
>> of the town and the road for night-flying bombers

When they come near they see that these
> are not street lights but many white stars
>> hanging low on the hills in this southern sky:

All night long trucks carry them
> through the darkness they do not know where
>> they are going but nevertheless understand;

With the passing of each kilometer
> the enormous certainty grows although
>> they hear no cannon, they sense that the hour is near.

Still in darkness the trucks stop:
> they have stopped before but this time they know:
>> no orders are given but the men drop to the ground

It is summer and the night air heavy
> with the scent of grape leaves; the warm earth
>> returns to the sun the heat it has taken up all day

If there are flowers in the villages
> each petal gives the night air its smell
>> which blows cool on the lines of marching men

The smells of cooking and of woodsmoke
        hold the far memory of distant dreams:
                the eyes of a cat seem like green gun-flashes:

Burdened with iron, travelling light
        and carrying much metal they become tired
                the singing and the talk fade and are gone

Each man walks alone with his thoughts
        every ear listens for what it must soon hear
                the men know that they are new, untried troops

The last crossroad lies far behind
        the last backward step has been taken
                the final decision made the last doubt thrown away:

Like a bridal procession and a
        funeral parade they march to the altar,
                the grave, the center of the worldwide stage

Too tired to speak or sing
        quick to tire but long in strength
                now too tired to curse, the men advance:

An order comes: they stop, fall:
        the place is high rough treeless
                false daylight has begun to lift

Cold as the echo of a magnesium flare:
        color, purple yellow and poison-green
                floats into the kindling fires of day

Down below in the valley is a village
        "Villanueva de la Cañada" the men whisper
                this town is Theirs but must be, will be Ours:

A sleeping town clean of war,
        every tree roof wall and window plant
                exactly patterned, perfect, sweet and still

The men understand that by sunset
        this town has to go, go up in blood-red
            sheets of flame and black fountains of dust:

And the sun comes up violently
        sending its rays like bars of music
            from great brass instruments and there is no sound:

Behind us our cannon fire three times
        three cannon clap like iron fists on a pine door
            advance! it is daylight! forward! day has broken!

Advance! leaving night and death behind
        we advance into light and life! advance!
            leaving the old world behind us we march into the new!

No one hears the shot but our first man has fallen.

Andalucía

Silence like light intense,
Silence the deaf ear of noise . . .
The hid guerrillas wishing to commence
The big war, the war of the full voice.
In rocks, knives, guns, and dynamite,
. . . Or the scratch of scorpions ticking in the night;
And at the church door near the altar boys
One in black frowns with a boy in white . . .

Andalucía, land of naked faces.
Country of silver and green sky; lonely country, country of throngs.
Arabia and Africa in gardens and in arid places.
Country of essential dances and the song of songs.
Andalucía, place of the wine yellow light;
Place of wind too lucid for hissing in small tones.
Andalucía, where our dead comrades are young bones,
The color of old rock mountains, bone yellow and white.

In Andalucía it is
Now a country of silences
Since the war; a hiss
Is the way of the wind,
And what a man says
Is also in his silences,
In the glance he gives behind
In Andalucía, land of naked silences.

Andalucía, you too will feel
The wide wind that unlocks systems:
Franco to skid his heels and reel,
Men to shudder on the cluttered Thames.
A great rushing across the planet drives
Breath into bodies. Shouts and arms awake.
Andalucía, country of silver and green, shake
Like a reclaimed cloak, hum like a city of hives.

In Andalucía it is
Now a country of silences
Since the war; a hiss
Is the way of the wind,
And what a man says
Is also in his silences,
In the glance he gives behind,
In Andalucía, land of naked silences.

1943

Spain

Then we could not praise them: they were prone
On the burning hills with their guns, and thermite
Drenched their houses. The battle was the pulse of beaten lands.

The year has flattened the unmarked graves, the bones
Are white under the invisible flowers in the thoughts
Of distant strangers, nourished by workers in their bleak gardens.

They did not die for flowers, nor memories to be pressed
In the archives of another war. They wanted to end indignity,
They fought for life and its continuance. We are that life.

We do not praise the valor of these fathers. We respect
That time and place: there was light in men, their women were beautiful.
Respect is not enough: we are the sons they could not have,
The daughters they did not see. We inherit graves and guns.

Elegy for García Lorca

There was a man.
He opened his eyes and said
I perceive the dawn;
now he is dead.

He said: I perceive the dawn
walking upon the tops of mountains,
setting its feet upon rooftops,
putting its fingers upon windowpanes to make their dust sparkle.
He said: I perceive the dawn arising in the heart of man.

They did not kill him for the dawn on mountains
because they have come to terms with mountaintops
out of whose gold and iron they can make a good thing.
They did not kill him because of many profitable rooftops.
They did not kill him in the name of dust; they love dust
and they would like his words to make it useful gold.
They killed him for the heart of man with which they can not come to terms.

He was born in the morning
and by nightfall he was a dead man;
he was reborn today
and tomorrow he will be born again;
he who is not dead will be reborn daily with the rising sun.

First Love

Again I am summoned to the eternal field
green with the blood still fresh at the roots of flowers,
green through the dust-rimmed memory of faces
that moved among the trees there for the last time
before the final shock, the glazed eye, the hasty mound.

But why are my thoughts in another country?
Why do I always return to the sunken road through corroded hills,
with the Moorish castle's shadow casting ruins over my shoulder
and the black-smocked girl approaching, her hands laden with grapes?

I am eager to enter it, eager to end it.
Perhaps this one will be the last one.
And men afterward will study our arms in museums
and nod their heads, and frown, and name the inadequate dates
and stumble with infant tongues over the strange place-names.

But my heart is forever captive of that other war
that taught me first the meaning of peace and of comradeship

and always I think of my friend who amid the apparition of bombs
saw on the lyric lake the single perfect swan.

Moonlight in Valencia: Civil War

Moonlight in Valencia:
The moon meant planes.
The planes meant death.
And not heroic death.
Like death on a poster:
An officer in a pretty uniform
Or a nurse in a clean white dress—
But death with steel in your brain,
Powder burns on your face,
Blood spilling from your entrails,
And you didn't laugh
Because there was no laughter in it.
You didn't cry PROPAGANDA either.
The propaganda was too much
For everybody concerned.
It hurt you to your guts.
It was real
As anything you ever saw
In the movies:
Moonlight. . . .
Me caigo en la ostia!
Bombers over
Valencia.

Guernica

(Holy City of Spain destroyed by Fascist bombs)

Dead. Dead. Every child. Shriek out
from the stormed park, the smothered school-yard! Shout!
because this quiet shocks the sky as much
as the first roar of the bombers.

                         Noise became
expected: ears survived. Even the touch
of shadows changing, that had stayed the same
for hundreds of holy years, became expected.

But the planes went, and all unresurrected
lies the city: not one sudden wonder
has risen to mock the bombs. Are you afraid?
Those were no eagles; all their titan thunder
was made by human hands.

                        Grant Icarus shade
or he will fall again! Mothers, grow wild,
shriek out! Dead. Dead. Every child.

Barcelona Celebrates Three Years of Franco

Over the sunless ways of Barcelona
Franco rides upon a proud white horse.
Behind him come the generals, that force
the blackness of their banners on the breeze.

Mother, this day is not for counting beads.
How can you lock your door, while Barcelona,
flushed like a maiden with festivities,
throws flowers at the leader's lifted head?

Three years ago the ways of Barcelona
opened themselves to Franco's triumph-tread,
and on the gutters empty guns lay dead.
Always counting your beads, have you forgotten?

Even the lock upon my door, the cotton
stuffed in my ears, allow this day no dimming.
Here is the room my bravest son was shot in.
He fell on the same day with Barcelona.

Let Franco fill his eyes with crowds of women
that dream of spitting where his horse has gone!
This room's the temple that I sing my hymn in,
and here I count the beads for Barcelona.

How glad I am that not a ray of sun
blesses the flag of Franco! Oh great owner
of farm and city—when our counting's done
we'll drive your shadow out of Barcelona!

To Eugene J. Loveman

(Gandesa)
We used to roam along the Gravesend shoreline, poking
through the piles of driftwood and debris looking for
something—treasure, or some strange sea-thing cast up on the
beach after storms. Old women came down with sacks to gather
the dead fish, and children came with wagons to cart away
loads of broken, tarred timber. We filled our pockets with
smooth round stones as white as moons, and sat on the ruined
walls of an old prison, and watched the liners sailing through
the Narrows, down the Jersey coast past Sandy Hook. We knew
all the bells and lights, and all the signal sounds and channels.
We were always looking for something.

On the sea fringe
where the waves
wash umber on the crusted rocks,
sand whispers in scoured shells
and sea gulls poise
to plummet under surf
for silver little fish

Here where Columbus smiles
when steamers vanish
downhill in the east
we lit the driftwood fires,
and in the sharkteeth flames
saw naked dancers on a jungle shore
worshipping weird idols and their gods.

We traced the lonely latitudes
where sad Magellan sailed,
and felt the tremor
of the other shore
beneath our feet
when giant combers fell.

The years have curtained down
behind the Jersey hills,
and now while you sleep
in the other shore of Spain
boys, as we were, wander here again

and scan the sea-lanes
where the cargoes ride
to lands where guntongues
bellow heavenward;
and when evening
drifts in from the east
they light perennial fires

And constant watchers
feed the phoenix flames
that flicker on the margins of the world.

In Memory of the Spanish Poet
Federico García Lorca

Where the white bridge rears up its stamping arches
Proud as a colt across the clatter of the shallow river,
The sharp guitars
Have never forgotten your name.

Only the swordspeech of the cruel strings
Can pierce the minds of those who remain,
Sitting in the eyeless ruins of the houses,
The shelter of the broken wall.

A woman has begun to sing:
O music the color of olives!
Her eyes are darker than the deep cathedrals;
Her words come dressed as mourners,
In the gate of her shadowy voice,
Each with a meaning like a sheaf of seven blades!

The spires and high Giraldas, still as nails
Nailed in the four cross roads,
Watch where the song becomes the color of carnations,
And flowers like wounds in the white dust of Spain.

(Under what crossless Calvary lie your lost bones, García Lorca?
What white Sierra hid your murder in a rocky valley?)

In the four quarters of the world, the wind is still,
And wonders at the swordplay of the fierce guitar:
The voice has turned to iron in the naked air,
More loud and more despairing than a ruined tower.

(Under what crossless Calvary lie your lost bones, García Lorca?
What white Sierra hid your murder in a rocky valley?)

Blood and Sand

If there ever was a spoiled darling,
It was you, García-Lorca.
The sensation of three continents,
That was you, García-Lorca.
You were asked to dinner everywhere.
You were divine, Federico.
What went on in you, Federico,
Orestes doubling for Dwight Fiske?
Everyone threw his love at your head,
Those ailing loves, Federico,
With the channering worm in their garlands.
Hot Spain showed you her bare belly.
You saw the black solar plexus
Hollow with maggots. No love there.
No love. You made a concert program
Out of synonyms for agony,
The frightful parching agony
Of the lovers of Lot's wife.
You bore your own caesarian
Children daily, and all black stones.
They kept you pregnant, Federico,
With the chemicals of their unlust,
With their ugly devouring sperm,
With their pustulant, corrosive blood.
You watched the monster, Federico,
That Yeats saw stirring in the desert.
You never took your eyes off it.
It watched you, García-Lorca.
Then one day it walked. It never
Noticed you again, Federico.

Spanish Sequence

I

He stands against the brick wall,
or in the open field, and ten rifles
converge upon the liquid beating heart.

He waits behind the blindfold of his eyes,
shouts at the onrushing dark
as he falls, and his blood slowly dies.

Such is the man we now come upon.
Such is the verdict we have yet to meet,
and many of us are still young.

Now, with fire controlling their cities,
and sky controlled by accurate planes,
honor, like a sun, dawns over the Pyrenees.

Now, when runners arrive stunned
from their coast's bombardment:
now, beginning this intimate season

when Spring with its punctual grass
prepares an arbor for lovers; today,
at last, we meet the shape of our years.

Turn, dreamer, to the burnt fields
where they wait calmly in trenches,
those who are first to fall, and least famous.
Turn where your own life may hold or fail.

II

Spain, the body,
and in its center
calmly beating
the great heart, Madrid.

Weep,
for the children are gone
the houses are gone
but the heart
still beats.

Listen:
over the roar of planes
above the wail of death
feeding its defenders
the heart beats.

Madrid!
Burning in the night
bleeding in the night
but still standing.

They have thrust all year
at the center of this man.

The heart of a people can bleed
but not to death
never to death.

III

A pall of smoke is rising over the city.
For days now they have been burning the bodies,
piled high, clothed in blue and red,
a thousand bullet-riddled men and women.

In Badajoz, the day the fascists came in,
all the civilians with rifle-marked shoulders
were led into the huge bull-ring.
dressed as they were in simple blouses.

Some ran screaming towards the hot guns,
many of them tried to scale the walls,
others tried to pray, but no one escaped,
no one remained standing.

All through the night this went on
and in the morning the burning began,
and a pall hung over the brown hills,
and the odor of burning flesh.

It was said on that day the blood
covered the arena like a robe;
the blood was said to be palm deep
that terrible day in Badajoz.

IV

"The assassins are at the gates of Madrid.
Let us go out to meet them.
Tear out the fascist claws and fangs,
and break his wings! Fight like men!"

Pasionaria speaks, and the silence
is greater than the soaring of birds.
O voice of these poor and proud,
tongue of the bitter bleeding mouth:

We were yoked as oxen, our backs bent;
we lived in the darkness of our labor;
we were bled for the wine of the manors.
The priests comforted us with poverty.
Hovels were our houses, disease our first born.
Now we cast off the weight of centuries
and take our place among the proud nations!
Let us stand as firm as our mountains.
We fight with Time at our backs, and alone.
The people of the world shout in their cities:
Planes for Spain, guns for Republican Spain,
and the people will find their way to us!

To resist is to win!
No pasaran: Pasarémos!

And the huge hall is listening;
in the sky, patrolling the coastline;
in the wet desperate trenches
and beneath the seas, listening . . .

V

Boldly the Pyrenees supported the sky
and they were in the foothills by dawn.
The last cold stars clung to the peaks,
flashed for a bright moment, then faded.

They climbed slowly towards the south
through the mountain footpaths,
led by a silent ragged Spaniard.
They felt snow at their throats
sweeping down from the giant crags.
Higher than the usual birds,
with the morning calm on their faces

and the freeze of air in the blood
they climbed, travelers from other cities,
strangers following another stranger
into a strange land, greeted by wind.
Suddenly below: the tremendous valley.
And the voice of the guide calling far
Viva España! Salud y victoria!

Huddled in thin coats, wide-eyed
on this Mount Olympus, they stood
as Cortez once did, in another century;
and, descending, alive in air,
the guards run to them shouting *Americános!
Amigos! Salud compañeros!*
And they are not frightened any more.

VI

From Figueras they boarded the train
smelling of cattle, bound for Barcelona.
The locomotive lunged with its hot wheels
and after a few hours the track curved
like a bow, seaward, and on the window
the blue Mediterranean was a thin line.

Marty came into the compartment:
I report after a quick reconnaissance
that on this garbage scow there are

deposited in various layers
Poles, Czechs, Slovaks, Greeks, Frenchies
and 57 other varieties—including
a guy from Brooklyn with a banjo whom
I strictly ignored. Herb said, Good work,
this is no time to fraternize with the enemy.

All through the long hot afternoon
they talked, and evening came quietly
with a wind that could kill a man
but leave the candle burning.

Steve sang *Drink to me only with thine eyes.*
Frank still had three good strings
and we joined with his guitar
in the Hoboken to Barcelona Blues:

> *start prayin', General Franco*
> *'cause you ain't got much time*
> *start prayin', old man Franco*
> *'cause you ain't got much time*
> *I've got a five cent bullet*
> *gonna ease your restless mind*

Marty imitated a bullfighter:
The bull charged but Marty (fast boy)
stepped to one side like a dancer,
tripped the bull, grabbed his tail
and heaved him over the bleachers
out of the park, Cheers!
    "I owe it all to
good clean living and Lydia Pinkham."
    Applause!

Then the transfer to trucks, grinding
towards the dark hills, without lights,
moving like a belt over the silent land.
Bill whispered, Are you afraid, Steve?

I think of how we had to sneak past
the Statue of Liberty to get here.
I think of these people standing up

without guns, and fighting, and holding,
and I know why I'm here. Afraid?
Jesus, yes . . . I sweat all the time.

It began to rain after a while
and the men were silent, listening,
huddled against one another for warmth,
locking arms and legs, dreaming of sleep.

They smoked and more talk, and the rain
drummed on the tarpaulin over their heads;
their city loomed in the night and
the new noise was not thunder, but war.

VII

Were there stars in the sky, Federico,
when the ignorant rifles struck you down
without even a sheet to cover your body?

      (in the evening, the dark evening)

Were there dancers in your brain, Federico,
when you faced the singing of the fields
and the cold fanatic faces of the Moors?

      (in the evening, the murderous evening)

Lorca, friend, did you smile perhaps
when death appeared in that poised moment
and called you by your first name?

      (in the evening, that terrible evening)

Evening, the warm loam of earth;
and beyond, the waters of Málaga
slowly turn red with his blood.

Who would have said it were true?
Who would have said that his great body,
ringed with poems, could so swiftly be broken?

Federico, did you wish it a silver thing,
the dagger of the moon, a luminous death?
Did you wish it to come as a horseman,
or sleep, or the failure of sunlight?

Or death as a woman, white and wonderful,
whose breasts at your mouth were grapes?
It was the bullet, Federico.
It was the bullet made of lead.

Ask the stones of Granada to shield you!
Command that the air become armor!
Call down the stars to blind them
for their rifles are raised, Federico!

Sky, be blue over his hill.
Earth, turn more gently now.
For Lorca is gone, and his wisdom.
He fell with the roar of pistols in his head.

He lies on no slab of stone,
nor are there pennies on his eyes;
he sleeps in the alkaline dust
and worms destroy his sacred lips.

He is in the great arena of silence
where heavenly bulls pierce the matador
with their bloodless horns, and angels
weep in the stands like little children.

His poems are frozen in the skull
and no Spring shall ever thaw them.
How shall we find his voice again,
and his guitar, which the wind now plays?

VIII

In Guernica the dead children
were laid out in order upon the sidewalk,
in their white starched dresses,
in their pitiful white dresses.

On their foreheads and breasts
are the little holes where death came in
as thunder, while they were playing
their important summer games.

Do not weep for them, *madre*.
They are gone forever, the little ones,
straight to heaven to the saints,
and God will fill the bullet-holes with candy.

IX

Many of them wept for the first time
as they paraded through the warm streets
fragrant with sunlight and flowers.

Silently with heads bared, the people
of Barcelona looked on in great wonder,
their lips moving *hijo mio* my son my son.

Silently, in their torn faded blouses,
the International Brigades marched:
the well, the healed, the wounded.

They were the pitiful few, fighters
with bare hands and eyes of their country,
seekers of truth in a time of treachery.

They came here singly by a hundred roads,
crossing frontiers in the darkness;
the young with their slogans and laughter,
and those remembering the dungeon and whip.

These men, offering their simple lives,
their names not even written down,
learning the strange words *hoy mañana
resistir y fortificar es vencer!*

Jim Lardner, Bill Schultz, Ralph Neafus,
the anonymous and lost, the thousand names.
In the warm valley or the snows of Teruel,
at Guadarrama or the rolling Guadalajara,

do not be lonely, you who remain forever
in this dry alien ground, far from home.

Death has only one language.

X

Generalissimo Francisco,
the man of God, the pope's choice,
voted most likely to succeed . . .

Approach, friend, and be recognized.
Greetings! We rejoice with you!
The State Department on this occasion
of your victory takes your bloody hand
in most fraternal greetings. Welcome
into the christian brotherhood of nations!
May you be blessed with crops and obedience.
May your reign be long and prosperous
and overflowing O with great goodness
and charity holy in the name of holiness . . .

We assume the German and Italian troops
will leave as quietly as possible.
let everything take place quietly.
Let the political prisoners be shot quietly
and the bleeding be as internal as possible.
Let the firing squads perform with silencers.
Let the barbed-wire camps be quiet.
Let Guernica sleep, and the children there.
Let darkness come down like a robe
to cover this infamous year.

To die, and die, and yet to lose;
to bleed, to give life as freely as water
and still lose! How bitter the day is.
Let this day be bordered in black forever.

                              Man's heart

takes on the definition of iridium,
and he spits upon this whore, Justice,
and tears the cloth from her eyes
and casts her out as a leper.

Remember this, betrayer;
remember this, you who feared;
you the sleeper, the doubter,
the diplomat with white gloves,
all who struck with the same knife.

The earth turns and turns.
History has written it down.
Time will not forgive.

Long Past Moncada

Nothing was less than it seemed, my darling:
The danger was greater, the love was greater, the suffering
        Grows daily great—
And the fear we saw gathering into that Spanish valley
Is rank in all countries, a garden of growing death;
Your death, my darling, the threat to our lifetime
        And to all we love.

Whether you fell at Huesca during the lack of guns,
Or later, at Barcelona, as the city fell,
        You reach my days;
Among the heckling of clocks, the incessant failures,
I know how you recognized our war, and ran
To it as a runner to his eager wedding
        Or our immediate love.

If I indeed killed you, my darling, if my cable killed
Arriving the afternoon the city fell,
        No further guilt
Could more irrevocably drive my days
Through the disordered battles and the cities down
In a clash of metal on murder, a stampede of
        Hunger and death.

Other loves, other children, other gifts, as you said,
"Of the revolution," arrive—but, darling, where
        You entered, life
Entered my hours, whether you lie fallen
Among those sunlight fields, or by miracle somewhere stand,
Your words of war and love, death and another promise
        Survive as a lifetime sound.

From Letter to the Front

IV / SESTINA

Coming to Spain on the first day of the fighting,
Flame in the mountains, and the exotic soldiers,
I gave up ideas of strangeness, but now, keeping
All I profoundly hoped for, I saw fearing
Travellers and the unprepared and the fast-changing
Foothills. The train stopped in a silver country.

Coast-water lit the valleys of this country—
All mysteries stood human in the fighting.
We came from far. We wondered, Were they changing,
Our mild companions, turning into soldiers?
But the cowards were persistent in their fearing,
Each of us narrowed to one wish he was keeping.

There was no change of heart here; we were keeping
Our deepest wish, meeting with hope this country.
The enemies among us went on fearing
The frontier was too far behind. The fighting
Was clear to us all at last. The belted soldiers
Vanished into white hills that dark was changing.

The train stood naked in flowery midnight changing
All complex marvelous hope to war, and keeping
Among us only the main wish, and the soldiers.
We loved each other, believed in the war; this country
Meant to us the arrival of the fighting
At home; we began to know what we were fearing.

Reflect our nations' fears; we acted as changing
Cities at home would act, with one wish, fighting
This threat or falling under it; we were keeping
The knowledge of fiery promises; this country
Struck at our lives, struck deeper than its soldiers.

Those who among us were sure became our soldiers.
The dreams of peace resolved our subtle fearing.
This was the first day of war in a strange country.
Free Catalonia offered that day our changing
Age's hope and resistance, held in its keeping
The war this age must win in love and fighting.

This first day of fighting showed us all men as soldiers.
It offered one wish for keeping. Hope. Deep fearing.
Our changing spirits awake in the soul's country.

V

Much later, I lie in a white seaport night
Of gongs and mystery and bewildered mist
Giving me a strange harbor in these white
Scenes, white rivers, my white dreams of peace.
And a ship lifted up on a sign of freedom.
Peace sharp and immediate as our winter stars.
A blue sailor with a cargo of guitars.

I saw a white ship rise as peace was made
In Spain, the first peace the world would not keep.
The ship pulled away from the harbor where Columbus
Standing on his black pillar sees new worlds;
And suddenly all the people at all the rails
Lifted their hands in a gesture of belief
That climbs among my dreams like a bird flying.
Until the world is lifted by one bird flying
An instant drawing to itself the world.

VI

Home thoughts from home; we read you every day,
Soldiers of distances. You wish most to be here.
In the strange lands of war, I woke and thought of home.
Remembering how war came, I wake and think of you,
In the city of water and stone where I was born,
My home of complex light. What we were fighting for,
In the beginning, in Spain, was not to be defined.
More human than abstract, more direction than end.
Terror arrived intact, lit with the tragic fire
Of hope before its time, tore us from lover and friend.
We came to the violent act with all that we had learned.

But now we are that home you dream across a war.
You fight; and we must go in poetry and hope
Moving into the future that no one can escape.
Peace will in time arrive, but war defined our years.
We are like that young saint at the spring who bent
Her face over dry earth the vision told her flowed,
Miring herself. She knew it was water. But for
Herself, it was filth. Later, for all to come
Following her faith, miraculous crystal ran.

O saint, O poet, O wounded of these wars
To find life flowing from the heart of man.
We hold belief. You fight and are maimed and mad.
We believe, though all you want be bed with one
Whose mouth is bread and wine, whose flesh is home.

Among the Fallen

The midnight herons, the filling station pumps
Roost in the moonlight. My feet on the familiar walk
Are lonely, again paused at the headlined news rack:
Billy, in Spain, has fallen. Beyond the ramps
Of the garage a street of porches dreams: I hear,
From the smoking swings, idling of night, talk,
From the bowl-lit face hanging in the dark
A slumbering of words, no shrapnel knowledge of fear.
Billy has fallen. On a thousand racks, all day,
I have read it. On ten thousand racks these men
Sleeping, I have seen fallen, below and above—
The sewermen, riveter—I have seen—who can say—
What cities of men fallen who must learn, risen
Raging, an anger more kind than love.

Lorca

Winter, in the delicate cold days brittle with detachment,—
far from summers of hot color, awnings, oranges at the door—
coolly reminds us that justice is the one on top.

In a time of faction and counteraction, when friends
are enemies, and enemies, friends, expedience
is the bracing morning exercise, the evening's tired regret;
and poetry is a Chinese game that will never be more,
until, like the Greeks' it is action.

Lorca was one who made his imitators write words:
He was dragged out and beaten.
He was often cold and hungry;
but who, leaning on a cloud,
was never poorer than he imagined.
Fugitive from a foreign literature,
he was forgiven poetry by the people.
Much of the witch hunting is done by the witches:
When Lorca was taken from the empty house of friends,
empty of friends, that old, biting Spanish dust swirled up
and whispered *Blood* and *Death,* and above all keep
Pride: magic is what's alone.

Is there anything as incurable as death?
Predicament of those among whom there can be
no shrines without a martyrdom.
Weep for the lost blood that can never be returned!
But weeping for spilled milk, the flavor is the same.
With Lorca all is well. His end was a Spanish afternoon,
a Goya aquatint, a parasitic life in death:
A literature crept in.

A Federico García Lorca

Ten years have passed since I found in a book shop in Albacete,
The paper-bound case of jewels which I treasure still, the book *Romancero
Gitano,*
And turned to the first poem, the "Romance de la Luna, Luna,"
And read and found fabulous peace in the midst of the war.

Later, in Madrid, the lads of the guerrilleros
Crossed the midnight lines from madness to the light of the Casa de Alianza.
And told us (Langston was there, and Rafael, and María Teresa)
That they came from the choked south, from your buried city, Granada.

And they told how they met in the streets the people who told them in
whispers
Of the way you died, with surprise in your eyes, as you recognized your
assassins,
The men with the patent-leather hats and souls of patent-leather.

c. 1948

Elegia

Madrid   Madrid   Madrid   Madrid
I call your name endlessly, savor it like a lover.
Ten irretrievable years have exploded like bombs
since last I saw you, since last I slept
in your arms of tenderness and wounded granite.
Ten years since I touched your face in the sun,
ten years since the homeless Guadarrama winds
moaned like shivering orphans through your veins
and I moaned with them.
                              When I think of you, Madrid,
locked in the bordello of the Universal Pimp,
the blood that rushes to my heart and head
blinds me, and I could strangle your blood-bespattered jailors,
choke them with these two hands which once embraced you.
When I think of your breathing body of vibrancy and sun,
silently I weep, in my own native land
which I love no less because I love you more.
Yet I know, in the heart of my heart, that until your liberation
rings through the world of free men near and far
I must wander like an alien everywhere.

Madrid, in these days of our planet's anguish,
forged by the men whose mock morality
begins and ends with the tape of the stock exchanges,
I too sometimes despair. I weep with your dead young poet.
Like him I curse our age and cite the endless wars,
the exiles, dangers, fears, our weariness
of blood, and blind survival, when so many
homes, wives, even memories, are lost.

Yes, I weep with Garcilaso. I remember
your grave face and your subtle smile
and the heart-leaping beauty of your daughters and even
the tattered elegance of your poorest sons.
I remember the gaiety of your *milicianos*—

my comrades-in-arms. What other city
in history ever raised a battalion of barbers
or reared its own young shirt-sleeved generals?
And I recall them all. If I ever forget you,
Madrid, Madrid, may my right hand lose its cunning.

I speak to you, Madrid, as lover, husband, son.
Accept this human trinity of passion.
I love you, therefore I am faithful to you
and because to forget you would be to forget
everything I love and value in the world.
Who is not true to you is false to every man
and he to whom your name means nothing never loved
and they who would use your flesh and blood again
as a whore for their wars and their wise investments,
may they be doubly damned! the double murderers
of you and their professed but fictional honor,
of everything untarnished in our time.

Wandering, bitter, in this bitter age,
I dream of your broad avenues like brooks in summer
with your loveliest children alive in them like trout.
In my memory I walk the Calle de Velasquez
to the green Retiro and its green gardens.
Sometimes when I pace the streets of my own city
I am transported to the flowing Alcalá
and my footsteps quicken, I hasten to the spot
where all your living streams meet the Gateway to the Sun.
Sometimes I brood in the shadowed Plaza Mayor
with the ghosts of old Kings and Inquisitors
agitating the balconies with their idiot stares
(which Goya later knew) and under whose stone arches,
those somber rooms beneath the colonnades,
the old watchmaker dreams of tiny, intricate minutes,
the old woman sells pencils and gaudy amber combs,
dreaming of the days when her own body was young,
and the rheumatic peasant with fingers gnarled as grapevines
eagerly displays his muscat raisins;
and the intense boys of ten, with smoldering aged eyes,
kneel, and gravely, quixotically,
polish the rawhide boots of the soldiers in for an hour

from the mined trenches of the Casa de Campo,
from their posts, buzzing with death, within the skeleton
of University City.
                            And the girls stroll by,
the young ones, conscious of their womanhood,
and I hear in my undying heart called Madrid
the soldiers boldly calling to them: Oye, guapa, oye!

I remember your bookshops, the windows always crowded
with new editions of the Gypsy Ballads,
with *Poetas en la España Leal*
and *Romanceros de los Soldados en las Trincheras.*
There was never enough food, but always poetry.
Ah the flood of song that gushed with your blood
into the world during your three years of glory!

And I think: it is a fine thing to be a man
only when man has dignity and manhood.
It is a fine thing to be proud and fearless
only when pride and courage have direction, meaning.
And in our world no prouder words were spoken
in those three agonized years than *I am from Madrid.*

Now ten years have passed with small explosions of hope,
yet you remain, Madrid, the conscience of our lives.
So long as you endure, in chains, in sorrow,
I am not free, no one of us is free.
Any man in the world who does not love Madrid
as he loves a woman, as he values his sex,
that man is less than a man and dangerous,
and so long as he directs the affairs of our world
I must be his undying enemy.

Madrid   Madrid   Madrid   Madrid
Waking and sleeping, your name sings in my heart
and your need fills all my thoughts and acts
(which are gentle but have also been intimate with rifles).
Forgive me, I cannot love you properly from afar—
no distant thing is ever truly loved—
but this, in the wrathful impotence of distance,
I promise: Madrid, if I ever forget you,

may my right hand lose its human cunning,
may my arms and legs wither in their sockets,
may my body be drained of its juices and my brain
go soft and senseless as an imbecile's.
And if I die before I can return to you,
or you, in fullest freedom, are restored to us,
my sons will love you as their father did
Madrid   Madrid   Madrid

Incident at Guernica

The bomber stuck to the sky like a burr to the earth—
Drone of motors, glint of sun on steel,
Immobile in space and fixed on the retina of time
For the instant at which the forked bloodstreams converge.
No swoop to break the spell—but the bottom eye of the ship winks
And a teardrop rolls down the sky's pocked cheek.
Encased chemicals under a silk parasol,
Falling stealthily, rape the innocent sky.
Discernment sees a flak-rimmed Manet
And kill-joys see the shape of sudden death.
Into a baby-carriage (occupant ascertained), it delicately falls,
Into the white folds of the bedding it nestles,
While people say the usual things——
"*Sacre bleu*"—"*Madre nuestra*"—"Holy cow!"
"Well, I'll be hog-tied, a three-point landing,"
And pray through their knees, their lips laboring with fear.
An idiot laughs, an old man leers at the fate of Oedipus,
And a mezzo-soprano who sings Brunnhilde every ten years
Revels in her Big Moment and hits high C
As reality explodes into Walpurgis.

For My Dead Brother

The moon was full that night in Aragón . . .
we sat in the black velvet shadow
of the hazel (called *avellano* there);
the men lay sleeping, sprawled on the packed earth
in their blankets (like the dead). . . .

With dawn we'd move in double files
down to the Ebro, cross in boats,
and many lying there relaxed
would lie relaxed across the river
(but without their blankets).

He said: "You started something, baby—"
(I was thirty-four; he ten years less;
he was my captain; I his adjutant)
"—you started something, baby," Aaron said,
"when you came to Spain."

Across the yellow river
there was a night loud with machine guns
and the harmless popcorn crackle
of hand grenades bursting pink and green,
and he was gone and somehow Sam found me in the dark,
bringing Aaron's pistol, wet with blood.
He said:
            "The last thing Aaron said
            was, 'Did we take the hill?'
            I told him, 'Sure.'"

Aaron, we did not take the hill.
We lost in Spain. Aaron,
I know, finally, what you meant that night
under the black shadow of the *avellano,*
sitting here in prison twelve years later.

We did not take the hill, *mi commandante,*
but o! the plains that we have taken
and the mountains, rivers, cities,
deserts, flowing valleys, seas!
You may sleep . . . sleep, my brother, sleep.

The Dead Past

For all of thirteen years
we have made speeches
in dusty half-filled halls, in private houses
     (a handful there),
called meetings, passed out leaflets,
picketed the consulates with picket signs that read:
     NO DEALS WITH SPAIN
     SAVE THE PRISONERS IN FRANCO'S PRISONS
     LONG LIVE THE REPUBLIC and
     MADRID WILL BE THE TOMB OF FASCISM!
For thirteen years . . .
                and there are those who say:
     Why live in the past? Why so much emphasis
     on what is dead and gone and lost and dry
     when the present is here, the future bursts the clock,
     so many things to do, so little time?

Is it the past and is it dead and gone
and was Spain lost or does the battle sound?
And is it dry or is it only the tears that are dry
on the faces of children, light streams through
dirt on cheeks and lips, and isn't the blood still wet
on the dirty concrete floors of the cells
in the model prison on the hillside?

There is a village I remember
where in the house on the narrow street
there were only the grandfather and his wife
and the daughter-in-law and the children
     (the one son dead in battle
     the other son dying in hospital)
and I lay crippled—not by wounds but
by the absurdity of rheumatism in battle,

where every night before I went to bed
        (their bed, they sleeping
        on the flagstone floor)
the old woman rubbed my legs and arms
with an old woman's remedies and when
every time I left the house
        I found a present on return:
        (a handful of hazelnuts,
        a glass of wine, dried figs
        or fresh figs)
a present for a stranger in a foreign land
because they knew why I was living in their house
and wanted to say (but did not have the words):
        We love you for coming
        for fighting
        for suffering for us
        (if only from rheumatism)
Are they dead and gone and dry (they were dry then);
The children had never seen a toy
in all their born days and did not know
what to do with one I imported for them
from Barcelona . . .
        are they lost
because the cause was lost (or said to be
by important people who knew better than
these poor *analfabetos* who knew only how to love
and how to fight?)
        Too much emphasis?

But tell us now, today
that the war is done,
the wounded healed and the dead are buried;
tell us now that the children's faces
are clean and fat
and their bellies flat instead of swollen
and the jails are empty and cobwebs are spun
in the corners of the cells
and
the blood has finally dried on the concrete floor
and cannot be distinguished from the red dust
of the arid soil;

and tell us the soil is no longer arid
but dark and damp and stirring
with the life of the vines
and the vats of olive oil are full
and the oil cheap and chickpeas plentiful
and meat is to be eaten instead of dreamed about
and the patent leather hats are green with age
in the museums and the fat sodomist
has gone to his reward at the feet of God—
then we will stop talking about
the past and laying so much emphasis
on what is dead and gone and lost and dry,
and return to the present that has grown out of
this past and cannot be separated from it.

Tomorrow's Seed

Proud banner of death,
I see them waving
There against the sky,
Struck deep in Spanish earth
Where your dark bodies lie
Inert and helpless—
So they think
Who do not know
That from your death
New life will grow.
For there are those who cannot see
The mighty roots of liberty
Push upward in the dark
To burst in flame—
A million stars—
And one your name:
      Man
Who fell in Spanish earth:
Human seed
For freedom's birth.

To Spain

Jarama, Teruel, Guadalajara—
who does not remember?
Their sounds tap on the mind's window
till memory wakes and the air is hollow with knocking—
the urgent hands of a hunted brother outside in the dark. . . .
Badajoz, Manzanar, Santander—
who does not remember?
Who has forgotten holy Guernica?

Sun, and the blood of the brigades soaked your battlefields.
They came, the brigade brothers
and left their young bones on your ancient soil.
The brigades died, and the land died with them—
but you went down fighting.

My forefathers too were Iberian,
a people gentle and proud,
like your people dark-browed, dark-souled
speaking the same tongue.
In my bones I know your sun-scarred hills
wrinkled brown and dry like the face of an old woman;
there grows the scraggly olive, covered with a fine gray dust.
In my veins I know your untamed rivers
born amid steep and lifeless crags,
dancing a wild *jota* down to sunbaked plains
and sudden green groves of citron and of lemon.
And in my mind I know your vast uplands,
bleak and harsh as the fate of your people,
where never the song of a bird is heard—
it is too lonely there, too windswept, too naked of trees.
Old is your land, old
with the wine-grapes of Carthage and the silver olives of the traders from
    Tyre.
Often have I pondered the classic names of your cities:
Toledo, Zaragoza, Valladolid;

Granada, Córdoba, Castille.
O cities of Lorca, your nightingales are silent now, your bells are stopped with
    dust!
O cities of El Greco, you stand on a harsh and lonely plain,
bathed in the green light of storm!

People of Lorca—
I remember how you were learning to read.
Between battles, with your bayonets,
you scrawled the letters of the alphabet in the dust.
As the war progressed, the day came when you could write your name entire,
and proudly you signed the post-card to the Ministry of Education:
Today for the first time in centuries, I Sancho Panza, soldier of the Republic,
was able to write my name.
Thank you, dear Republic,
for not keeping me ignorant.
But now it has all been taken from you,
they want you ignorant as animals,
your work-twisted hands must know neither pen nor bayonet.

And they want you poor,
poor with the poverty of centuries.
A heavy cross of gold, laid on your backs, crushes you to your knees.
For the tearing cramps of hunger you are given incense to eat.
The droning of parish priests drowns out the vast groaning
from cell and dungeon-keep.
The *Caudillo* struts in his leather boots—
his paramours long since lie
under the Reichstag, in a criminal's grave in Italy;
yet, with mincing steps, he tramples on your dreams.
And still, while the parish priests drone orisons,
while leather jackboots click on cobbled streets,
an eye speaks to an eye;
a heart turns over its treasure in the deep and lonely night:

They say
El Caudillo knows—
there are men in the hills who have never surrendered!
They live there as the eagles do,
they bide their time as Boabdil. . . .

Dear land
your children are scattered far:
from Perpignan
where welcoming arms of barbed wire awaited them,
to far-flung continents.
But deep underground are the shoots of the dream,
in the high pinnacles of your hearts you have never surrendered,
and eagles soar there still in lonely flight.

Ours is an age of exiles,
of lands bereft and hunted men.
Yet, from the high Pyrenees, as from the mountains of Macedonia,
the unconquered shall return.
The children of Perpignan shall have their land again.
Ibarruri—you shall embrace your beloved miners.
And from far continents, from lands of friendship and from hostile lands,
from all the island abattoirs
that dot the fair Aegean,
from all the barbed-wire hells—
salud, my brothers! We shall meet again!
We shall all come home!

Activist Miliciano

As he felt the wall against his back and against
the back of his head, he suddenly thought: The glint
of sun I see on those rifles is the last
glint of sun I shall see on rifles or
on anything else.

       The thought
seemed to him too personal for this moment,
which, with three hundred others coming
after him, the counteroffensive broken, and the loss
of four towns, was more than merely individual.
But he was no theoretician, had no last words, and even
when he heard the snick of the bolts clicking
into place, all he could think was:
I did the best I could. So it's all right. But
after a life at it, it's hard not to be here
to see how it all came out.

Lorca

     Split ears of morning earth green now,
Love and death twisted in tree arms,
     Come love, throw out your nipple
to the teeth of a passing clown.

Spit olive pits at my Lorca,
Give Harlem's king one spoon,
At four in the never noon.
Scoop out the croaker eyes
     of rose flavored Gypsies
Singing García,
In lost Spain's
Darkened noon.

Eisenhower's Visit to Franco, 1959

. . . we die of cold, and not of darkness.
—Unamuno

The American hero must triumph over
The forces of darkness.
He has flown through the very light of heaven
And come down in the slow dusk
Of Spain.

Franco stands in a shining circle of police.
His arms open in welcome.
He promises all dark things
Will be hunted down.

State police yawn in the prisons.
Antonio Machado follows the moon
Down a road of white dust,
To a cave of silent children
Under the Pyrenees.
Wine darkens in stone jars in villages,
Wine sleeps in the mouths of old men, it is a dark red color.

Smiles glitter in Madrid.
Eisenhower has touched hands with Franco, embracing
In a glare of photographers.
Clean new bombers from America muffle their engines
And glide down now.
Their wings shine in the searchlights
Of bare fields,
In Spain.

Into Darkness, in Granada

O if I were not so unhappy
I could write great poetry!
Dusk falls through the olive trees
Federico García Lorca
leaps about among them
dodging the dark as it falls upon him
O if only I could leap like him
and make great songs
Instead I swing about wildly
as in a children's
jungle gym
in a vacant lot by Ben Shahn
jump up suddenly
upon the back of a running horse
in the face of a plains' twister
And paddle away slowly
into total darkness
in a Dove boat

All Elegies Are Black and White

to Robert Motherwell

When Villon went to his college
he wore a black gown
he put his hood up when
he went out on the black streets.

He ate black bread
and even drank a kind of black wine,
(we don't have any longer)
it wasn't that good Beaune
his skill taught him how to steal,
a disappearing drink also.

The sky was white over Paris,
until it fell in the streets,
like a sky over mountains,
disturbing and demanding.

When you are in Spain
you think of sky
and mountain where the forest
is without water.
You think of your art
which has become important
like a plow
on the flat land.

There are even a few animals
to consider.
And olives.

Do you regard them separately?
The forms of nature,

animals, trees
That bear a black burden
whose throat is always thirsty?

I know of Seville of black carriages
one factory
one river
the air is brown.

Alas we have fair hair, are *rojo.*

Throw a mantilla over your face
rojo of the light,
walk only in the white spaces.

The trains that cross back and forth
the borders of Elegy
sleep all afternoon, at night
lament the lost shapes.

I think when you oppose
black against white,
archaeologist you have raised a dream
which is bitter.

The white elegy
is the most secret elegy.

One may arrive at it
from the blue.

The sky in Spain is high.
It is as high as the sky
in California.

When one begins with white and blue
it is necessary for one's eyes to darken.
One may have fair hair in Spain,
yet the trouble of blue eyes!
Unless one can always live
sparsely as in Castille.

(How wise you are to understand
the use of orange with blue.
"Never without the other.")

And what courage to allow oneself
to become black and blue!

It is necessary that eyes be black
so the white may deepen
in them the white may sink,
it can then be constant, as music
is constant, or a marriage, or fountains,
or a palace whose shadow is constant.

To make an Elegy of Spain
is to make a song of the abyss.

It is to cut a gorge into one's soul
which is suddenly no longer private.
This privacy which has become invaded
straightens itself up, it sings,
"I am proud as a cañon."

Can you imagine the shock over the world

against which two enormous black rocks roll

this world that looks like a white cloud

shifting its buttocks?

                    When the guitar strikes

A procession of those tasters of ecstasy
the thieves of dark and light

beginning with Villon

whose black songs are elegies
whose elegies are white

                    Dios!

In Memory of a Spanish Poet

Take leave of the sun, and of the wheat, for me.
—Miguel Hernández, written in prison, 1942

I see you strangling
Under the black ripples of whitewashed walls.
Your hands turn yellow in the ruins of the sun.
I dream of your slow voice, flying,
Planting the dark waters of the spirit
With lutes and seeds.

Here, in the American Midwest,
Those seeds fly out of the field and across the strange heaven of my skull.
They scatter out of their wings a quiet farewell,
A greeting to my country.

Now twilight gathers,
A long sundown.
Silos creep away toward the west.

The Spanish Civil War

Thirty years ago tonight
        this bitter night
the spanish civil war began
        o my dear

someone
        we see dimly
        having now remembered him
was wound up tight
with a key in his back
        too tight

But notice the moon glowing on snow
on the palegray snow where it creeps
at the edge of the palegreen pasture
        in the season of going under
and the gray moon shining thirty years ago
on the palegray lemon grove where earth
sparkled with mica and a few bees buzzed
in the dark
        a few latewandering bullets

someone very stiffly crawling
shaking his stiffened head
moves like a black toy on the appalling
earth   and someone
moves at the edge of the pasture
coming this way
        to bed

to bed my dear
for the spanish civil war
spread and spread
        always spreading

and the armies gathered
        always gathering
        in every gathering place
and the world creeps
        the whole world always creeping
to the lemon grove
        our neighbors creeping gathering
        vicious and cruel with eyes like mica

My dear this is my song
of a country
        that it was lovely in the dawn
        that it was garlanded an ox for a lady
        that it was a clear call musical in the field
        that it was a wall but not too high to see over
        that it was rebellious as much of the old as the young
        that it was inquisitive
        that it was a welcome
        that it was born in the woman who lives in the stone
        that it was built by the men who could hew and finger

that it   began even so in a space ravaged from
            a noble people and that it proceeded
            in the only course open to such beginning
            a study and cultivation of death and of
            all manner of degradation and that it
            is a brain rotted in cowardice a heart
            squirming and white
that it is venality   avarice   and the selling
        of authority
whereby the hands of cowards are strengthened
        for cowardly ends
while the old rage in dark houses and the young
        parade   shadows in the streets
and the protestation of murder has been made
        a sin

that it is

o my dear
        in this thirtieth
            year of awakening

my song is
> bitter as the night
> > and exhausted

What was born then has no ending
> has come nearer and nearer
like the contagion in the forest
> like the disequilibrium of the seas

Remoteness
and death in the lemon grove
> under the gray moon
have crept homeward
> turning my tears to stone

Truly my life has been lived in an evil time

Look
the dark man creeping
where snow drives its blunt edge across the pasture
> in our november
moving stiffly   jerking his head
> like a broken toy
moving with difficulty toward our window
lighted by the palegray moon
> in this forgotten corner of the land

soon
he will be in your bed
in your warmth and privacy

Perhaps finally he will not know what to do
and then you must decide
> quickly
> for you had not thought this would happen
how you will receive the last shred
> of the love of the world.

Word of Mouth

I / *THE RETURN*

Westward from Sète
                      as I went long before
along my life
            as I went
                   wave by wave—
the long words of the sea
                     the orange rooftop tiles
back to the boundary
              where I had been before.

Spain.
            Sex of cactus and of cypresses,
Tile-orange, green;   olive;   black.   The sea.
One man.   Beethoven radio.   War.
Threat of all life.   Within my belief's body.
Within my morning, music.   High colored mountain
along the seacoast
              where the swallows fly.

Prolonged
beyond your cries and your cities.
Along my life and death backward toward that morning
when all things fell open and I went into Spain.

One man.   Sardana music.   This frontier.
Where I now come again.
               I stop.
                    I do not pass.

NOTE: *The country is the Catalan border of France and Spain.*
The two times are July, 1936, the beginning of the war,
and the time of my return to the border in 1963.

Wave under wave
              like the divisive South
afire in the country of my birth.

A moment of glass.   All down the coast I face
as far as vision, blue, memory of blue.

Seen now.   Why do I not go in?   I stand.
I cannot pass.   History, destroyed music.

I need to go into.
              In a dream I have seen
Spain, *sleeping children:*
                   before me:
                          as I drive
as I go
        (I need to go into
                  this country
of love and)
             wave after wave
                   they lie
in a deep forest.
             As the driving light
touches them
             (I need this country
                     of love and death)
they begin to rouse.
             They wake.

II / *WORD OF MOUTH*

Speeding back from the border.
                    A rock came spinning up
cast from the wheels of a car.
                   Crackled the windshield glass.
Glitter before my eyes like a man made of snow
lying over the hood, blind white except for glints
an inch of sight where Languedoc shines through.

You on my one side, you on the other!
What I have is dazzle.   My son; my friend;
tell me this side and tell me that side,
news of the road near Agde.

Word from this side, word from the tree-side—
Spain at our back : agony : before me, glitter,
                                        today
blinding my eyes, blind diamonds, one clear wound.

Something is flying out of the sky behind me.
Turning, stirring of dream, something is speeding,
something is overtaking.

Stirrings in prisons, on beds, the mouths of the young,
resist, dance, love.   It drives through the back of my head,
through my eyes and breasts and mouth.
I know a harvest : mass in the wine country.
A lifetime after, and still alive.

Something out of Spain, into the general light!
I drive blind white, trusting news of this side,
news of that side, all the time the line of the poem:
Amor, pena, desig, somni, dolor.*
The grapes have become wine by the hand of man.
Sea risen from the sea, a bearded king.

The seaward cemetery risen from the sea
like a woman rising.
                    Amor.
                            Phases of sun.
The wine declared god by the hand of man.
Pena.
                A rumor given me by this side and that side.
We drive in brilliant glitter, in jungle night, in distant war,
in all our cities, in a word, overtaking.
                                Desig.

*NOTE: *The line is from a Catalan poem in* Cantilena *by Joseph*
Sebastien Pons. Love, agony, desire, dream, suffering.

A cry received, gone past me into all men,
speaking, into all women.
                              A man goes into the sea,
    bearded fire and all things rise from this blaze of eyes,
living, it speaks, driving forth from Spain,

                                        somni, dolor,
These cliffs, these years.   Do we drive into light?
Driven, live, overtaken?

                    Amor, pena, desig.

The Cartridges

You sleep weightless on my palm, the revolver
I smuggled across eleven borders
hidden in my raincoat, hidden from my wife,
my children, myself. But now we are

alone with the radio and its cries
in the off-season villa by the shore,
so into this chapel of banalities
I give you my hand, I give you my life.

Six little .22 long-rifle slugs
golden-haloed like guardian angels,
their glum faces grease-smeared, are on the table
posed on a sheet of pure typing paper.

At home in California in my rifle,
closeted now and bandaged in a torn sheet,
they would mean nothing, the final opening
of a rabbit brain, the release of clichés,

the release of gases, animal pain,
or the tearing of glass. Nothing at all.
Here in my numbed fingers, one by one,
I take them up and give them to their stations.

First you, my little American, you bring
reports of everything I left behind,
and you, the hope of middle age, the game
I play with sleep when sleep is everything.

And you, stupid, are a black hole in the air
and nothing more. I refuse to explain.
And you, all of whose names are simply Spain,
are every pure act I don't dare.

This one has no name and no nation
and has been with me from the start. And you,
finally, you have a name I will not name, a face
I cannot face, you could be music, you

could be the music of snow on the warm plain
of Michigan, you could be my voice
calling to me at last, calling me out of Spain,
calling me home, home, home, at any price.

To P. L., 1916–1937

a soldier of the Republic

Gray earth peeping through snow,
you lay for three days
with one side of your face
frozen to the ground. They tied your cheek
with the red and black scarf
of the Anarchists, and bundled you
in canvas, and threw you away.
Before that an old country woman
of the Aragon, spitting on her thumb,
rubbing it against her forefinger,
stole your black Wellingtons,
the gray hunting socks, and the long
slender knife you wore
in a little leather scabbard
riding your right hip. She honed it,
ran her finger down the blade, and laughed,
though she had no meat to cut,
blessing your tight fists
that had fallen side by side
like frozen faces on your hard belly
that was becoming earth. (Years later
she saw the two faces
at table, and turned from the bread
and the steaming oily soup, turned
to the darkness of the open door,
and opened her eyes to darkness
that they might be filled with anything
but those two faces squeezed
in the blue of snow and snow and snow.)
She blessed your feet, still pink,
with hard yellow shields of skin
at heel and toe, and she laughed
scampering across the road, into

the goat field, and up the long hill,
the boots bundled in her skirts,
and the gray hunting socks, and the knife.
For seven weeks she wore the boots
stuffed with rags at toe and heel.
She thought she understood
why you lay down to rest
even in snow, and gave them to a nephew,
and the gray socks too.
The knife is still used, the black handle
almost white, the blade
worn thin since there is meat to cut.
Without laughter she is gone
ten years now,
and on the road to Huesca in spring
there is no one to look for you
among the wild jonquils, the curling
grasses at the road side,
and the blood red poppies, no one
to look on the farthest tip
of wind breathing down from the mountains
and shaking the stunted pines you hid among.

Spain—The Modern Phoenix

*"Most of today's youth, I fear, knows far too little about the
Spanish Civil War for us to accept this." So wrote a young
kinsman, an editor of a "youth" weekly, of an earlier version that
lacked the Prologue.*

1. PROLOGUE

To you, born far too late
for what was once to us, now ancient mariners,
the daily source of singing glory or of flaming indignation
over the seesaw battles tearing Spain's newborn Republic of the Thirties,
let me remind you that the latest headlines herald
new storms of protest in the old bullring of nations.

Back in our time, our veins volcanoed when four traitor-generals
heiled Hitler, Mussolini and two Popes to win
legions of flying, clanking, and preaching crocodiles.

Since Dante put some Papal monsters deep in his *Inferno,*
let us highlight the infamy of those two Holy Fascists
with the assumed name of that "Infallible" Pius who battled
Risorgimento's heroes with foreign forces
to keep slave states in central Italy.

The first, Achille Ratti, Pius the Eleventh, embraced
the assassin Mussolini to roll back the clock
a century and rob their countrymen for priestly profits.
Then Ratti and his crime-collaborator,
slick Cardinal Pacelli, later Pius Twelfth,
the Pope who would permit the slaughter of Jews,
vowed to restore Spain's Holy Inquisition.
Like vultures' claws, their long black arms reached
into the great non-Catholic nations, all but one,
and forged in time a mongoloid alliance between
the modern Genghis Khans and the great "democracies"

that still persists, four decades after the Nuremburg trials of war criminals,
with one of Europe's Fascist Trinity.

Now that the seething Seventies repeat the rebellious Thirties,
the times demand an aging poet
recall the earlier age
and celebrate the brave ones slain,
who should not be unknown
to our rebellious, knowledge-thirsty youth.

Let's turn back to the Dark Era when Fascists
rode like the crazed Four Horsemen through
Spain's fragile new republic.

With Foreign Legionnaires, mainly deluded Moors from Africa,
with midnight execution squads at home,
with Mussolini's tank-armed Legions
and Hitler's bombing hordes
they daily filled new graveyards.

The embattled workers, given new strange arms,
the bloodied Loyal regiments retreating, facing rout,
sent forth a call for aid from freedom lovers everywhere
and so the International Brigades were born.

2. THE BRIGADES ARRIVE IN 1936

They came with the four great winds in their leaf-green youth.
They were students with quicksilver minds, more footloose,
more sensitive to the barometer of history than
tenured teachers. They were the disillusioned
unemployed, frayed victims
of the Great Depression, deciding it was time to act.
They were the young colts of the prairies, the dreamers who still read poetry
instead of doping Daily Doubles and Three-Horse Parlays;
the tailors from sweatshops who still bled at the prick of needles;
belt-line assembly robots from Detroit who rebelled
at obsolescence planned in chrome-plated coffins.
They were miners long accustomed to coughing out their lungs and
    protesting
but willing to be jolted now in cattleboats five thousand miles
to set off dynamite blasts for a better world.

They came to this strange land of the questing Don Quixote
and that doomer of all dreams, black-hooded Torquemada.
They came when monsters like the nightmares of Goya
eclipsed the once bright skies. The gallant fools
were anti-Fascists far too early—in November, 1936.

Listen to the trumpet names under which they march:
Abe Lincoln, that brigade of blacks and whites
from the sweet land of segregated liberty.
Here are the refugees from Hitler,
the Ernst Thaelmann Centurions who honor
a long-jailed Communist. They're led by Ludwig Renn, who pilloried war in his
     novels.
Look up! French aviators under another novelist,
André Malraux, light up the Pyrenees like daybreak.
Here tramp the Commune de Paris Battalion,
the Dombrowsky Battalion of Poles; the Russians
with future Marshals Rossovsky, Malinovsky, and Koner;
the Garibaldi Battalion led by the anti-clerical Republican Pacciardi and the
     Socialist Nenni,
the flower of English shires, of South American jungles, and of Yugoslavian
     mountains
singing *The Internationale, Bandiera Rossa,*
The Rising of the Moon, The Marseillaise,
The Four Insurgent Generals and *The Peat Bog Soldier.*
John Brown's body lies a-moldering in his grave
But his soul goes marching on!

Madrid is doomed! Three quarters of University City has fallen
to General Mola's Foreign Legion, to the hireling Moors, the Nazis, and
     the Fascists.
The moderate government of "fair weather" liberals has fled,
leaving only the untrained common people, unaccustomed
to rifles, half-scared of their own hand grenades;
their allies—anarchists from Barcelona who scorn all discipline
but somehow follow that scarred old metal worker, bookseller, and terrorist,
     Buenaventura Durruti;
their allies—the Communists with that firebrand, La Pasionaria of the flashing
     eyes;
their allies—these green International volunteers with a couple of weeks of
     drilling;

just a ragtag collection with an old Republican general,
José Miaja Menant, brought out of retirement
to command the rabble and their lost city.

The skies spew death from bombers of dear Adolf Hitler's Condor Legions of
    Guernica glory.
Four columns of Emilio Mola Vidal are pounding against the great city and
    Mola boasts
a Fifth Column of secret Fascist sympathizers sharpen
knives for a dark night of assassinations.
The world asks: "Has Madrid fallen yet?"
They are battling in University City. Millán Astray, founder of the Foreign
    Legion, voices
the slogan for the attackers: "Down with Intelligence!"
The Foreign Legionnaries seize the School of Architecture;
the battle surges to the Hall of Philosophy and Letters.
Has the city fallen yet?
A women's battalion fights to hold the Segovia Bridge
and mud-smeared children help build barricades.
The casualties are ghastly; all ages and conditions
have losses. Half of those green Internationals
lie dead in the Groves of Academe but the hireling Moors
are driven from Philosophy and Letters.

The headlines of an incredulous world proclaim:
Miaja is still holding Madrid.
No pasaran! They shall not pass! For two more years
Miaja's motley crew commands the city.
Madrid foils all onslaughts of the world's Fascists.
It is a portent of things to come:
not of the soft and zoftig whore, La Paree, surrendered quickly and offering
    perfumed arms,
but Target London, mark for all the furies of aerial and buzz bombs;
of Target Moscow, battered, ever-menaced;
of Leningrad with its full million dead; of Stalingrad
in shambles, all metropolises that broke surging hordes
of stenching crocodiles.

3. ELEGY ON THE DEAD

No pasaran! But heavy is the toll of those
who came to this strange land of the questing Don Quixote
and that doomer of all dreams, black-hooded Torquemada.

Alas, it is a paradox of nations where the executioner,
the Minister of War, Varela, will name Our Lady,
The Virgin of Segovia, a full Field Marshal.
It is the land where the Dark Ages' Inquisition
continued into modern times, then was renewed;
the country of Bull Ring savagery, the nation where
fanatics of the Right have never worried,
about spots staining queenly hands as long
as there is Holy Water and the Virgin's smile.

Now beat drums slowly. It is two years later.
It is the Year of Munich, of Liberal sellouts,
of great surrenders, the year that Stalin panicked.
Here is the crucial battle where the River Ebro
flows through Aragon, where olive groves hang heavy with their spicy fruit.
Here is the grim, relentless drive to hack
French-bordered Catalonia from the heart of Spain.
Alas, the River Ebro flows bloodred through Aragon.
Mourn for our dead who fall under ten thousand
bombs daily for five pulverizing months
while Liberal sellouts Roosevelt and Léon Blum permit
the fleets of Mussolini to blockade Spain's seaports
and deny arms to a recognized republic.
What balm is there for youths and the old men
who clutch their blasted guts, grip severed arms
where River Ebro flows below Mount Picoso,
where Gandesa, a mountain city, crumples in ruins,
where Ebro meets the Mediterranean near Tortosa's shambles.
Alas for the great Spain of the Moslem Renaissance,
alas for the land of Cervantes, Baroja, and Lorca,
also for modern Spain that almost threw off the Holy Trinity
of ignorance, superstition, and oppression.
It ends with Beads and Holy Water, with Shekels, Marks, and Dollars,
with new conspiracies, Colonel Casado holding out
false hopes of leniency under a regime of surrender.
It ends with a long-continuing new Holy Inquisition
with dark nights of proscription by modern Torquemadas.
It ends with the weeping of women and the firing squads,
with short-range bursts that spatter blood against
the ancient walls of churches, jails, and farmhouses.

4. ALMOST FORTY YEARS

With Beads and Holy Water, with Shekels, Pounds, and Dollars
the Generalissimo Franco goes on for almost forty years.
Does he ever have nightmares of Mussolini and cuddly Clara (Blessed)
      Petracci
strung up by their heels from lampposts in Milano?
Does he awake before dawn seeing old Champion Hitler
and cooing Eva Braun poison themselves in the ruins
of a Berlin that did not rule for a thousand years?
Did he shudder when his bombing Condor Legion general,
Von Sperrle, met his doom by hanging at Nuremburg?

Ah, no! Take a Knights of Columbus tour of a truly Catholic nation.
Fly jumbo jet to see Old Glory waving over
our nuclear Air Force buttressing the terror of Franco.
Do you think we devastated Europe and Asia to end dictators?
Your anti-Fascists are no longer fashionable
with the Pentagon or the C.I.A.'s octopus-armed plotters.
Go visit the sacred shrine of Our Lady of Fatima
and spread her message calling for a New War—on Communism.
Enjoy the beaches where we've cleaned up, perhaps, the nuclear fallout.
Don't rile old wounds! Don't mention those allies like Hitler and Mussolini!
The Spaniards and the Internationals who sought
to make the great peninsula the grave of Fascism
have moldered in unhonored graves for almost forty years.
It's different now. The Church is Progressive,
Neo-Fascism is Liberal and everybody loves
the long peace of the Generalissimo except . . .

Keep quiet! Hush it up about those stubborn Basques
of Guernica, El Ferrol, the northern ports and mines,
Granada, Seville, Barcelona and those students
who are igniting torches as if it were the Thirties.
They're spouting gross sedition of a day
when all the statues of Franco will be toppled down,
when Our Lady of Segovia will be stripped of her Field Marshal's baton
and when those glorious fools, the sons of Don Quixote,
will be honored in a thousand villages
and where the River Ebro flows through Aragon,
where olive groves hang heavy with their spicy fruit.
The day is coming when marimbas and guitars

no longer will twang just melancholy strains
from Pyrenees white-crested to vineyards of Málaga,
and when another Renaissance will see
the dead of both the Loyalists and Internationals
be honored with new names of avenues and parks
throughout a bright Madrid of heads held proudly
and faces like Spring blossoms.

Neruda, the Wine

We are the seas through whom the great fish passed
And passes.   He died in a moment of general dying.
Something was reborn.   What was it, Pablo?
Something is being reborn : poems, death, ourselves,
The link deep in our peoples, the dead link in our dead regimes,
The last of our encounters transformed from the first
Long ago in Xavier's house, where you lay sick,
Speaking of poems, the sheet pushed away
Growth of beard pressing up, fierce grass, as you spoke.
And that last moment in the hall of students,
Speaking at last of Spain, that core of all our lives,
The long defeat that brings us what we know.
Meaning, poems, lifelong in loss and presence passing forever.
I spilled the wine at the table
And you, Pablo, dipped your finger in it and marked my forehead.
Words, blood, rivers, cities, days.   I go, a woman signed by you—
The poems of the wine.

On the Murder of Lieutenant José del Castillo
by the Falangist Bravo Martinez, July 12, 1936

When the Lieutenant of the Guardia de Asalto,
heard the automatic go off, he turned
and took the second shot just above
the sternum, the third tore away
the right shoulder of his uniform,
the fourth perforated his cheek. As he
slid out of his comrade's hold
toward the gray cement of the Ramblas
he lost count and knew only
that he would not die and that the blue sky
smudged with clouds was not heaven
for heaven was nowhere and in his eyes
slowly filling with their own light.
The pigeons that spotted the cold floor
of Barcelona rose as he sank below
the waves of silence crashing
on the far shores of his legs, growing
faint and watery. His hands opened
a last time to receive the benedictions
of automobile exhaust and rain
and the rain of soot. His mouth,
that would never again say "I am afraid,"
closed on nothing. The old grandfather
hawking daisies at his stand pressed
a handkerchief against his lips
and turned his eyes away before they held
the eyes of a gunman. The shepherd dogs
on sale howled in their cages
and turned in circles. There is more
to be said, but by someone who has suffered
and died for his sister the earth
and his brothers the beasts and the trees.

The Lieutenant can hear it, the prayer
that comes on the voices of water, today
or yesterday, from Chicago or Valladolid,
and hangs like smoke above this street
he won't walk as a man ever again.

Madrid, May 1977

Spain will surprise you.
—Suarez

Tooting down the Gran Via,
tossing out bundles of loose white leaflets,
the campaign caravans roll.
At nine in the evening
leaflets snow on the heads and shoulders
of Madrilenos at sidewalk cafes
and cover their plates of hot, fried churros,
while those in the paseo scuff through leaflets stained with
streetdust and churro grease.
Mornings, out of each porteria pops
a porter with broom like a jack-in-the-box
to bare his section of the street
for a few hours until the tooting begins
again, and the paper snow.
It is a serious carnival.

The waiter who speaks English
and looks like a sad prizefighter
sets down my plate of langostinos
and says, "Yes, we have learned
very quickly how to disagree.
The hardest thing we must learn now
is how to disagree without violence."

Off the main streets we walk in a city
of paper walls, one hundred
and fifty-nine parties have built these surfaces
of pasted paper and print.
Like bears on hind legs sharpening their claws,
men and women stand by the walls
and scratch with their fingernails
at the campaign posters they disagree with,

ripping tiny strips from the print.
We pass a five-year-old,
scraping with his nails at a poster.
This is a new game.
Only people over sixty-two have
ever played it before.

In the evening stroll, young lovers in jeans,
twined together like churros,
writhe through double-breasted businessmen,
past posters of La Pasionaria,
past bare breasts blooming on news kiosks,
past movie lines for uncensored sex.
For good or ill, America strolls up the street.

At midnight, coming from supper,
we stop at a gray clump on the sidewalk.
It is a pile of puppies.
They are asleep,
cuddled together on the pavement
in a litter of leaflets.
Off to one side, their owner
dickers with three possible customers,
each of whom has for a moment forgotten
that, in a few weeks, having placed
a slip of paper in a plastic urn,
into his empty hand will fall
responsibility for his own life
and a share of responsibility for the world.

Journey to Madrid

At last, the museum and Hieronymus Bosch!
I'm trapped within a flaming room,
Nightmare of delicious reds and blues,
His Garden of Delights, O paradise
Of men and animals, blindly devouring
One another: I know where I am.
Franco's garden, the world's garden.
Yes, I thought. Yes, at last,
That swift and true revelation!

My first walk on the Calle de Goya
(My lips sang), the morning a climate
For the Rising: here I had traveled,
Was crucified, but not yet risen.
Once fallen, can we rise?
Is the Phoenix a myth?—ashes to dust,
As with all flame, all gardens?
Ah, but morning on these stones
Blinding me: could this be Spain?

That other Spain, my youthful snare,
Stirs as I walk down the Plazas,
Touching the fountains, the sacred water,
Toward the Museo del Prado, the center
Where my history whirled, as now
A roaring ring of cars, and girls
On the backs of bikes, skirts ablaze,
The present Garden of Delights lies
Taunting me: yes, it is Spain.

Oblivious of language, my lips sang.
After Bosch, Velazquez, Goya,
I walked the city and dreamed a time
When flame called and held me bound,
That other Spain that was my thorn:

The drop of blood the rose denies
But bleeds the hand, the head, heart—
All that yearns to be given,
As poems I gave to feed a thirst.

I am the ghost calling back
His drop of blood from that cauldron.
Ghost of those songs, *No Pasaran.*
That blood stayed red for thirty years.
And now, the city alive, the sun
Blazing (O garden, flame), I said
I will be free—and flew up
Into my former grace, released,
Radiant, ignorant, and redeemed.

I let the drop of blood flow back
Into the man on the motorbike,
The girls whose arms hold him fast:
Their kisses cancel out the dead.
I see my dream fade beyond
The flush of war, my singèd past.
I wave. They don't know who I am.
Why should they know? The day throbs.
I pass among them as a wraith.

I forgive you, lovers, workers,
Forgetful, alive. Our time crosses.
I free you, I free myself.
That's the Phoenix, the true Rising,
To join the blind god of History,
Of his wrath and pity born,
Who devours our youth for a future good.
Now to the bullfight where the sword drives
To the heart, to draw fresh blood.

In Barcelona You Tried to Scream

to Susan

You had spent the day looking at paintings.
The real park was too green, still dappled
at twilight. The crippled children sat
too quietly. Someone had dressed them
in lace and gabardine, like the antique
figures you'd seen through a haze of fatigue.
You covered your daughter's eyes.
You stared at the children under the trees
who stared at nothing, their incurable lives.
Their deaths seemed to rise inside them
like the sleep of the newly-born.
Their nurse gazed over the pond.
Your husband said JUST DRIVE
and you held the wheel like a pair of shoulders.

Tonight you dine in Paris. Without turning
you know the street outside glitters,
that people speak cheerfully into the wind.
If you close your eyes, you can see the women's
faces floating like orchids. Your husband
offers you a light, and you lean forward
in your fragile chair, in the middle of Paris.
In an invisible France, people you'll never meet
are lighting lamps for their frightened children,
or driving too fast, or selling everything.
In Barcelona you tried to scream.
In Paris your husband offers you a light
and his hands carve themselves in one motion
behind your eyes.

Francisco, I'll Bring You Red Carnations

Here in the great cemetery
behind the fortress of Barcelona
I have come once more to see
the graves of my fallen.
Two ancient picnickers direct
us down the hill. "Durruti,"
says the man, "I was on
his side." The woman hushes
him. All the way down
this is a city of the dead,
871,251 *difuntos.*
The poor packed in tenements
a dozen high; the rich
in splendid homes or temples.
So nothing has changed
except for the single
unswerving fact: they are
all dead. Here is the Plaza
of San Jaime, here the Rambla
of San Pedro, so every death
still has a mailing address,
but since this is Spain
the mail never comes or
comes too late to be of use.
Between the cemetery and
the Protestant burial ground
we find the three stones
all in a row: Ferrer Guardia,
B. Durruti, F. Ascaso, the names
written with marking pens,
and a few circled A's and tributes
to the FAI and CNT.
For two there are floral
displays, but Ascaso faces
eternity with only a stone.

Maybe as it should be. He was
a stone, a stone and a blade,
the first grinding and sharpening
the other. Half his 36
years were spent in prisons
or on the run, and yet
in that last photograph
taken less than an hour before
he died, he stands in a dark
suit, smoking, a rifle slung
behind his shoulder, and glances
sideways at the camera
half smiling. It is July 20,
1936, and before the darkness
falls a darkness will have
fallen on him. While
the streets are echoing
with victory and revolution,
Francisco Ascaso will take up
the hammered little blade
of his spirit and enter for
the last time the republics
of death. I remember
his words to a frightened
comrade who questioned
the wisdom of attack: "We
have gathered here to die, but we
don't have to die with dogs,
so go." Forty-one years
ago, and now the city stretches
as far as the eye can see,
huge cement columns like nails
pounded into the once green
meadows of the Llobregat.
Your Barcelona is gone,
the old town swallowed
in industrial filth and
the burning mists of gasoline.
Only the police remain, armed
and arrogant, smiling masters
of the boulevards, the police
and your dream of the city

of God, where every man
and every woman gives
and receives the gifts of work
and care, and that dream
goes on in spite of slums,
in spite of death clouds,
the roar of trucks, the harbor
staining the mother sea,
it goes on in spite of all
that mocks it. We have it here
growing in our hearts, as
your comrade said, and when
we give it up with our last
breaths someone will gasp
it home to their lives.
Francisco, stone, knife blade,
single soldier still on
the run down the darkest
street of all, we will be back
across an ocean and a continent
to bring you red carnations,
to celebrate the unbroken
promise of your life that
once was frail and flesh.

For the Fallen

In the old graveyard behind
the fortress of Montjuich
side by side are buried
the brothers Ascaso and
Buenaventura Durruti.
If you go there and stand
in the June sun or under
the scudding clouds
of November you will
hear neither the great wail
of the factories nor the sea
groaning into the harbor
laden with goods and freckled
with oil. You will hear
the distant waves of traffic
in the late afternoon rush
and maybe the yellowed grass
eating, for this is that
time in Barcelona, you
will hear your own breath
slowing and time slowing
and then the death of time
because it stops here. You
can go down on your knees
and pray that the spirit
of men and women come back
and inhabit this failing flesh
but if you listen well
your heart will ask
you to stand, under
the fading sun or
the rising moon, it
doesn't matter, either
alone or breathing as you
do now the words

of the fallen and the slow
clouds of diesel exhaust.
Look at your hands. They
are not scarred by
the cigarettes of the police,
and the palms are soft,
the fingers long but
slightly kinked, the hands
once of a boy stained
with the ink of dull reports
the day they laid
Buenaventura beside Francisco
Ascaso and thousands gathered
weeping or somber. The nails
were bitten down then.
The comrades must have known
it was over, and Joaquín
Ascaso, staring at the earth
that had opened so quickly
for his brothers, must
have whispered *soon*.
Soon the boy rose
from his desk and went
into the darkness
congealing in cold parlors
or in the weariness
of old pistons, in the gasps
of men and women asleep
and dreaming as the bus
stalls and starts on the way
home from work. And Joaquín,
who had never knelt, rose
and went home to prepare,
knowing he was all
of them, as you know
they are all that gathers
in your hands, all
that is left, words
spoken to no one
left, blurred in
the waves of the old sea,
garlands of red roses

that tattered, chips
of light and dark, fire
and smoke, the burning
and the cold that were
life and can still
shiver these two stiff
and darkening hands.

Granada: The Rose

You leveled with me, Granada;
you didn't once overcharge;
you walked out of your way to show me my way;
you really meant it when you said *De nada!*
—so I'll level with you.

Of course I loved your beauties—Lorca taught me how;
but neither Alhambra's picturesque wealth
nor Albaicin's picturesque poverty brought me,
neither the gypsies' hot freedom on their hill
nor the cold imprisonment of Fernando and Isabella.
I came, after forty years,
to find the center of Lorca's life
and leave a rose there.

At eleven this morning I shall board the bus for Málaga
having left no rose,
although I know where it should be placed.
Perhaps it was the fahrenheit that stopped me,
or my wife's plea that I do nothing "controversial."

But in fact at the end it grew clear
that Lorca needs no flower;
his name bursts richer than the gardens of the Generalife.
It was I who needed to bring it and find its proper place
—I, whose mouth opened because his was shut,
I, whose weakness feeds on his strength.

And you, Granada, you need it
—though I am a small poet, seldom anthologized,
and one rose more or less is perhaps not important
in a city of many roses.

When you have erased the name of Valdes
from that street behind the post office,
when you have finished with the statue of José Antonio,
when you have renamed the Square for him whose eyes caressed it
at all hours from the Acera del Casino window,
whose shoes increased its price each time he stepped across it—
then I will come again;
I have learned how to wait, but this time
it will not be for long.
I will come to you, Granada,
and place my rose at the feet of his statue,
for whatever one rose is worth.

García Lorca and the
One-Legged Schoolteacher

No one sings here,
no one cries in the corner.

The luck of an old priest.
He wins a morning's sleep
because he believes:

today no one will be executed.

He sleeps a mile away
from the hill
where they shoot people.

He hears only bells
against the wind
and dreams

of the fountain and the boy
herding goats at dawn.

To Fuente Grande and the olive grove,
to the fountain filled with goat bells.

In the roadhouse the poet and Gonzalez,
the one-legged schoolteacher, waste
their last minutes arguing
with guards who must kill them.

There will be no confessions.

Now the sleeping priest
dreams a trumpet
and shots in the distance.

Now three soldiers
as young and soft as angels
empty their pistols
in the soft necks of gourds.

The sun shifts along the hill
and lights up the grey shale.

The priest waking
believes the shots have come

because of the laughter and the beauty
of girls. He goes to the fountain
and hears from the boy he loves:

how he watched two girls bathe
under the shade of the olive trees;

how he heard flies and cried,
recognizing the one leg
of the dead schoolteacher.

The priest hears the goat bells
and dips his hand in the waters.
He thinks of the kindest words:

God forgives
those who die under olive trees.

What men notice, he thinks,
is you live with one leg
and your death spreads,

like the buzz of children
when one of them finds a dead rabbit
and brings it in a sack to school.

The Valley of the Fallen

*In this Valley of the Fallen, one finds the soul of Spain, beautiful
and severe. When the great bronze doors—eleven tons each—
swing open for state ceremonies, ten thousand worshippers can
assemble there at a time. . . . Only Franco and his intimates
know the cost of this monument with its adjacent Benedictine
monastery and its lavishly fitted center for social studies. . . .*
—Benjamin Welles

1

My new friend, Maisie, who works where I work,
A big, pleasant woman, all elbows and peasant skirts,
Has a young child, and debts, and struggles on her own.
Not twenty-one, I am her confidante.
Gallant, intrepid, she soldiers on;
But in the ladies' restroom, or when we munch
Our sandwiches at our adjoining desks,
Her bitterness erupts: the bum! the bum
Who, when she was pregnant, knocked her down,
Stole money from her purse to spend on drink,
And still harasses her with drunken calls
In 1946.
One day I have to ask,

"Maisie, why did you ever marry him?"
Gazing into her large, pale-blue eyes
That brim with rue: "Well, you see,
He fought in the Abraham Lincoln Brigade."
"Oh," I say. I would have done it too.

2

When I say I wouldn't go to Spain
Till Franco died, I've told a whole
Biography: my age, my politics,
My Red—and red-haired—mother whose green eyes
Sparked at the sins of tyrants anywhere;

My father, who was counsel for the poor
And radical, against the bigot and the hater,
Burnt up the courtroom with his tongue of flame
(McCarthy got around to us much later).
So Spain burst in while I was still a child:
My introduction to the world.

At seventeen, my first love, Frank,
Gave me some records, battered seventy-eights,
The off-key songs of the International Brigade.
I still sing them, remember all the words
In Spanish, French and German:
The Peat Bog Soldiers, accompanied by harmonica
In a Barcelona basement; "*Freiheit!*" we sing
To a guitar. You can still hear
The thuds of the bombardment.
I sing and listen till the tears run down.
That's forty years of tears.

> *Seven hundred men worked every day for ten years to dig this*
> *place, and many of them were political prisoners of the regime.*
> *Franco lies now in a tomb before the high altar; and all day long*
> *the monks, the nuns and the soldiers file through. . . .*
> —*Jan Morris, 1979*

3

My husband and I shudder a bit and smile—
He's an architect, has seen photographs
Of Franco's grandiose memorial,
The Valley of the Fallen.
At first the thought appalled, but we've decided
It's part of architecture, part of history too,
So we drive the road from the Escorial,
Climb tiers and tiers of stairs,
Take in the view.

The whole vast place is virtually empty
Save for a handful of tourists like ourselves.
Down the long gloomy hall, not as grotesque
As we expected; muted lights;
Chisels score the vault so that we'll know

They tunneled through the mountain,
Franco's slave labor, some the very men
Who fought him.
                    But at least they buried him!

We reach the circular altar with its flame;
First, the grave of José Antonio,
Primo de Rivera, who fathered the Falange,
On it a huge ugly wreath
From the Italian Fascisti.
I wouldn't be surprised if asps crawled out
Beneath its leaves of artificial bronze,
But still—at my age—am surprised
That the old evil lives.

Behind this, the Caudillo's stone.
I say, "I'm going to spit upon his grave."
John tilts his head towards the honor guard,
Impassive, armed, white-gloved.
He knows me well enough
To know I just might do it. But instead,
I speak a curse: *Franco, I spit upon your grave.*

On the way out, we use the men's room
And the ladies' room, try to buy postcards
But it's closing time;
Then drive back to Madrid,
Where I read poems to the kids
At the University,
In a classroom scarred with revolutionary slogans
Four years old, that no one's bothered to erase.
I sing of Lorca, Chile, and Neruda
And the wars we lose.

> *The Valle de los Caidos can be included in your trip to the*
> *Escorial. . . . Like a modern-day Valhalla, the crypt is cut through*
> *853 feet of living rock and surmounted by a 492 foot cross of*
> *reinforced concrete faced with stone (with an elevator to the*
> *top). Admission 75 pesetas with two in a car; 100 pesetas for*
> *more than two. Open 9–7:30.*
> *—Fodor's Spain, 1984*

Ingathering

The poets are going home now,
After the years of exile,
After the northern climates
Where they worked, lectured, remembered,
Where they shivered at night
In an indifferent world.
Where God was the god of business,
And men would violate the poets' moon,
And even the heavens become zones of war.

The poets are going home
To the blood-haunted villages,
To the crumbling walls, still pocked
With a spray of bullets;
To the ravine, marked with a new cross,
Where their brother died.
No one knows the precise spot where they shot him,
But there is a place now to gather, to lay wreaths.
The poets will bring flowers.

The poets are coming home
To the cafés, to the life of the streets at twilight,
To slip among the crowds and greet their friends;
These young poets, old now, limping, who lean on a cane:
Or the arm of a grandchild, peer with opaque eyes
At the frightening city, the steel and concrete towers
Sprung up in their absence.
Yet from open doorways comes the odor of grapes
Fermented, of fish, of oil, of pimento . . .

The poets have come home
To the melodious language
That settles in their heads like moths alighting,
This language for which they starved
In a world of gutturals,

Crude monosyllables barked by strangers.
Now their own language enfolds them
With its warm vocables.
The poets are home.

Yes, they have come back
To look up at the yellow moon,
Cousin of that cold orb that only reflected
Their isolation.
They have returned to the olives, the light,
The sage-scented meadows,
The white-washed steps, the tubs of geraniums,
The sere plains, the riverbanks spread with laundry,
The poppies, the vineyards, the bones of mountains.

Yes, poets, welcome home
To your small country
Riven by its little war
(as the world measures these events),
A country that remembers heroes and tears;
Where, in your absence, souls kept themselves alive
By whispering your words.
Now you smile at everything, even the priests, the militia,
The patient earth that is waiting to receive you.

They Shall Not Pass

Above me, the sky is all Atlantic
and I taste vinegar, salt,
and those hot yellow peppers
Natividad used to eat
with tamales and beer.
And the sweat above her lip—
I can taste that too.
And I have to remind myself
why I left Mexico,
why I'm dying here in Madrid
when I should be standing,
thumbs hooked in my belt loops,
a Lucky Strike caught in the corner of my mouth.

I was a Wobbly like my father
and like him, I always bought two drinks:
one for myself and one for the ghost
of universal brotherhood,
with his tattered suitcase, checkered tie,
and a thirst for handshakes and hammers,
always leaning at the bar when I'd arrive,
with his *Joe, buy me a drink, just one more.*
He was in Vera Cruz the night I left,
he stood on the deck with me before I sailed,
squinting at the dock, pointing out the ones
who were his,
while I stood there, empty of everything
but what I believed:
that your brother was your brother
and you had to spare a dime,
that when you went down,
the next man would stand up,
hand in his pocket,
that there were angels
who walked among the honored dead

carrying red sickles,
that Joe Stalin sat like Ole King Cole
top of the world
and I'd sit next to him someday
with the back pay of a thousand years
in my own hands.
I had a heart like a goddamn sponge.
You could fill me
with slogans, with songs and marches,
with dead men—
like Sunshine.

He was next to me
when he split up the middle,
out of luck, out of dimes;
when there was terror no one told me existed:
betrayers, idealists—hysterical and uneven fighters.
Only this: They shall not pass.
I said it over and over to myself
as we defended the University of Madrid,
even as I took this slow glide down,
my blood like thick bolts of cloth,
hitting the ground as I fell,
while the layers of ice and ash
floated down from kingdom come.

A chrome ship slides across the sky's smooth surface
and Franco himself lifts the Stars and Stripes sail.
My whole face is numb.
I wanted to hit the coast of Spain
like a fist ramming an old man's belly,
but instead found what's-his-name
in the first bar I stepped into,
wearing a Saint Patrick's Day smile:
Cold sober, Joe, he said, and he spat on the sawdust floor.
I'm my own man, first time in years.
You should try it.
Then he told me
a man can kill without hate,
that that's how it's done,
that Jesus Christ is the bullet
that makes everything right.

But it doesn't matter
now that the glorious perfumed air
is filled with butterflies
which have men's faces, men's feet,
now that the cocoon of flesh
that held me splits apart
and I step left, right, left,
and what's-his-name swaggers head of the line
and his voice floats over us
like the Holy Ghost:
Victory, friends, brothers;
as we march
all in a row
into the motionless sea.

Maria

18 November 1941

In Salvador and China, in Spain and Nicaragua
risings began.
                    Sandino said,
"When the people are satisfied with freedom,
let the ants bring me the news underground."
I could no longer use a camera—no one face,
no mass of sombreros was enough in number.
I was one of a mass whose horizon I couldn't see.
I focused on the daily task. I let love
set my limits, when I could. I let the body,
whose discipline is pain, choose a generous
death.
            Now I was Maria,
Mexico's name for each of its alien poor.
I took the name, studied in Moscow, traveled
long roads in hunger. I said to the sun,
you lead me. Somehow a modest life grew.

We had a world, we said, to wash clean, minds
to renew. I was one of the many drops of rain
on the clear pane elegant tyrants erect as a shield
between themselves and the poor. This glass,
I felt, we will wash it clean, break through—
and if in the heat of love or hate
we dry on the glass—blood spatter, rain spatter,
wine—well, we do.
                    I was not afraid.

I lived level to the need to stop blood, carry water,
make soup. Before Spain, I loved best
the work away from desks, the wordless work
of fields and floors—digging or washing or gathering
wheat in. In Spain I lived with Carlos. I thought,
he has organized an army: his will. And I can still

see the 5th Regiment,
their caps thrown into the air, the last bars of
"La Internacional" lingering in the shouts to be on
with it, a massive surge of faces, blended and composed—
tidal music, centuries of repression breaking free
at last, we thought. It was a time that compares
to music, to a harmony of will and sacrifice so valid
it feels as if the world is spinning in your hand,
and in that rhythm we moved, firm in the principles
and demands of the time, inviting our ancestors, all
those who suffered, to be there in the impersonal
intensity of our blood. We had, for a time,
great power. And as always with great power,

we were tested.

Madrid

23 November 1941

In the first days of Madrid, when the city was the front,
Mamma was in my head—I couldn't get her out—
as if she'd given me her energy to use. I felt
protected. In a break in the bombing, so quiet
it seemed morning, I took keys to the supply room,
a pail and a mop, strangely happy—content
the way children are, not knowing why they're here
but sure of their right to be, not knowing how the world
unfolds but trusting the movement, the way I'd follow
close on Papa's whistle, not knowing the tune
but there with him note for note, as if I knew.
I splashed the stone floor with water, and they were
Udine's stones in the piazza when we cleaned
winter off and the barrels of last wine were rolled in.
The town was then one family. Today, Mamma teased,
everyone's papa is yours, everyone's husband is mine.
Work or no work, life was fine.

I flung the last of the water into a corner, between
cabinets, and then—I'd heard nothing, seen nothing—
I knew. I took the gun from my coat pocket,
demanding the shadow walk out of the shadow.
Three times, more. But he bolted, tumbled into me,
past me, stumbling at the door as I shot. He fell.
The blood welled, ran over his collar, filled
the cracks between stones, the crooked stones.
Stunned, I watched them fill, inch by inch—
the floor a map of Europe, this a school, these
the rivers down to the common sea.
                    Who was he?
I searched him for papers. He was blank. Ours, theirs—
I never knew. Carlos said, "No matter.

Supplies are low. He was stealing food.
You know what the Party demands."
                              I knew.

And this was the source of my calm thereafter:
I owed a death. My place would be filled.
I had reached the final edge of choice, and as
I stood there, ready in the larder that had been
Udine in spring and a sharing of wine, I willed
one thing only—purity intense as earth's,
a boundless cup into which all blood would sink,
valued equally, and by the compassionate chaos
of time lie hidden from view.
                              In me this was
sentiment. But in Badajoz, Seville, Granada—
fascists gave commands. *Limpieza,* purity so
impersonal, it was ironic, grand. "Give them coffee,
lots of coffee." Then a burst of shells, and cups,
coffee cups, thousands, shattered their brown blood
on the ground. On stones it drained, stained,
seeped from view. There was in the rhetoric
at dawn more blood. Loudspeakers spat it,
radios waved wet *banderas,* blood on the air,
and these rained down new rumor, blood in the streets.
Young men who rode trams to the front, women
in the factories heard of *limpieza.* Anarchist,
priest, communist—all of us knew this wish
for purity—that victims be invisible, be coffee
steamed into the ground.
                              Briefly I hated the dead.
Hated them, loved them, all in the dead man
at my feet. I held his blood in the lines of my hand,
watched it dry. Who was he? He was me. He was mine.
I needed the blood—here, in my hand. Stronger
than any caress, more mute, it said *yes.*
I was bound to claim him—
                              else be lost
in violence, too free, possessed.

The fascists stacked our dead,
El Mundo Obrero balled in their mouths,

the flesh of their most private moments cut off,
scattered. They were to be icons of our impotence,
syllables in a debate that daily grew unspeakable.

Carlos said—you are so silent.

I am, I said. Yes, I am.

From a Single Center . . .

21 December 1941

we tried to live. That's as it should be.
Now there's argument and doubt.
The center shifts, the line falls back, allies
unmask themselves, or mask; A few dry apologists
argue the war, they justify by numbers—how many
of ours were taken for *paseos,* how many of theirs;
how many cells were filled, emptied and filled,
by mistake how many; whether the ears
that hear confession now detect through their sleep,
faint and shrill, ululations the Africans made
when they fell on young women, how many at a time. . . .

What is counting but the wish for distance?
I counted, too—lentils, so scarce we doled them out
like pills; children who needed succor; Franco's
columns, four, and that mysterious fifth, the spies.
By Málaga I hoped never to see another war—
and then Guernica, Brunete, Teruel, Tarragona,
Barcelona yet to come. I could, in the last year,
no longer tell the color of an armband,
so many were blood, no longer measure loss
or honesty—they are not flour that sifts or bandages
that fold. They are open wounds down a corridor,
you want to close your eyes.
                              Lines that fled
the burning town I counted by cart and car and mile.
We had to be calm—was there time to feel?
My heart was sealed, a cask of wine let down a well
to keep from thieves, to age in the dark and cool.
Thirsty, or longing to be drunk, I'd send down
a grappling hook and hear the echo of a thump,
the scrape of stone and metal. Because I had learned
to hold a gun, to shoot, I saw in my hand,

as if in a smoking mirror or a lake burned off
by sun, the Aztec signature of war unfold,
the blossom at the tip of the detached god's bone.
You can't ask what is cruel or kind.

Was I blind?
         In the war I saw up close—so close
a mountainside of stark trees against snow could seem
an old man's face, unshaven. A rose was an urgent
smear, red down a wall. When we had time
for a personal love, Carlos and I,
we used our bodies like braille.

Events are our minds turned inside out.
In Madrid, in heroic November, the wounded
were loaded in on stretchers, in the trunks of cars,
or slung in carts like sheaves of torn hay.
In the kitchen a cauldron of thin garlic soup,
some beans. Bread came stale—in burlap sacks
long skinny loaves, floured "bones" without feet.
Their knobs blued with mold in the larder,
the leftovers stacked there, too tough for jaws
that stammered and mewed cold breath like gauze,
then locked in a final freeze of pain.
                 "Maria,"
they called—the urge for last words so strong
that almost, almost in the conscious ones I'd see
words gather speed, change, shake free
like sweat on muscle. Nearly impersonal,
finally beautiful, they told their last stories,
their lives, keeping alive in their whispers
what never can be lost. . . .

Sometimes there is no time—it cascades
and eddies, flows backwards, spews future, past,
and present in a mix. In San Martín, a jolt
of the ambulance over the ruts of the field sent me
a glimpse of a face—I saw a child, gentle and sad.
He belonged nowhere, and he stood exactly there,
in the red dirt, dried garlic looped in the window
behind him, the smoke on the white walls ashen.
He held a broken puppet by a string, something

human or animal carved from a gourd. I looked,
looked again, but had to go on—to Madrid,
to beds where young men left their words in blood,
where fever smudged the sheets with visions
of their children, born and unborn, orphaned
to the cradles of the mud.

If we could look into the future, would we go there?
In the spiral of hunger's discontent, would we go?

Somehow we go. New societies are born,
much wider than our minds. And if for a moment
we doubt, our bodies remember. They believe.
We make our bodies available to death,
and therefore live. It is the hero's way—

every woman knows it.

Retreat to the Future

1 January 1942

As the Republic's last Cortes disbanded,
and the stones of Figueras shook in the echo of bombs,
our people, frantic, were shoved from the winter roads
by our own troops, disregarded. They only watched
as national treasures, paintings huge in their gold
frames, took their places, cradled
in the last trucks going out. No one cried,

What have you done? What more can you give?

No theory marshaled the suffering of Spain
to right order. I felt its weight
as I watched in disgust. I felt love shudder
from power and change to an endless debt.
Offered a ride, I refused and walked the other way,
to the Plaza. There, I sat at a café table to wait—
for what?
            The town was empty. A bit of sun,
soured like the rind in the dirty glass on the dirty
table, was left. It hung limp on an ancient oak,
the city's center.

Through this Plaza men for the Brigades had passed.
Overhead a black bird screamed—the jolted
town an ambulance, stuck in a ditch.
I watched the shadows of the old oak lengthen.
My shadow stretched in the dust to sleep.
I closed my eyes and saw the after-lines of branches
turn blood in the cracks of crooked stones.
I wanted to float in these—I knew
where they went.
But I drifted down
to Udine, a day when Papa nailed wood at right angles.

He built a frame, stood it on end as if to ask
what next? what more? holding that window up to the sky,
squaring off part, the air lens enough,
the frame his telescope.
Then I drifted, years,
and in the darkroom this window of Papa's hovered,
parting known from unknown as a human face,
seen clear enough to honor, washed
mutely into view—
a beggar's gaunt face.
She didn't move her lips, but I heard her say,
"You will hang my sorrow on a wall?" She spat
and turned away. "Don't pray to it."

Startled, I shook
awake. I felt a sudden joy. I stood and felt
the muscles in my thighs—they were strong. I breathed
in, and in. I flung the dirty glass to the roots of the old
oak, watched it flash and shatter. And I followed
the people I loved across the border, a tatter of retreat,
refugees by the thousands crossing from Catalonia
to the French camps, to bitter charges,
countercharges—to the scourge of our better
natures, defeat.

When Carlos found me,
he had words from Machado ready on his lips—
*Y cuando llegue el día del último viaje . . .**
When the day of my last journey arrives,
and the ship, never to return, is set to leave,
you will find me on board with few supplies . . .
casi desnudo, almost naked, like the children
of the sea. He smiled, looked mostly ahead,
without reprisal, proud. "It is not our last
battle," he said.
                    Was he right?
Was there hope? I hoped. Arms limp at my sides
as he held me, too tired then to say or be anything

*NOTE: *The first line of the last stanza of Antonio Machado's
"Retrato" (Portrait), which is translated in Gibson's next four-and-
a-half lines.*

more than a bookmark closed in the book of his body,
the future unread. It was a relief
not to be dead—that strengthened me. Regret
is one blindness I've refused. Without that,
the least life is good.

I have seen light quicken
across silent faces, *de repente,* sudden as lightning
across a solid sea, then thunder stir deep passion,
and the dead—I mean
those who have lived without history, more silent
than fossils—awaken,
ready to live and die that their children might live
and die in dignity. They fix their eyes on that.

With such men and women I live.
And if it often seems we have the choice of fire
or fire, and the cities burn, the children scream,
and the war, a hired taxi with no driver, stalls
between burning walls and burning trees
in whose roots real serpents crawl—
I can grow still and wait
until Papa's frame floats up, a focus. Then I see
clear
              a simple human face.

I can follow that.

Rusia en 1931

The archbishop of San Salvador is dead, murdered by no one knows who. The left says the right, the right says provocateurs.

But the families in the barrios sleep with their children beside them and a pitchfork, or a rifle if they have one.

And posterity is grubbing in the footnotes to find out who the bishop is,

or waiting for the poet to get back to his business. Well, there's this:

her breasts are the color of brown stones in moonlight, and paler in moonlight.

And that should hold them for a while. The bishop is dead. Poetry proposes no solutions: it says justice is the well water of the city of Novgorod, black and sweet.

César Vallejo died on a Thursday. It might have been malaria, no one is sure; it burned through the small town of Santiago de Chuco in an Andean valley in his childhood; it may very well have flared in his veins in Paris on a rainy day;

and nine months later Osip Mandelstam was last seen feeding off the garbage heap of a transit camp near Vladivostok.

They might have met in Leningrad in 1931, on a corner; two men about forty; they could have compared gray hair at the temples, or compared reviews of *Trilce* and *Tristia* in 1922.

What French they would have spoken! And what the one thought would save Spain killed the other.

"I am no wolf by blood," Mandelstam wrote that year. "Only an equal could break me."

And Vallejo: "Think of the unemployed. Think of the forty million families of the hungry. . . ."

In Hiding

*After Franco's victory, Manual Cortes, socialist and soldier of the
Republic, spent thirty years in hiding in the attic of his home.*

From the attic's shutter crack I watch
Juliana recede down the road to Málaga,
            her egg baskets aglow in dawnlight,
and I turn from yesterday's papers, the radio

            humming low so the neighbors won't hear:
Franco guiding Eisenhower through
            the NATO base at Torrejón, a marching band,
the B-47s grumbling as they rise

            laden with napalm and atom bombs, the way,
in '37, the Nazi Heinkels rumbled over Guernica,
            our battalion, the 101st, peering up
from the trenches as the bombs surged down,

            and if not for the noise it looked
like a man shelling peanuts on a sidewalk,
            innocent litter that pigeons would eat
on a sun-drenched day in the spring, when you smell,

            as you can today, the lemon blossoms—but yellow smoke
laddered the sky, and the faces
            of the dying in Cathedral San Xavier
we could only imagine, like images

            remembered from a film seen years
before. So much one can only *imagine:*
            this attic room unchanged for decades,
and Conchita now with a child of her own,

and Juliana tells me all along
the road from Torremolinos to Málaga
            the villas of the rich, Americans
and Madrillino doctors, gaze out

        on the sea, Hollywood men, their women
precious stones, sunning themselves
            each afternoon on the balconies.

        * * *

But isn't this also a life of leisure?
            I weave, some mornings, mats of esparto grass
                Juliana will sell in the city,
and some nights try to read again

the difficult chapters of *Kapital.*
            Even those mornings when De Valente's
                Guardia Civil, all of them drunk,
would ransack Juliana's wardrobe, tear

her slips and nightgowns from the dresser
            to find some evidence of me,
                my waiting here, only this wall
between me and the firing squad—was leisure.

I counted time, like a blind accordionist
            tapping his boot to the music,
                his ears by now so acute
he still can hear his heartbeat

among the loud notes of his reel.
            Time, it comes down to, and timing.
            As mayor, as soldier, I believed in
The People, in bread for them, and land.

To believe in them now, I believe
            in this waiting, asking to keep
                the waiting holy, uncompromised by memory,
though some nights I'm still faltering

knee-deep through snow in Catalonia,
            my boots turned rags, the wound
                        in my neck, where the bullet passed,
stanched with a scarf, my comrade

a Jewish corporal from Mérida,
            moaning for his sweetheart on my back,
                        the dark hole in his chest
all night dampening my shoulder.

            * * *

            Last year Conchita, my only child,
married the village postal clerk,
a man who does not know I exist. With my
            smuggled champagne I stared through the shutters

            at the wedding dance in the courtyard below,
and wept, not for her, but for my own absence,
the way a ghost must weep, continually,
            for things it lived with and touched.

            But later, I found myself humming
to the band as it yelped its tunes,
yet softly, so no one would hear.
            Then the guests were home, yellow lights

            still strung in the olives. The musicians,
ties and jackets draped on wicker chairs,
wiped sweat from their brows and gently placed
            in their cases the heavy accordions.

            Always people say you walk
ahead into the future, though in truth
you walk backwards toward it, and only
            the past spreads its vista before you,

            though always, my friends, it is fading.
And you try to remember what it is that you
believed in. You try very hard.
            You wait. You watch until it's gone.

Madrid: July 1978

All day I staggered about, unable to shake off those three
visions of Goya: the white-bloused Palace defender, arms wide,   about
to join his comrades heaped under conqueror bayonets;
the Infant Time beheaded by his father's teeth; the things of night
leering their black mass of triumph . . .

All day I staggered about, unable to shake off the posters
summoning Spain's "New Force" into Madrid,
into the bullring wide as Saturn's jaws
to tear at the frail new day, to hymn July 18th: when bayonets
pointed at the north, the Palace.

Now, back in bed, I am reached
by a rumbling from a region, of a kind, unknown.
You might call it the whir of nightlife traffic;
for me it is once more the insurgent artillery
closing in on the city . . .

But a loudspeaker reaches me too—enflamed, enflaming—
protesting yesterday's army attack on Pamplona,
passionate as that which bloomed through the last nights in '39,
saying there's sap in it yet; after thirty-nine years
it could bloom again!

And I, who came to salute ghosts, salute Time instead:
Saturn's new child, unawed by his brothers' fate.
If, as the graffiti around the corner threatens,
the army will strike again, the "Fuerza Nueva," rumbling
even now into Madrid
in caravans of cars trailing red and gold streamers,
black-massing even now in the bullring, tucking chains
and batons into their trousers along with what's already
there risen and ready, Time's new city
will not lie back and take it.

Barcelona: The Last Night

I am lying past midnight
thinking not of a woman but of a city.
I have always been susceptible to cities—not all:
some I hate outright: the arrogant ones,
the ones who want my money,
the man-eating ones—
from them it is bliss to escape!
some I both hate and love,
including the one that cradled me:
of those I love
I touch not a hair
—they never suspect I am there.

It is not blind love, Barcelona.
I took note of the driver
who doubled my fare,
the guard at the beach gate
who denied me a glimpse of the sea.

But inside the cathedral a Sunday handful responded
in sweet Catalan (forty years outlawed)
to the priest's chant;
while out in the square, hands linked,
defying a hostile high noon,
four rings of gentle sardañas
revived with each cool flow
from the gaily umbrella'd musicians;
and the side-street one-man show:
juggling oranges four at a time,
blowing Ping-Pongs ten feet high
and homing them in his mouth like doves,
coaxing frail melodies
from Catalan veins around him,
catching them one by one in his trumpet
and blaring them back full-fledged

into the veins that had nested them;
and the multicolored cartoons
turning old walls into young screams for freedom;
and the lad in the bookstore, the crone at the hotel,
eyes flashing, back stiffening:
"Of course I am Catalan!"

My Mother with Purse the Summer
They Murdered the Spanish Poet

Had she looked out the window she would have seen a quiet street,
each house with a single maple or elm browning in the sun
at the end of summer, the black Fords and Plymouths gleaming
in their fresh wax, the neighbor children returning home
dark suited or white frocked from their Christian studies.

Had she looked out she would have seen the world she crossed
the world to find. Instead she unclasps the leather purse
to make sure she has everything: mirror, lipstick, billfold,
her cards of identity, her checkbook with the week's balance
correctly entered, two monogrammed, embroidered handkerchiefs

to blot and hold the tears, for—dark veiled—she's on her way
to meet her husband, gone three years now into the sour earth
of Michigan. Can the long white root a man in time becomes
talk back to one who chose to stay on the far shore
of his departure? Before the day ends, she'll find out.

She will hunch over tea leaves, she will open her palms,
first the hardened hand of the wage earner, then the soft one
that opens to the heart. To see, she will close her eyes;
to hear, she will stop her ears, and the words will be
wrong or no words at all, teeth striking teeth, the tongue

doubled back upon itself, the blackened lips vanished
into the hole of the throat. But for now she looks up.
It is summer, 1936. The first hints of autumn
mist on a row of curtained windows that look in on us
as my mother, perfumed, leans down to brush my mouth with hers,

once, to say my name, precisely, in English. Later
two women will pretend they have reached two other worlds,
the one behind and the one ahead. As they keen

in the darkness perhaps only one will pretend, perhaps
neither, for who shall question that we most clearly see

where no eye is? Wide-eyed he sees nothing. White shirt
worn open, dark trousers with no belt, the olive skin appalled.
When the same wind he loved and sang to touches his cheek
he tries to rub it away. There are others, too, walking over
the flat, gray stones to where a line of men smokes and waits.

The trees have stilled. Had she looked out the window
my mother would have seen each house with its elm or maple
burning, the children drowning in the end of summer, the mist
blurring the eyes of our front windows, the shale hills
above Granada where all time stopped. Her purse snaps shut.

My Night with Federico García Lorca

(as told by Edouard Roditi)

It happened in Paris.
Pepe asked me over to dinner
to meet a guy named Federico
who was on his way to New York.
I was nineteen years old.
Federico was eleven years older
and had just finished
a relationship in Spain
with a sculptor
who had been rotten to him.
Federico only had two lovers—
he hated promiscuous queens.

We were both Gemini.
Since astrology
was very important to him,
Federico took an interest in me.
We spoke in Spanish.
I had learned it
from my grandmother, a Sephardic
Jew, who had taught me
sixteenth-century expressions.
Federico was amused by all this.

We drank a lot of
wine that night.
In the morning, when I woke up,
his head lay across my nipples.
Hundreds of people
have asked me for details:
Was Federico fabulous in bed?
I always give them my standard answer:
Federico was emotional

and vulnerable; for him.
the most important thing wasn't sex
but tenderness.

I never saw him again.
The following day he left for England
then New York and Cuba.
Later, the second love
of his life was murdered
defending the Republic.

All this happened in Paris
almost sixty years ago.
It was just a night of love
but it has lasted all my life.

The Carpenter Swam to Spain

For Abe Osheroff
and the veterans of the Abraham Lincoln Brigade

The ship hushed the waves to sleep at midnight:
Ciudad de Barcelona, Ciudad de Barcelona.

In the name of the aristocrat strolling through his garden
Franco's tanks crawled like a plague of smoldering beetles;
in the name of the bishop and his cathedrals
the firing squads sang a stuttering mass with smoke in their throats;
in the name of the exiled king and blueshirts on the march
bombers with swastika fins sowed an inferno
in village market places and the ribs of the dead.
At Guernica an ancient woman in black stumbled
across a corpse and clawed her hair;
at Víznar, where the spring bubbles, a poet in white shoes
coughed the bullet's blood onto his white shirt,
gypsy sobbing in the cave of his mouth.

Ciudad de Barcelona: The ship plowed the ocean,
and the ocean was a wheatfield thinking of bread.
And the faces at the portholes thinking: Spain.

In España, the carpenters and miners kneeled with rifles
behind a barricade of killed horses,
the peasant boys cradled grenades like pomegranates
to fling against the plague of tanks, the hive of helmets.
Elsewhere across the earth, thousands more laid hammers
in toolboxes, holstered drills, promised letters home,
and crowded onto ships for Spain:
volunteers for the Republic, congregation of berets,
fedoras and fist-salutes for the camera, cigarettes and union songs.
The handle of the hammer became the stock of the rifle.

The ship called *Ciudad de Barcelona* steamed
across the thumping tide, hull bearded with foam,
the body of Spain slumbering on the horizon.

Another carpenter read the newspapers
by the tunnel-light of the subway in Brooklyn.
Abe Osheroff sailed for Spain. Because Franco's mustache
was stiff as a paintbrush with his cousins' blood:
because Hitler's iron maw would be a bulldozer,
heaving a downpour of cadavers into common graves.

The ship of volunteers was *Ciudad de Barcelona,*
Abe the carpenter among them, and for them
the word Barcelona tingled like the aftertaste of a kiss.
Two miles from shore, they saw the prop plane hover
as if a spectre from the last war,
the pilot's hand jab untranslated warning.
Then the thud, a heart kicking in spasm,
the breastbone of the ship punctured
by a torpedo from Mussolini's submarine.
In seven minutes, the ship called *Ciudad de Barcelona*
tilted and slid into the gushing sea,
at every porthole a face trapped,
mouth round and silent like the porthole.

Eighty mouths round in the high note of silence.
Schultz, captain of the Brooklyn College swim team,
pinned below deck and drowned,
his champion's breaststroke flailing.
Other hands that could swim burst through the wave-walls
and reached for the hands that could not. The boats
of a fishing village crystallized from the foam,
a fleet of saints with salt glistening in their beards,
blankets and rum on the shore.

Abe swam two miles to Spain,
made trowels of his hands
to cleave the thickening water.
His fingers learned the rifle's trigger
as they knew the hammer's claw.
At Fuentes de Ebro, armageddon
babbled and wailed above the trenches;

when he bled there, an ocean of shipwreck
surged through his body. Today, his white beard
is a garland of clouds and sea-foam,
and he remembers Schultz, the swimmer.

Now, for Abe, I tap these words
like a telegraph operator
with news of survivors:
Ciudad de Barcelona, Ciudad de Barcelona.

The Search for Lorca's Shadow

I've seen the hillside. A soft wind moved
through the leaves of the olive trees. Yes,
this is a poem about historic death,
it would be incomplete without hillsides
thick with olive trees, their leaves turning
silver as the land wind shivers them.
The earth, by which I mean the soil, the dirt,
is a metallic gray covered here and there
by a loamy dust which may or may not
shift in the breeze. The ants come and go
doing their dull work. They are alive,
they are going about the business
of their lives, building their dwellings,
providing, eating as best they can.
They do not remember the victim.
They did not even know his name, his voice
which rings still in the voices of others,
his dark hair fallen across one eye,
his rages and jealousies, his body
clothed in worn cotton garments sewn by hand.
(Were he alive he could look carefully
at the bloodstained shirt, count the stitches
that attached the cuffs, and tell you, "No,
that is not the work of my grandmother.")
Forgive the ants, they are merely ants,
though they are alive and he is not,
though they would surely eat him if they could,
if in fact anything were left to eat—
the bones are here as clean as porcelain,
for the earth has long ago eaten all
there was to eat. First forgive the ants
or we'll get nowhere in this useless search
for the darkness he was and the darkness
he became. It is August. The noon sun
pours down on this merciless landscape

that watched with its thousand eyes hidden
in the gashed trunks and the undersides
of gray stones and did nothing. Someone
wrote, "The crime was in Granada,"
though actually it was here among ants,
stones, dust, olive trees, fallen fruit, the boots
of armed men, the cries of women and men
where now there is only silence and no
darkness we can say is his, Federico's.

GLOSSARY

Acera del Casino: García Lorca's street in Granada, just off the Puerta Real and across from the Avenida José Antonio.

Albaicin: The only section of the old quarter in Granada that was spared from demolition when Isabel and Fernando drove out the Moslems.

Alcalá: A major highway that heads east from its origin in the Puerta del Sol, the central plaza in Madrid.

Almería: Capital of the province of the same name in southern Spain, located on the Mediterranean, about 110 miles south of Valencia.

anarchists: One of the major political forces in Spain, particularly through the anarcho-syndicalist trade union federation, the CNT. Opposed to all forms of centrally organized government and believing in direct action, they were especially important in Andalusia, Catalonia, and Aragon. The CNT organized militia units into columns that saw action on the Aragon front. There was a constant struggle between the forces of the radical Left (the CNT, FAI, and POUM) and the rest of the supporters of the Second Republic (principally the Spanish Communist party and various liberal democratic parties) over the conduct of the war. The radical Left argued for a working-class revolution, the other supporters of the Republic for a Popular Front democracy. This conflict continues to divide historians of the Left.

Andalucía (Andalusia): A large agricultural region in southcentral Spain, portions of which were captured by Franco early in the war.

anestex: An anesthetic.

Aquel rincon de la Mancha de Cuyo nombre no quiero acordarme: That corner of La Mancha that I don't want to remember (translated line from Langston Hughes's "Song of Spain").

Aragon (Aragón): An arid, sparsely populated province in northeast Spain. It was the site of several major battles during the last half of the war, among them Teruel, Belchite, and the Ebro campaign.

Ascaso, Francisco (?–1936): A leading anarchist figure in Catalonia. His brothers Domingo and Joaquín were also active in the movement. Ascaso had been a carpenter but evolved into a strike leader and political activist who believed in assassination as a political weapon. He was killed in the opening days of the Spanish Civil War, July 1936, fighting to put down the right-wing military rebellion in Barcelona. He was a reflective, capable leader, and his death was a significant loss for Spanish anarchism.

Badajoz: The capital of the province of Badajoz in southern Spain. After its capture by the Nationalists in August of 1936, reports spread of a major massacre there.

banderas: Spanish for "flags."

Barcelona: The capital of the province of the same name as well as the autonomous region of Catalonia. Spain's primary port, it was the capital of the Second Republic from November 1937 and the object of intense bombing (as many as twenty raids per day) by the Nationalist air force. Barcelona was the stronghold of the CNT and the POUM, and the conflicts there between the Republican factions were particularly intense, leading to the "May Days" (May 3–8, 1937) street fighting. Barcelona fell to the Nationalists on January 26, 1939.

Belchite: A small town about twenty-five miles south of Zaragoza. It was the site of one of the battles fought by the members of the Abraham Lincoln Battalion in the Aragon offensive of August 1937. It was notable for its intense house-to-house fighting.

Bilbao: The chief city of the Basque provinces and the second-largest port in Spain. Important for its shipyards, steel mills, and nearby iron mines, it fell to Nationalist forces on June 19, 1937.

Blum, Léon (1872–1950): A French Socialist politician who lead the Popular Front government in France from June 4, 1936, until June 22, 1937, and again briefly from March 13 to April 10, 1938. Blum wanted to help the Spanish government but vacillated because of his fears of a broader war in Europe. He also worried about whether he could count on his own military to act against Franco. He thus followed an ambivalent policy—allowing volunteers to cross the border into Spain but generally supporting nonintervention.

Bolshevik: The faction of the Russian Social Democratic party led by Lenin from 1903. After the success of the Bolsheviks in the October Revolution of 1917, it was the dominant party in the country. It became the Communist party in 1918 and took control of the Soviet Union.

Bonnet, Georges Etienne (1889–1973): The French foreign minister at the time of the Munich crisis of 1938.

Brunete: A town approximately fifteen miles west of Madrid. The Battle of Brunete was a series of battles that took place over three weeks, from July 7 to July 26, 1937. The campaign was an attempt by the Republican army to encircle the Nationalist forces besieging the capital. Even after vicious fighting and extensive casualties, the battle lines would change little.

camión: Spanish for "truck."

Casa de Alianza: The Madrid office of the Alliance of Antifascist Intellectuals, where poems, broadsides, and posters were produced and where artists and intellectuals met during the Spanish Civil War, among them Rafael Alberti and María Teresa León. The Americans Edwin Rolfe and Langston Hughes spent time there as well.

Casa de Campo: A sprawling wooded park northwest of the city that was the scene of major fighting during the attacks on Madrid. Its hills and scrub brush made rapid troop movement difficult but provided excellent cover for the Nationalist troops. In the summer of 1936, when terror reigned in both Nationalist and Republican cities, the Casa de Campo was the scene of frequent summary executions.

Casado López, Segismundo (1893–1968): A Republican army officer best known for his political role at the end of the war, when he tried to negotiate a compromise with Franco by offering to remove Communists from the government.

Caspe: A town and railroad center in Aragon first captured for Franco and then retaken by anarchists from Barcelona, despite the fascist use of a human shield of wives and children from union families. The town was defended by American volunteers in 1938 until they were overwhelmed by a much larger fascist force.

Castile: The area of north-central Spain that includes Madrid.

Catalonia: The region in most northeastern Spain, bordered by France on the north and the Mediterranean on the east. Catalonia and its capital, Barcelona, have traditionally sought independence from the rest of Spain. Autonomous during the Spanish Civil War, it was the site of many significant battles, particularly during the last year of the war. The fall of Barcelona to the Nationalist armies in January 1939 meant the war was essentially over.

Caudillo, el **(Spanish):** Literally "leader" or "chief" of all political parties, the title Franco assumed in 1937.

Celadas: Frozen heights where the International Brigades fought during the battle for Teruel early in 1938.

Chamberlain, Neville (1869–1940): Prime minister of Great Britain from 1937 to 1940. He was known primarily for his appeasement of Hitler in signing the Munich Pact of September 1938, a pact that effectively killed any hopes of British or French help for the Republic.

Chatos: A Russian fighter plane (Polikarpov 1–15) used by the Republican air force and flown largely by Russian pilots. Nicknamed Chatos (snub-noses) because of their shortened fuselages.

chofers: Spanish for "drivers."

CNT (Confederación Nacional del Trabajo): Founded in 1911, the CNT was one of the two important labor groups in Spain (the other was the UGT), both having around a million members. Often referred to as anarchist, the CNT practiced a form of syndicalism based in industrial unions and eschewed any belief that there could be anything but continuous class conflict between employers and workers. Independent of any political party, it often called on its members to boycott elections, but it was the absence of such a boycott that contributed to the electoral victory of the Popular Front in 1936. The CNT advocated a revolutionary strategy for winning the war and the revolution, a policy strenuously opposed by not only the Republican parties but also the Communists.

Columbus: A statue of the famous explorer overlooks the Barcelona harbor.

commissar: A feature of the Republican army, modeled on the Soviet Red Army. A political commissar worked alongside the military officers at every level of command. These commissars were primarily responsible for morale and political education.

Condor Legion: Over nineteen thousand German military personnel participated in the Spanish Civil War in support of the Nationalists. The amount of material contributed by the Germans was immense and extremely important for the Nationalists' victory: advanced bombers, fighters, tanks, anti-tank and anti-aircraft guns, artillery, transports, communications, and seaplanes. The personnel was regularly rotated and new techniques tested, including one of the most infamous maneuvers of the war, the destruction of Guernica by firebombing.

Córdoba (Cordova): Capital of the Córdoba Province in Andalusia, about 150 miles east of Sevilla. Like most cities in Andalusia, Córdoba fell almost immediately to the fascist rebels when the uprising started in July 1936.

Cortes: The parliamentary body of the Spanish Republic.

Daladier, Edouard (1884–1970): A French Socialist politician, who was the minister of war from 1936 to 1940 and served as prime minister from 1938 to 1940. He supported appeasement and signed the Munich Pact. He built his support in France by exploiting anticommunism and antiwar sentiment. Although sympathetic to the Spanish Republic, he was often vacillating and advocated neutrality and nonintervention.

difuntos: Spanish for "deceased."

Durango: A tiny village in northern Spain that was the first unarmed community to be bombed from the air. Hitler's Condor Legion struck it in March 1937, a month before the bombing of Guernica.

Durruti, Buenaventura (1896–1936): Perhaps the most famous Spanish anarchist during the Spanish Civil War. He died while commanding a militia battalion on the Madrid front at University City on November 20, 1936, only four months after the war began. He remains to this day a potent symbol of the pure political revolutionary.

Ebro: A major river in northeast Spain that flows southeast almost five hundred miles from the Cantabrian Mountains near Bilbao to the sea near Tortosa. Many significant battles in the last half of the war were fought around the Ebro region between Zaragoza and the Mediterranean coast.

Escorial, El: An enormous building north of Madrid, part palace, part convent, and part mausoleum.

Espada: Spanish for "swordsman."

Ethiopia: An ancient nation located in east-central Africa. It was invaded by Italy in 1935 as part of Mussolini's imperialist dreams. A black soldier in Oscar Hunter's short story "700 Calendar Days" explains why he volunteered for Spain: "I wanted to got to Ethiopia and fight Mussolini. . . . This ain't Ethiopia, but it'll do" (in *The Heart of Spain,* ed. Alveh Bessie [New York: VALB, 1952], 29).

FAI (Federación Anarquista Ibérica): The group of theoreticians and activists who made up the ideological vanguard of Spanish anarchism. Its paramilitary cadres were responsible for some indiscriminate violence in the early days of the war. Historically somewhat at odds with the CNT, it modified its position enough so that its members came to hold positions of leadership in the CNT. Barcelona was its primary site of influence; its presence in Madrid was minimal. One of the major slogans of the CNT-FAI was "The war and revolution are inseparable."

fascism: A twentieth-century phenomenon that emerged first in Italy after World War I with the rise of Benito Mussolini. It was a counter movement to socialism and democracy and championed extreme state power, the abolition of individual rights, and aggressive nationalism. It typically idealized dictatorial leaders, promoted ethnic and religious hatred, and encouraged violence against opposing philosophies and political parties. Virtually all Lincoln Battalion members would have said they went to Spain "to fight fascism."

Florida: One of two hotels in Madrid—the other being the Gran Via (across from the Telephonica building)—where journalists frequently gathered during the war. Hemingway stayed there when he was in Madrid in 1937, taking one of the large (and now inexpensive) rooms in the front that faced the fascist artillery.

Gandesa: A small town on the western edge of the province of Tarragona, about sixty-six miles south of Lleida. During the retreats of March and April 1938, many members of the Lincoln Battalion, including Robert Merriman, were lost around Gandesa. During the Ebro offensive in the first days of August 1938, the Lincolns were stopped just outside Gandesa. Two weeks later, the Lincolns would begin a ten-day stint overlooking Gandesa from Hill 666, just east of the town, that would be some of the most brutal days of the war.

Garcilaso de la Vega (1501–36): A soldier-poet. His poetic output was small but highly polished, so that he became the undisputed classic poet of the Golden Age of Spanish literature.

Gateway to the Sun. See Puerta del Sol.

Gautier, Théophile (1811–72): French poet and writer.

Granada: A province located in southeastern Spain on the Mediterranean. Its capital, Granada, was captured by the Nationalists early on, while the rest of the province was the site of considerable military conflict thereafter. The Nationalists instituted a reign of terror to suppress the working classes there.

Gran Via: The major east-west avenue in Madrid. During the first months of the war, the fascist general Emilio Mola announced that he would be having coffee on the Gran Via by October 12. The general did not keep his rendezvous. It was down the Gran Via that the International Brigades marched in November of 1936 on their way to the front on the outskirts of Madrid.

Guadalajara: A town in central Spain located about thirty-five miles northeast of Madrid on the road to Zaragoza. It was here that, beginning on March 8, 1937 (and lasting for about ten days), approximately 35,000 Italian and 15,000 Spanish troops began a campaign to attack Madrid from the north. The Republican army, aided considerably by the International Brigades, among them the Italian Garibaldi Battalion, decisively defeated the Italians. The propaganda value to the Republic, in being able to demonstrate that organized Italian units were being used by the insurgents, was considerable.

Guadarrama winds: Winds sweeping down off the Guadarrama Mountains that are a distinctive characteristic of Madrid's climate. Madrid is situated on a 2,120-foot high plateau, and is encircled by the Guadarrama Mountains to the north.

Guardia, Francisco Ferrer (1859–1909): A famous Spanish anarchist educator executed by the state during the "Tragic Week" of July 1909, an outburst of rioting and church-burning triggered by popular resentment against the Moroccan War. The week raised before the privileged classes the specter of a proletarian revolution, a possibility that would haunt Spain's wealthy and galvanize its poor for decades.

Guernica: A historically important but militarily insignificant Basque town of 7,000. On April 26, 1937, over forty German aircraft of the Condor Legion appeared over Guernica. Within a few hours, most of the city center was in ruins, and over a thousand civilians were dead. Its fame enhanced by Picasso's painting protesting the bombing, this raid has become one of the signal events of the war.

Halifax, Edward Frederick Lindley Wood (1881–1959): Succeeded Sir Anthony Eden as foreign secretary under British Prime Minister Neville Chamberlain in March 1938. He helped implement Chamberlain's appeasement policy. Halifax's visit with Hitler at Berchtesgaden on November 17, 1937, was the first concrete step in putting the policy into effect, and he played a large role in negotiating the Munich Pact in 1938. From 1940 to 1945, he was Britain's ambassador to the United States.

Hernández, Miguel (1910–42): A Spanish poet who fought in the Communist Fifth Regiment in the Spanish Civil War. He died in a fascist jail in Alicante.

Hijar: A Spanish town where American and other international volunteers fought in the spring of 1938. Fascist assaults reduced it to a pile of rubble.

Huesca: A province in northern Spain. Captured by Franco, it was fought over throughout the war.

"The Internationale": The anthem of the international working class. It was written by Eugene Pottier in Paris in 1871 to celebrate the Paris Commune, March–May 1871, which was set up at the end of the Franco-Prussian War in opposition to the humiliating peace agreements the French government at Versailles had arranged with the Prussians. At the end of May the military triumphed, and in the aftermath over seventeen thousand men, women, and children were executed. Here is one version of the first stanza and the chorus:

> Arise ye prisoners of starvation!
> Arise ye wretched of the earth,
> For Justice thunders condemnation;
> A better world's in birth . . .
> > 'Tis the final conflict,
> > Let each stand in his place,
> > The International Party
> > Shall be the human race.

José Antonio. See Primo de Rivera, José Antonio.

Jarama: A valley south of Madrid that was the site of major battles where the International Brigades helped prevent the capital from being encircled early in 1937.

Lérida: A Republican province in northern Spain.

limpieza: Spanish for "cleanliness," "purity," "honesty."

Llobregat: A region in Catalonia. In 1934, illegal strikes in the Llobregat potash mines were broken by mass detentions and firings.

Machado, Antonio (1875–1939): A major Spanish poet who supported the Republic and died on the Spanish frontier in February of 1939.

Madrid: Capital of Spain, located at the geographic center of the country. The inhabitants of the city stormed the military barracks and in hand-to-hand combat saved the city for the Republic in July of 1936. The International Brigades were thrown into combat in Madrid, and the government moved to Valencia. Madrid was the focus of several failed Nationalist attempts to capture the city. Madrid finally fell to the Nationalists in the last days of the war.

Majorca: The largest of the Balearic Islands southeast of Barcelona. It was overtaken almost immediately by the Nationalist forces and served as an important naval and air base during the war, especially for the Italian forces.

Málaga: A significant port city on the southern coast of Spain. It was taken by the Nationalist army on February 8, 1937, after the Republicans abandoned the city without much of a fight. Some of the most brutal reprisals of the war took place immediately afterward.

Malraux, André (1901–76): A celebrated French novelist who wrote *La condition humaine* (1933), a novel about the Chinese Communists' struggle against the invading Japanese. He was an ardent supporter of the Spanish Republic. Early in the war, he procured airplanes and organized the Escaudrilla España, a group of international volunteers and mercenaries who flew for the Republic. His novel *L'espoir* (1938) would be one of the most important literary works to emerge from the war.

Moncada: A town in Catalonia, about fifteen miles from Barcelona at the time of the civil war. Rukeyser's train from Paris stopped there in 1936.

Mandelstam, Osip (1891–1938): A Russian modernist poet and literary critic, whose second volume of poetry, *Tristia* (1922), was attacked by Communist party critics because he was reluctant to espouse the revolution in his work. Arrested for writing an epigram on Stalin and reading it to friends, he spent a few years in exile. He returned to Moscow but was arrested again and died in custody at a transit camp near Vladivostok.

Maxim: A British-made machine gun used extensively in the Republican army.

Miaja, General José (1878–1958): A career military man who was an ambivalent supporter of the Republic. He was, nonetheless, given the role of defending Madrid from Franco's advancing forces when the government moved to Valencia in November 1936.

milicianos: Members of the largely untrained volunteer militias that rose up to defeat the fascist rebels in such cities as Madrid and Barcelona.

Motherwell, Robert (1915–91): An American artist, one of the pioneers of abstract expressionism, who began a major series of over a hundred paintings in 1949 that were inspired by the Spanish Civil War. The series was entitled *Elegy to the Spanish Republic* and was dominated by the dramatic use of black on white.

Mundo obrero: The official newspaper of the Spanish Communist party throughout the civil war.

Mussolini, Benito (1883–1945): The Italian dictator who was the founder of Italian fascism. He was a socialist in his youth, but after fighting in World War I, he organized fellow veterans into the strongly nationalistic Fascist party. Having imperialistic designs, he conquered Ethiopia in 1936 and annexed Albania in 1939. Siding with Hitler, he sent thousands of Italian troops to support the Nationalists against the Republican government.

Nationalists: The forces of the Right, opposed to the Second Republic, who supported a military coup to overthrow the democratically elected government. They were also referred to as insurgents, fascists, rebels, and the Burgos junta, among other terms. General Francisco Franco became their head of state on October 1, 1936.

Non-Intervention Committee: A committee made of representatives from every European country except Switzerland organized to supervise the workings of the Non-Intervention Pact, a pact created in the fall of 1937 by the European countries and the Soviet Union regarding the Spanish Civil War. The committee came to be viewed by many as an exercise in hypocrisy, as France and Britain's appeasement of Germany and Italy allowed Hitler and Mussolini to strongly support the rebels.

"No Pasaran" (They shall not pass): The rallying cry raised by the people of Madrid early in the war as Franco's armies threatened their city. The phrase came to represent the fighting spirit of the people of the Republic.

paseo: A leisurely stroll or promenade. On Sunday many people dressed up for a traditional promenade along major streets or through public squares. During the war it also became the name for the journey to an execution.

La Pasionaria (1895–1989): Dolores Ibarruri, a well-known Spanish Communist who was the party's spiritual leader during the war. She was given the name La Pasionaria (the passion flower) because of her power as an orator. Reared a devout Catholic in the Basque provinces, she married an Asturian miner and began her ascent to the top of the Spanish Communist party. Closely connected with the Soviet Union, she went into exile in Moscow at the end of the war. She returned to Spain after Franco's death to take back her seat in the Spanish Parliament.

Plaza Mayor: A beautifully proportioned, rectangular, seventeenth-century, cobbled, arcaded square from which the streets of Old Madrid radiate. The Plaza Mayor is located off Calle Mayor, a few blocks from Puerta del Sol.

Perpignan: A city in southern France near the Mediterranean just north of the Spanish border. Many in the Lincoln Brigade would spend a few days there getting organized before they crossed over the Pyrenees into Spain.

Poetas en la España leal and Romanceros de los soldados en las trincheras: Two of a number of poetry anthologies issued in Spain by Loyalist supporters during the war.

POUM (Partido Obrero de Unificación Marxista): The Revolutionary Communist party. The smallest of the four major left organizations, the POUM was anti-Stalinist and was closely linked with the CNT in wanting a prompt anticapitalist revolution. Its insistence on the immediate establishment of the revolution was at odds with the Communist party's insistence on winning the war first. In addition, the leader of the POUM, Andrés Nin, had been a secretary of Leon Trotsky, so the Communist party accused the POUM of Trotskyism. After the POUM's participation in the antigovernment disturbances in Barcelona, its days were numbered. In June 1937 the Republic outlawed the POUM and arrested many of its leaders.

Primo de Rivera, José Antonio: Founder and leader of the right-wing Flangist party. He was executed by firing squad on November 20, 1936, thereafter becoming a fascist martyr and eventually a cult figure. A statue of him is located in Granada across from García Lorca's window.

Puerta del Sol: The central plaza of Madrid.

Quinto: A small town about twenty-five miles east of Zaragoza. It was the first town taken by the Lincoln Battalion during the Aragon offensive of August 1937, a brutal battle in which much of the fighting was literally door-to-door. The Lincolns took about a thousand prisoners, and the Lincolns' losses were relatively small.

Ramblas: The street in Barcelona leading down to the harbor. It is a major shopping area.

refugios: Air-raid shelters.

Reid, Arnold: A classmate of Edwin Rolfe at the University of Wisconsin. Rolfe describes his death in *The Lincoln Battalion: The Story of the Americans Who Fought in Spain in the International Brigades* (New York: Veterans of the Abraham Lincoln Brigade, 1939): "On a hill adjacent to the Lincoln position another American—one of the most competent and mature and kindly of all in Spain—died as he directed the fire of a machine-gun in his company. He was Arnold Reid, a twenty-six-year-old American who had worked for many years in South and Latin America, and who had joined the Spanish battalion of the Fifteenth Brigade in order to strengthen the work of the many Latin Americans in its ranks. The Spaniards, especially the young *quintos,* had loved the quiet young man who had become commissar of their machine-gun company; who knew their language and songs and traditions as well, if not better, than any of them" (267).

Renn, Ludwig (1889–1979): A Communist novelist from an aristocratic background. Born Arnold Friedrich Vieth von Golssenau, he served as a captain in the German army in World War I. In Spain, he served first as the commander of the Thaelmann Battalion and then later as chief of staff of the Eleventh International Brigade.

Retiro: One of Spain's most beautiful parks, located in the middle of Madrid. It encompasses a lake and a number of distinct squares, open spaces, and formal gardens. Laid out in the seventeenth century, the park's 320 acres originally served as a royal retreat (*retiro*).

Romancero gitano (Gypsy ballads): A 1928 book of poems by Federico García Lorca.

Salamanca: A city and province northwest of Madrid, Franco's headquarters during the assault on Madrid.

Salud: Spanish word meaning "health." It is the popular greeting used by members of Spain's working classes, the Left, and supporters of the Spanish Republic.

Saragossa. See Zaragoza.

Second Republic: Came into existence in 1931 after municipal elections throughout Spain returned victories for Socialist and Republican candidates, demonstrating that the monarchy had lost popular support. The Republic was known as *La niña bonita* (The beautiful maiden) because of its widespread support, but it was weakened by political, economic, and social strife. The Republican coalition lost the elections to a right-center coalition in 1933. When the Republican forces won the Popular Front elections of February 1936, the forces of the Right organized a military coup that precipitated the Spanish Civil War in July 1936.

Telephonica: The large modernist-style telephone building, which served as the headquarters of Spain's telecommunications company. Standing on the Gran Via on the highest ground in the center of Madrid, it was the city's highest building when it was erected in 1929. It was shelled repeatedly by the rebels and also used as a reference point to aim shells up the Gran Via.

Teruel: A city located about ninety miles northwest of Valencia in east-central Spain. Just before Christmas 1937, the Republican army took the city in a battle that Edwin Rolfe describes as "Spain's Valley Forge." By the end of February 1938, however, with vastly superior firepower, the Nationalist forces had retaken Teruel.

Thaelmann Battalion: One of the first international battalions and originally placed in the Twelfth Brigade. Primarily political refugees from Nazi Germany, they fought heroically throughout the war and were vital in the defense of Madrid during the winter of 1936–37. They would be later transferred to the Eleventh Brigade, which was reborn as the Thaelmann Brigade, named for Ernst Thaelmann, a German Communist leader imprisoned by Hitler.

Toledo: A city and province south of Madrid, the scene of heavy fighting early in Spain's civil war.

torero: Spanish for "matador."

Torquemada, Thomas (1420–98): The head of the Spanish Inquisition, responsible for the burning of heretics and for the expulsion of the Jews from Spain.

Tortosa: A town near the mouth of the Ebro River, where it flows into the Mediterranean. Located about 120 miles south of Barcelona, it fell to the Italian forces in April 1938, cutting Catalonia off from the rest of Republican Spain.

Udine: The city in northern Italy where Tina Modotti was born.

UGT (Unión General de Trabajodores): A socialist-led trade union, and one of the most powerful in Spain, numbering around a million members. Its leader at the beginning of the war was Largo Caballero, who quickly become the Republic's prime minister.

Unamuno, Miguel de (1864–1936): One of Spain's most notable modern writers. When the Spanish Civil War began, he was sympathetic with the Nationalists, but his position shifted shortly thereafter. On October 12, 1936, at a ceremony held at the University of Salamanca, in Nationalist territory within a hundred yards of Franco's headquarters, Unamuno dramatically criticized Millán Astray, the Nationalist general who had founded the Spanish Foreign Legion and who shared the platform with him that day. Unamuno thereafter remained under house arrest until his death two months later.

University City: The hillside campus of the University of Madrid, which was the scene of dramatic fighting during the struggle for the city. After being halted by the people's militias, Franco's troops were preparing additional attacks on the city when the International Brigades marched through Madrid on November 8 to take up positions in their first major battles. On November 9 International Brigade troops spearheaded a counterattack among the gum and ilex trees of the Casa de Campo. In a series of bloody bayonet charges ending in hand-to-hand combat the International Brigades helped retake portions of the park, though Nationalist troops remained entrenched there. A week later, the International Brigades engaged in hand-to-hand combat in University City, much of which was reduced to rubble in the process. Buildings were sandbagged; doors and windows were barricaded; machine guns swept all the open approaches. At one point, the ground floor of one building was held by the Thaelmann Battalion and the other floors by Franco's Moors. On another day one room in the Hall of Philosophy changed hands four times. The battle for University City continued until November 23, when the fascist advance was stopped, but University City remained divided between the opposing armies for the rest of the war. The grounds were deeply entrenched, tunnels were dug under streets exposed to fire, and various buildings remained in either Nationalist or Republican hands.

Valdés Guzmán, José: The fascist commandante in Granada. He was the officer most responsible for García Lorca's death.

Valencia: One of Spain's largest cities, located on the Mediterranean east of Madrid. Near a major agricultural region and noted for its port, Valencia became the refuge of the Republican government after November 6, 1936, when Madrid seemed ready to fall to Franco's advancing army.

Valladolid: A politically conservative province (and capital city) in north-central Spain, where Nationalists gained control and murdered about nine thousand citizens judged to be Republican sympathizers.

Vallejo, César (1892–1938): A Peruvian poet and novelist, born in the Andean town of Santiago de Chuco. His *Trilce* (1922) was a volume of radical experimental poetry, some of it written in a Peruvian prison. He lived in Paris from 1923 to 1931, when he was deported, and then moved to Spain, where he joined the Communist party. He became active in the antifacist movement when the Spanish Civil War broke out.

Valley of the Fallen: A valley north of Madrid that Franco converted into a vast monument to himself and his regime.

Velasquez: The street in Madrid where the headquarters of the International Brigades was located (and where Edwin Rolfe edited the English language magazine of the brigades, *Volunteer for Liberty,* from 1937 to the beginning of 1938).

Velasquez, Diego de Silva (1599–1660): One of Spain's most important painters. He was the court painter to Philip IV and was known particularly for his portraits of the royal family and members of the court.

Villanueva de la Cañada: A small village about twenty miles west of Madrid. It was the site of brutal fighting during the Battle of Brunete in July 1937.

Wolff, Milton (b. 1915): The ninth and last commander of the Lincoln Battalion. An art student from Brooklyn and a member of the Young Communist League, he rose from a machine-gun company to lead the Lincolns in the Ebro offensive of the summer of 1938. His autobiographical novel of the Spanish Civil War, *Another Hill,* was published in 1994.

Zaragoza (also Saragossa): An old and important city in northeastern Spain, in the Aragon region, about two hundred miles west of Barcelona. A Nationalist stronghold, Zaragoza was an elusive goal the entire war for the Republican armies. Besieged early in the war by Buenaventura Durruti's anarchist column, it later was the target of the Aragon offensive of August 1937 and the Ebro offensive of July 1938.

ABOUT THE POETS

Ai (1947–) was born Florence Anthony in Albany, Texas. She did not learn her real father's identity until she was sixteen. Her father was Japanese American; her mother was black, Irish, and Choctaw Indian. She took the name "Ai," which means "love" in Japanese, to signal her heritage. Ai's childhood was spent in a variety of cities, including Tucson, Los Angeles, and San Francisco. She was educated at the University of Arizona and the University of California at Irvine. Although she has done short lyrics on both intimate and public historical topics, her specialty is the dramatic monologue, sometimes in the voices of invented personas, sometimes in the person of named public figures. Her speakers have included Marilyn Monroe, Leon Trotsky, Emiliano Zapata, John F. Kennedy, Joseph McCarthy, the Atlanta child murderer, and an anonymous *Kristallnacht* survivor. Some are corrupted seekers after power who fruitlessly try to justify themselves; others have been consumed by different appetites. Her language is vivid but rather matter-of-fact and unadorned. The voices of her speakers sometimes acquire an almost deadpan, driven passion. She has been obsessed, throughout her career, with the intersecting subjects of death, sex, history, and religion. Her poems seek to lay bare our most violent inner motives and the meaning of the desire behind them. Like Sylvia Plath, she has sought a way to write without holding anything back. In the process, especially when taking up real people and events, she has spoken brutal truths about public life with a clarity no other discourse can muster.

John Bensko (1949–) was born in Birmingham, Alabama, and educated at the University of Alabama and Florida State University, where he earned a Ph.D. He has taught at the University of Alabama and at Old Dominion University in Norfolk, Virginia. Bensko spent a year in Spain as a Fulbright professor at the Universidad de Alicante. He now coordinates the creative writing program at the University of Memphis. His books include *Green Soldiers* (1981), *The Waterman's Children* (1994), and *The Iron City* (2000).

Alexander F. Bergman (1912–41) was the pen name of Alex Frankel, who was born in Brooklyn, New York, in a room behind his father's small laundry. In 1917 the family moved to a farm outside Waterbury, Connecticut, but Frankel returned to the New York area for high school. Afterward he took a job in the bookkeeping department at the Consolidated Edison Company, where he worked the four-to-midnight shift until his resistance broke down and he developed tuberculosis. Frankel was confined to bed by early 1938. It was at that time that his close friend and fellow poet from high school, Eugene Loveman, was killed in Spain. Several of his poems were published in *New Masses;* Joy Davidman edited and introduced Bergman's poems in *They Look Like Men,* published posthumously in 1944.

John Berryman (1914–72) was born John Smith in McAlester, Oklahoma. When he was twelve, after his family had moved to Florida, his father shot himself to death outside his son's window. Berryman was educated at Columbia and Cambridge universities and became an influential teacher at Harvard, Princeton, and Minnesota, but he struggled with alcoholism and madness throughout his life. In the end, he leapt to his death from a bridge in Minneapolis.

Although he wrote short poems, a long poem, *Homage to Mistress Bradstreet* (1956), and a 385-poem sequence, *The Dream Songs* (1964–68), are his major achievements. In the latter work Berryman performs, exhibits, and burlesques his psychic struggles and his attitudes toward contemporary culture through a series of personae. Stylistically and rhetorically inventive, they are quite unlike anything else in modern poetry. His Spanish Civil War poem comes from his early intensely left-wing poetry.

Alvah Bessie (1904–85) was born in New York City and was educated at Columbia University. He survived the first years of the Great Depression digging potatoes for farmers in Vermont and selling his book reviews and short stories. His first novel, *Dwell in the Wilderness,* was published in 1935. He returned to New York to work for the *Brooklyn Daily Eagle* but soon quit to assist the Spanish Information Bureau in the same city. In 1938 he left for Spain in time to join the Ebro campaign. He fought with the Abraham Lincoln Battalion, and his book *Men in Battle* (1939) was the first personal narrative by an American volunteer. In 1943 he went to Hollywood to write screenplays for Warner Brothers, but four years later he was called before the House Committee on Un-American Activities, which sought publicity for its anticommunist campaign by holding hearings about the film industry. Like the other members of the Hollywood Ten, Bessie cited his First Amendment rights in refusing to testify. He was cited for contempt and sent to federal prison in Texas, where he wrote a series of poems about the

Spanish Civil War. A longtime victim of the blacklist, Bessie continued to write fiction but was barred from pursuing his Hollywood career.

John Malcolm Brinnin (1916–98) was born in Halifax, Nova Scotia, in Canada, the child of American citizens. He was educated at the University of Michigan, and he taught at the University of Connecticut and at Boston University. He was the editor of the left-wing literary journals *New Writers* and *Signatures* in the 1930s. In 1942 he began publishing the first of six volumes of poetry and eleven volumes of literary criticism and nonfiction, among them studies or memoirs of Dylan Thomas, Gertrude Stein, and Truman Capote.

Olga Cabral (1909–97) was born in Port of Spain, Trinidad, in the British West Indies. She began publishing poems in little magazines in the 1930s but abandoned poetry until middle age while she was writing children's books in the 1940s. Her books of poems include *Cities and Deserts* (1959), *The Evaporated Man* (1968), *Occupied Country* (1976), and *In the Empire of Ice* (1980). She married the Yiddish poet Aaron Samuel Kurtz in 1951.

Robert Bhain Campbell (1911–40) was born in Royal Oak, Michigan, and educated at the University of Michigan, where he twice won the Hopwood Award. According to some sources, Campbell tried to join the International Brigades to fight in Spain but was turned down. After doing graduate work at Columbia University, where he also met and became close to John Berryman, he returned to Michigan to teach at Highland Park Community College in Detroit. Campbell's *The Task* (1945), from which "Among the Fallen" is taken, was his only book; it was published posthumously with an introduction by Norman Rosten. Campbell died of cancer in 1940.

Hayden Carruth (1921–) was born in Waterbury, Connecticut, and was educated at the University of North Carolina and the University of Chicago. He served two years in Italy during World War II. He was poetry editor of *Harper's* magazine beginning in 1977 and taught for a number of years at Syracuse University. His nearly thirty volumes of poetry begin with *The Crow and the Heart, 1946–1959* (1959) and continue through *Scrambled Eggs and Whiskey: Poems, 1991–1995* (1996). Admired by many for his control of a wide variety of forms, he has mostly avoided intensely confessional poetry, the one exception being *The Bloomingdale Papers* (1975), a sequence written in the 1950s while suffering from the combined effects of alcoholism and a nervous breakdown. Carruth has also written extensively about other poets' work.

John Ciardi (1916–86) was born in Boston and educated at Tufts College and the University of Michigan. After service in the air corps during World War II he taught at Harvard and at Rutgers, until resigning in 1961 to pursue a career lecturing, writing, and running a weekly radio program on word histories. He published twenty books of poems, a respected translation of Dante, and several volumes of nonfiction.

Joy Davidman (1915–60) began publishing while she was still an undergraduate at Hunter College. *Poetry* began to publish her poems in 1936, and within a year or two she had joined the Communist party. *Letter to a Comrade,* the only collection of her poems, was published in the Yale Series of Younger Poets in 1938. She spent the latter half of 1939 in Hollywood as an assistant screenwriter for MGM, an experience that led to her writing film reviews for *New Masses* in the early 1940s. She contributed new poems to her massive anthology *War Poems of the United Nations* (1943) and to *Seven Poets in Search of an Answer* (1944), wrote two novels, and converted from Judaism to Christianity after a religious experience in 1946. She divorced her first husband, the Spanish Civil War veteran William Gresham, and married the British writer C. S. Lewis in 1956; the 1993 feature film *Shadowlands* tells a version of her relationship with Lewis.

Barrows Dunham (1905–95) was born in Mount Holly, New Jersey, and educated at Princeton, where he earned a Ph.D. in philosophy in 1933. He taught English at Franklin and Marshall College in Lancaster, Pennsylvania, from 1926 to 1937, then became a philosophy professor at Temple University in Philadelphia. He taught there until losing his job in the McCarthyite witch hunts in 1953. His several books include *Man against Myth* (1947), *The Artist in Society* (1960), and *Heroes and Heretics* (1964).

Martín Espada (1957–) was born in Brooklyn, New York, of Puerto Rican parents. His father was a photographer who illustrated his first book of poems. Espada now teaches at the University of Massachusetts, but his earlier experience is much broader. He was a night clerk in a transient hotel, a journalist in Nicaragua, a welfare rights paralegal, and later a tenant lawyer in Boston. In addition to writing his own poetry, he has edited collections of political poetry and the works of contemporary Latino poets. His political poetry is notable for making its points with great wit and bravado.

Kenneth Fearing (1902–61) was born in Oak Park, Illinois, a Chicago suburb, where his father was an attorney. The family broke up a year after Fearing was born, and he moved in with an aunt. He was educated at the University of Illinois and the University of Wisconsin and moved to New York in 1924.

There he supported himself with a series of brief jobs, usually working for only a few months. He sold pants in a department store and worked for the WPA, *Time* magazine, the United Jewish Appeal, and the Federation of Jewish Philanthropies. He also published pulp fiction, detective novels published under his own name, and soft-core pornography published under the pseudonym Kirk Wolff. From 1933, when he was married, to 1942, when the marriage disintegrated, his wife, Rachel, was the reliable breadwinner. Fearing himself was notoriously unkempt and a serious alcoholic.

From the time he arrived in New York he published poetry steadily and wrote serious fiction, placing over forty poems in such journals as *New Masses* before publishing his first book of poetry in 1929. With the advent of the Great Depression, he was drawn to the Communist Left, though he remained an irreverent and iconoclastic fellow traveler. His revolutionary and anticapitalist 1935 *Poems* helped define a dynamic relation between proletarian poetry and experimental modernism. It included several exuberant, Whitmanesque social satires focused on the mass culture of consumer capitalism and successfully employed modernist techniques for political ends. The book was also devoted to the poor, but Fearing was simultaneously ruthless about all the idealizations that drive self-delusion in modern culture. His one great commercial success was his 1946 novel *The Big Clock,* which was made into a film by Paramount. In his 1956 *New and Selected Poems* he attacked the anticommunist witch hunts in both prose and verse.

Lawrence Ferlinghetti (1919–) was born Lawrence Ferling in Yonkers, New York. The original family name of Ferlinghetti was restored in 1954. He was educated at the University of North Carolina, Columbia University, and the Sorbonne, where he earned the Doctorat de l'Universite in 1949. He was an officer during the World War II Normandy invasion. Ferlinghetti is the author of numerous plays and over thirty volumes of poetry, among them *A Coney Island of the Mind* (1958) and *A Far Rockaway of the Heart* (1997). He has been coowner of the City Lights Book Shop in San Francisco since its inception and is the founder of City Lights Press. He is one of the major figures of the Beat movement.

Sol Funaroff (1911–42) was born of Russian parents. His father died in Palestine after the family fled across Europe. While Funaroff's mother was working in a sweatshop in 1915, the tenement they lived in on New York's East Side burned down. Neighbors carried him gasping from the building, but his lungs were weak thereafter. As a child, he sold candy and fruit to garment workers and later worked in a matzo factory and an upholstery shop. During the depression he got part-time work as a relief investigator and as a reporter for the *New York World* and news services and did some editorial work for the *New Republic* and *Scribner's*. The WPA Writer's Project gave him some steady work in the late 1930s. Meanwhile he wrote poetry and became an important organizer for the proletarian poetry movement in the 1930s. He founded Dynamo Press, which published *Dynamo* magazine and books by Fearing, Rolfe, and Funaroff himself. His two poetry collections are *The Spider and the Clock* (1938) and the posthumous *Exile from a Future Time* (1943). Always ill, Funaroff died young. The title of his second book is taken from lines in the opening poem of his first collection. "I am that exile / from a future time," he writes, "from shores of freedom / I may never know."

Margaret Gibson (1944–) was born in Philadelphia and grew up in Richmond, Virginia. She was educated at Hollins College and the University of Virginia. Her books include *Signs* (1979), *Long Walks in the Afternoon* (1982), and *Memories of the Future: The Daybooks of Tina Modotti* (1986), a book-length poem-sequence from which the poems reprinted here are taken. The poems adopt the voice of Tina Modotti (1896–1942), an Italian-born actress who had a role in Erich von Stroheim's film *Greed* (1924) and then became a celebrated photographer, nurse, and revolutionary in Mexico and Spain. The book was also energized by Gibson's activist work on behalf of tenants' rights in the Puerto Rican community of New London, Connecticut.

Don Gordon (1902–89) was born in Bridgeport, Connecticut. His father had immigrated from Lithuania and traveled through the small towns of Connecticut on a horse-drawn dry-goods wagon. The family moved to Los Angeles in 1912, where Gordon's mother and sister both won small parts in movies and his father was admitted to the California bar. Gordon was educated at the southern branch of the University of California (now UCLA) and at Pomona College. Uncertain what direction to take, he became a reader for the movie studios, canvassing novels for possible film productions. In the 1930s he began publishing poetry and became active on the left. Gordon rose to assistant head of the story department at MGM, but in 1951 he lost his job and was blacklisted. After a series of minor jobs, among them driver for a day care center, Gordon retired in 1964 and devoted himself to poetry. His books are *Statement* (1943), *Civilian Poems* (1946), *On the Ward* (1977), *Excavations* (1979), and *The Sea of Tranquility* (1989).

William Lindsay Gresham (1909–62) was born into a southern family that was nostalgic for the lost cause of the Confederacy. After moving to New York at age eight, Gresham was drawn first to Coney Island as a boy and later to

Greenwich Village as a young man. He sang folk music at a café, served a term in the Civilian Conservation Corps, and returned to New York, where he met and married a wealthy woman. Gresham was determined to become a writer, but these plans were interrupted by fifteen months of service with the Anglo-American artillery battery in Spain. His marriage collapsed when he returned home, and he began to drink. He then married the poet Joy Davidman and worked as a freelance writer and editor, publishing a novel *Nightmare Alley* in 1946. A second novel, *Limbo Tower,* appeared in 1949, but his marriage failed, and he lapsed into alcoholism. Gresham took his own life after being diagnosed with cancer.

Barbara Guest (1920–) was born in Wilmington, North Carolina, and was educated at the University of California at Berkeley. She became well known as a writer in the late 1950s as part of the New York School of poets. Like others in the group, Guest had a sound background in modern painting, a background that influenced her poetry and led to collaborations with graphic artists. Robert Motherwell's abstract, elegiac series of Spanish Civil War canvases underlie the poem published here.

Robert Hass (1941–) was born in San Francisco and reared in San Rafael, California. He was educated at St. Mary's College and Stanford University, where he received a Ph.D. In addition to four books of poetry, he has written criticism and translated European poets into English, including several volumes by Czeslaw Milosz. He has also published *The Essential Haiku: Versions of Basho, Buson, and Issa* (1994) and has taught at several schools, including Buffalo and Berkeley. Unlike poets who hope to redeem the ordinary by finding the poetic in it, Hass sometimes begins with the poetic—a radiant detail, a moment of loveliness—and works to show its relevance to daily life. Yet as the poem included here shows, he is also deeply concerned with the struggle to live both morally and aesthetically and with the ways history and culture challenge such an effort. He has written about Vietnam, Native Americans, the American working class, and the collapse of American cities. These concerns are unified by a recurring interest in the relationship between language and material reality and by a meditative sadness of tone that pervades much of his work.

Langston Hughes (1902–67) was born in Joplin, Missouri, but grew up mainly in Lawrence, Kansas. Before enrolling at the historically black Lincoln University in Pennsylvania, he worked at numerous menial jobs but also saw Africa, Mexico, and Paris. He would later make trips to the Soviet Union and Spain during the Spanish Civil War. In addition to his poetry Hughes wrote several stage plays and musicals, numerous newspaper columns, an autobiography, and several collections of short stories. Jazz and the blues remained a strong influence from his first books to the masterful collage poem *Ask Your Mama* (1962). He wrote some of America's most telling indictments of racism but also reached out to the poor of all ethnic backgrounds. Moreover, he was one of the few male poets of his generation who could write persuasively both about women and within a female persona.

For several decades Hughes was simultaneously the foremost African American poet and the premier poet of the American Left. Without understanding that double identity and dual cultural role, one cannot fully appreciate his life and work. Few American writers have been at once so deeply loved and so viciously reviled. His poem "Let America Be America Again" became an anthem for a generation; memorized, read aloud, it symbolized at once their political aspirations and their historical memory. Yet at the same time extreme right-wing groups picketed his readings and distributed hate literature about him.

All this came to a head during the McCarthy period of the 1950s. Hughes had at the very least been a fellow traveler of the American Communist party (CP) since the late 1920s, which is hardly surprising. The American party had taken the cause of civil rights seriously almost from its inception, and it was hard to find a leading black intellectual or artist who was not a formal member or a close collaborator on a whole range of cultural issues. Hughes was active in the Young Communist League in the 1920s and thereafter published in CP newspapers and through CP imprints. In the 1950s, under pressure from the House Committee on Un-American Activities, Hughes offered a muted disclaimer for his radical politics and issued his *Selected Poems* (1959) that eliminated his most radical poems and even some of his stronger poems about racial injustice. This picture was not corrected until 1994, when *The Collected Poems of Langston Hughes* was published, though Hughes did put together the progressive collection *The Panther and the Lash* in an effort to right the balance in the year of his death.

Rolfe Humphries (1894–69) was born in Philadelphia, Pennsylvania, and educated at Amherst College. After taking a poetry class from Genevieve Taggard, he began to publish his own work, meanwhile teaching at Woodmere Academy on Long Island for thirty-two years. Active in the Communist party in the mid-1930s, Humphries was deeply concerned about the rise of European fascism. He coedited *And Spain Sings: Fifty Loyalist Ballads* (1937) and translated Garcia Lorca's *Poet in New York* (1940) and *Gypsy Ballads* (1953). In 1940 he signaled his disillusionment with the party in his poem "With a Resignation, Untendered." He taught writing and Latin at Amherst College from 1957 to 1965; by that time he had also become a major translator.

Randall Jarrell (1914–65) was born in Nashville, Tennessee, and educated at Vanderbilt University. He taught at a number of colleges and universities, meanwhile acquiring a reputation as a devastatingly witty reviewer of other people's poetry. After enlisting in the army air force in 1942, he was assigned to an aviation facility in Tucson, Arizona, where he became a celestial training navigator. It may well have been his very distance from the World War II front that made him an attentive listener to B-29 crews, other returning soldiers, and home front family members and led him to retell their stories so effectively. Influenced by W. H. Auden early on, he was inspired by the war to use a less intricate, more conversational idiom. Both then and later in his career he sometimes adopted a woman's persona to tell a gendered narrative. Overall, it is the body of poetry he wrote about World War II, partly anticipated by his work on Spain, that constitutes his most distinctive and important contribution to his country's literature. A 1954 novel, *Pictures from an Institution,* uses Sara Lawrence College as a model for its satire.

Robinson Jeffers (1887–1962) was born in Pittsburgh, Pennsylvania, where his father was a minister and a professor of biblical literature. The family moved to northern California in 1903, before the area was fully settled. Jeffers was educated at Occidental College in Los Angeles. His initial interests were in medicine and forestry, which he studied, respectively, at the University of Southern California and at the University of Washington. In 1914 he went to Carmel, California, where he built with his own hands a stone tower near his house overlooking the Pacific Ocean and devoted himself to writing poetry. Many of the landscapes that figure in his work are from the area in which he lived. Jeffers developed a philosophy he called "inhumanism," in which he urged us to "uncenter the human mind from itself," to turn away from technology and incapacitating social regulation and look to nature as a proper model of consciousness. In nature he found a way of combining a fierce will with stoical endurance, twin values symbolized by the hawk and the rock. He also found an indifference to human struggle—a view reflected in his Spanish Civil War poem—that seemed to him the only spiritually sound and rational response to a world obsessed, alternatively, with mass murder and commodification. Although he is justly famous for his lyrics about nature, which use a Whitmanesque line to celebrate nature and decry its destruction by civilization, he also wrote many poems about national and international politics.

Bob Kaufman (1925–86) was born in New Orleans. His father, who was half African American and half Jewish, worked as a Pullman porter for the railroad that ran between New Orleans and Chicago; his mother, a black woman from an old Martinique family, the Vignes, was a schoolteacher. "His Jewish surname and Creole-like features," the introduction to his selected poems notes, "were shared with twelve brothers and sisters. . . . Up until his death from emphysema in January of 1986, Kaufman was known as a mostly silent, wiry black man who walked the streets of San Francisco's North Beach district day and night, often appearing as a mendicant, madman, or panhandler. Yet various schools of American poetry have sung his praises." His working life began at sea when he became a cabin boy on the *Henry Gibbons*. Based in New York and San Francisco, he worked on Henry Wallace's 1948 Progressive party presidential campaign, during which he was arrested and thrown into jail. Early on he connected with the Beat poets and became one of the notable figures of the movement. At the end of the 1950s City Lights Books issued three of his broadsides, including the widely read "Abominist Manifesto."

Kaufman would declaim his poems and manifestos at poetry readings and in other public places; often enough the police would arrest him. Eventually he began to drink under the strain; back in New York he was arrested and given shock treatments against his will. After President Kennedy was shot, Kaufman took a vow of silence, maintaining it for a decade. Then he began writing again; the poems were rescued from a hotel fire by a friend and published as his third book in 1981. By the end, he had been a Beat poet, a surrealist, a sound poet, a jazz poet, and a poet of black consciousness.

Carolyn Kizer (1925–) was born in Spokane, Washington, and educated at Sarah Lawrence, with later work at Columbia University and the University of Washington. Her books of poems include *The Ungrateful Garden* (1961), *Mermaids in the Basement* (1984), and *Pro Femina* (2000). She has been a regular participant in California events honoring the Veterans of the Abraham Lincoln Brigade.

Aaron Kramer (1921–97) was a widely published, poet, essayist, and translator, who taught English for many years at Dowling College in Oakdale, New York. He wrote committed poetry all his life, generally aiming for a public, accessible diction that could reach a wide audience. Kramer started writing about Spain while still in his teens, declaring himself a "people's poet," and began to publish in *Young Pioneer,* a journal of the Communist party's youth organization. In the 1940s he joined Langston Hughes in poetry readings, and in 1949 he became the only white member of the Harlem Writers Club. After World War II, in the wake of the Holocaust, Kramer took up Jewish history as a regular subject. The following decade, still a young man, he joined the literary resistance against McCarthyism, though he broke with the Communist party in 1953. He received a Ph.D. from New York University in 1966 and published several scholarly books thereafter.

Philip Levine (1928–) was born in Detroit, Michigan, and educated at Wayne State University. He later studied at Iowa with Robert Lowell and John Berryman. Along the way he took a number of working-class jobs; those and the ruined industrial landscape of Detroit helped shaped the settings and political loyalties of his poems. For years Levine has looked to modern Spanish poets for inspiration, and he has written a number of poems about the Spanish Civil War, often embodying his special sympathy for the Spanish anarchist movement. Although Levine's work is pervaded by an eloquent rage at injustice, it also reaches repeatedly for a visionary lyricism.

Archibald MacLeish (1892–1982), born and reared in Illinois, was educated at Yale University and Harvard Law School. He lived in Paris in the early 1920s after frontline service in World War I. He was on both the editorial board of *Fortune* magazine in the 1930s and the executive committee of the League of American Writers, a Popular Front organization supported by the Communist party. MacLeish served as librarian of Congress and as assistant secretary of state in the Roosevelt administration. Despite the self-sufficiency of poetic form he argues for in "Ars Poetica," he often addressed political topics in poems or radio plays. His poetic drama *Panic* (1935) and his book *Public Speech* (1936) signal his endorsement of collective action.

Ben Maddow (1909–92) was born in Passaic, New Jersey, and educated at Columbia University. Best known as a Hollywood screenwriter and as the author or editor of numerous books on photography, Maddow wrote only one book of poems, *A False Autobiography: Poems, 1940–1990* (1991). His career began in the 1930s, when he published a limited number of poems in such journals as *Blues, Poetry,* and *New Masses,* and he scripted a number of politically radical projects for Frontier Films, among them *Heart of Spain, China Strikes Back, People of the Cumberland,* and *Native Land.* At first he published under the pseudonym David Wolff to keep his activities secret from employers. After military service in World War II he began working in Hollywood. His screenwriting credits included *Framed* (1947), *Intruder in the Dust* (1949), and *The Asphalt Jungle* (1950), but then he was blacklisted and unable to work under his own name from 1952 to 1960. He managed to do some poorly paid work under the pseudonym Philip Yordan, but such important projects as his coauthorship of *The Wild One* (1954) remained uncredited. After agreeing to testify in confidence for the House Committee on Un-American Activities, he was able to resume his career.

Sherry Mangan (1904–61) was an Irish Catholic from the industrial town of Lynn, Massachusetts. He was educated at Harvard, where he became president of the Harvard Poetry Society and began publishing poems in the *Advocate*. At the end of the 1920s he worked to establish himself as an independent printer, while also publishing the magazine *Larus: The Celestial Visitor*. A novel, *Cinderella Married or How They Lived Happily Ever After: A Divertissement*, appeared in 1932. *No Apology for Poetrie and Other Poems* was published two years later. It was not until the advent of the Spanish Civil War that Mangan became a revolutionary Marxist. After moving to Paris in 1938, he developed two identities, one for bourgeois society and one, associated with a series of pseudonyms, in which he wrote as a member of the Trotskyist movement. In Paris, and later in Argentina after the Germans occupied France, Mangan was a *Time-Life-Fortune* journalist under one name and an official representative of the Marxist Fourth International under another. He returned to France in 1944, but soon after that was demoted at *Time* as part of its effort to purge liberals from the staff.

Jaime Manrique (1949–) was born in Barranquilla, Colombia, moved to Florida with his family as a teenager, and is now a naturalized U.S. citizen. He was educated at the University of South Florida and has taught at a number of schools, including Goddard College, the New School for Social Research, and Columbia University. His poetry includes *Scarecrow* (1990), *My Night with Federico García Lorca* (1997), and *Tarzan* (2001). He has also written several novels, including *Colombian Gold* (1983) and *Twilight at the Equator* (1997). His work often challenges the homophobia and machismo that are part of Latin culture. His book *Eminent Maricones* (1999) includes an account of García Lorca's influence on his work.

Thomas Merton (1915–68) was born in Prades, France, the child of parents who returned to the United States the following year. Merton took courses at Clare College, Oxford, but completed his degree at Columbia University. After courses at Corpus Christi Church near Columbia, he joined the Catholic church in 1938. He entered the Trappist monastery near Bardstown, Kentucky, in 1941, thereafter publishing not only poetry but also a series of spiritual diaries, autobiographical reflections, and literary essays. In the late 1950s he began writing more broadly on such subjects as world peace and racial harmony.

Edna St. Vincent Millay (1892–1950) was born in Rockville, Maine, and educated at Vassar. In 1917 she moved to New York's Greenwich Village and joined the revolutionary mix of politics, modernism, and sexual experimentation that typified the community. She was consistently involved in political causes through World War II and regularly wrote poems about them, but her most important legacy is no doubt the witty, antiromantic sonnets she wrote in significant number. Their rhetorical dexterity and confidence reflects an adaptation of Elizabethan sonnet style, while the gender instability and reversal of conventional gendered roles embodies both her feminism and the rethinking of sexual identity that preoccupied modernist writers and the general public.

Martha Millet (1919–) was regularly visible as a writer on the left from the 1930s to the 1950s. She contributed poetry to such radical publications as the *Young Pioneer* and *Daily Worker* in the 1930s and was represented with a series of poems, among them an elegy to García Lorca, in *Seven Poets in Search of an Answer* (1944). She published *Thine Alabaster Cities,* a poem sequence, in 1952 and *Dangerous Jack,* a verse play, in 1953, and she edited *The Rosenbergs: Poems of the United States,* in 1957, meanwhile contributing to *Masses and Mainstream.* She moved to Boulder, Colorado, with her husband, the radical journalist Sender Garlin in 1980.

James Neugass (1905–49) grew up in a wealthy New Orleans family of bankers and industrialists but was nonetheless drawn to the Left. He was educated at Phillips Exeter, Yale, Michigan, Harvard, and Balloil College, Oxford, though he never stayed long enough at any of them to earn a degree. He then traveled and wrote in Europe for seven years before the depression forced him to return to the United States, where he wrote poetry and worked at odd jobs in the 1930s until volunteering for service in the Spanish Civil War. In Spain he drove an ambulance for the International Brigades at a series of battles—Teruel, Segura de los Baños, Belchite, and the Ebro. After returning home, Neugass took a series of factory jobs, meanwhile publishing six novels and a series of translations. His novel *Rain of Ashes* (1949) was accepted for publication shortly before his early death. After "Give Us This Day" was published in *Story,* the magazine issued it as a separate pamphlet with an illustration by Luis Quintinilla.

Kenneth Porter (1905–97) was born near Sterling, Kansas, and educated at Sterling College and Harvard University, where he received a Ph.D. in 1936. He taught history at several schools, ending his career at the University of Oregon. *No Rain from These Clouds: Poems, 1927–1945* (1946) includes work from earlier chapbooks. His nonfiction includes the two-volume study *John Jacob Astor* (1931), *Relations between the Negroes and Indians within the Present Limits of the United States* (1933), and *The Negro on the American Frontier* (1971).

Mike Quin was the name that Paul William Ryan (1906–47), a labor union activist and columnist for the *Daily People's World,* adopted for his political work. Born in San Francisco, he left school at age fifteen and worked in shops and offices until becoming a sailor in 1925. Upon his return from sea in 1929 he worked in a bookstore, joined the John Reed Club, became a labor activist, and wrote for the *Waterfront Worker* and other publications. Two important collections of his poems and columns are *Dangerous Thoughts* (1940) and *More Dangerous Thoughts* (1941). Also see *On the Drumhead: A Selection from the Writings of Mike Quin.* As Ryan, he wrote several mystery novels.

Kerker Quinn (1911–69) was born in Peoria, Illinois, and educated at nearby Bradley University. He was an editor of the literary magazine *Direction* in the mid-1930s and later of *Accent* (1940–60), a literary magazine published at the University of Illinois at Urbana-Champaign where Quinn taught from 1935 until his death, at which time he was head of the creative writing division.

Kenneth Rexroth (1905–82) was born in South Bend, Indiana, and moved to Chicago with his family at age twelve. Although he attended classes at Chicago's Art Institute and later at the Art Students League in New York, he was largely (and prodigiously) self-educated. He would learn several languages, translate poems from Chinese, French, Spanish, and Japanese, and exhibit his own paintings in several cities. He also worked early on as a fruit picker, a forest ranger, a factory hand, and an attendant at a mental institution. Later he was a columnist for the *San Francisco Examiner* and the *San Francisco Bay Guardian* and a teacher at several universities.

Rexroth's long career and interesting life are not easy to represent fully. He was a fellow traveler of the Communist party, a key figure in the West Coast anarchist movement, a conscientious objector in World War II, and a longtime Buddhist. His early political poetry is notable for its capacity for intellectual reflection; his nature poetry virtually established the genre in California. He championed a number of younger poets, including the Beats, and helped found several West Coast cultural institutions.

Edouard Roditi (1910–92) was born in Paris, France, of parents who held American citizenship. He was educated first at Balloil College, Oxford, and then at the University of Chicago. He published fifteen books of poetry from 1935 until his death and wrote hundreds of essays on art and literature and a number of short stories. He is one of America's most notable surrealists.

Edwin Rolfe (1909–54), who was born Solomon Fishman, grew up on Coney Island. He took the pen name Rolfe in high school and eventually adopted it as his only name. Both his parents were politically active, though they were committed to competing wings of the Communist party. Rolfe began writing revolutionary poems while he was still in high school and was soon publishing them in the party's newspaper, the *Daily Worker*. Along with Langston Hughes he read his poems at the party's "Red Poets Night" in 1928, but the following year, disenchanted with rigid party functionaries and alienated by the infighting that helped destroy his parents' marriage, he quit the party and enrolled at the Experimental College at the University of Wisconsin. Never abandoning his identification with working people or his theoretical devotion to international socialism, he returned to New York two years later, rejoined the party, and became features editor of the *Daily Worker,* though his decisions to quit and rejoin would forever mark him as untrustworthy to some party bureaucrats. When the Spanish Civil War broke out, he joined the Abraham Lincoln Battalion. In the summer of 1937 he went to Madrid to edit the English language magazine of the International Brigades and the following year joined his comrades in the field.

He had published his first book of poems in 1936, which was reviewed in the *New York Times Book Review*. It was the last mainstream attention he would receive until the *New York Review of Books* devoted a full page to his *Collected Poems* more than fifty years later. His first book focused on the Great Depression; his second, privately printed in 1951, centered on Spain and was pervaded by the haunting lyricism associated with the lost cause of the 1930s. By then Rolfe had been drafted for World War II service but was sent home when he became ill in training. He moved to Los Angeles in 1943, supporting his poetry writing by part-time work on the fringes of the motion picture industry. A breakthrough came in 1947 when Humphrey Bogart and Lauren Bacall were signed to star in a film based on one of his scripts, but within months the House Committee on Un-American Activities hearings began in Hollywood; Rolfe was blacklisted and his film abandoned by Warner Brothers. He then took up his last great subject, McCarthyism, writing stronger poems on the topic than did any other American. After Rolfe died of a heart attack in 1954, the poet Thomas McGrath assembled some of his poems for a posthumous volume, but a number of Rolfe's poems were not published until his *Collected Poems* of 1993.

James Rorty (1891–1973) was born in Middletown, New York, the son of an Irish nationalist who had fled British persecution. Rorty graduated from Tufts College and thereafter wrote advertising copy and worked at a settlement house before serving in the ambulance service in World War I. He returned a pacifist, moved to San Francisco, and began to write poetry, including *What Michael Said to the Census-Taker* (1922) and *Children of the Sun* (1926). His politics had been a mix of socialist and anarchist tendencies, but he became a founding editor of *New Masses*. By 1932 he was secretary of an organization promoting the Communist party's candidates for president and vice-president, but he became disillusioned with the party. From 1933 to 1935 he was active in the American Workers party, which sought to offer a radicalism "rooted in American soil," aiming to be more militant than the Socialists and more practical and flexible than the Communists. Rorty's books include *Our Master's Voice* (1934), an exposé of the advertising industry; *Where Life Is Better* (1936); *American Medicine Mobilizes* (1939), an attack on the American Medical Association; and *McCarthy and the Communists* (1954), an anticommunist book that nonetheless denounced extremism and supported civil liberties.

Norman Rosten (1914–95) was born in New York and educated at Brooklyn College and New York University. During the 1930s he worked for the Federal Theater and published regularly in *New Masses*. In addition to his poetry, Rosten wrote novels, nonfiction, and a series of plays, including a number of radio plays for Armed Forces Radio during World War II. *The Big Road* (1946) is a book-length poem about road building in Alaska.

Muriel Rukeyser (1913–80) was born and reared in New York City and educated at Vassar College and Columbia University. During the 1930s Rukeyser regularly wrote for such Communist party publications as *New Masses*. She was in Spain to cover the antifascist Olympics in Barcelona when the Spanish Civil War broke out. She described that experience in the long poem "Mediterranean," first published in *New Masses,* and returned to the subject throughout her life. Years later, in 1975, she went to South Korea to protest the poet Kim Chi-Ha's imprisonment and anticipated execution; the poem sequence "The Gates" grew out of that trip.

From the outset Rukeyser was at once a political poet and a visionary. At times, those qualities were intensified, and in those moments she was simultaneously a revolutionary and a mystic. To grasp the forces that drive her work, we have to come to terms with a visionary impulse rooted in time, embedded in a struggle with lived history, and understand the larger notion of politics that underlies all her poetry. She understood early on what so many of us could not: politics encompasses all the ways that social life is hierarchically structured and made meaningful. Politics is not only the large-scale public life of nations but also the advantages, inequities, and illusions that make daily life very different for different groups among us. She understood that race and gender are integral parts of our social and political life. Never officially a feminist, she nonetheless devoted herself to voicing women's distinctive experience throughout her career. Rukeyser meditated on her poetics in *The Life of Poetry* (1949). She also published a novel, *The Orgy* (1966), as well as two biographies, *Willard Gibbs* (1942) and *The Traces of Thomas Harriot* (1971).

Morton Seif (1928–) was born in Brooklyn, New York, and educated at the University of North Carolina and New York University. He published his book of poems, *The Broken World,* in France while he was taking courses at the University of Aix–Marseille. He would later teach at several American schools, while writing reviews for a number of magazines and doing research on modern American writers and on American-Dutch relations. He settled in Berkeley, California, in the 1980s. By that time he was using the name Morton Philip Van Mappes Seif.

Vincent Sheean (1899–1975), born in Pana, Illinois, would become a well-known journalist and author. He recounts his early life in *Personal History* (1935), which details his adventures in the Middle East, his sympathy for anti-imperialist movements in China, and his growing concern over the rise of European fascism. He was a correspondent in Spain during the civil war and wrote about his experience in *Not Peace but a Sword* (1939). "Puigcerdà" was part of a group of Spanish Civil War poems Sheean published in *New Masses.* He also published a number of novels.

Walter Snow (1905–73) was born in Gardner, Massachusetts. He was a frequent contributor to such radical publications as the *Daily Worker* and *New Masses* in the 1930s and helped Jack Conroy edit the radical literary magazine *Anvil.* He was also an organizer for the American Newspaper Guild and the American Labor party. Like a number of writers on the left, he supported himself in part by writing popular fiction. He published his first detective story in the 1930s and returned to the genre two decades later. At that point he turned against the Communist party and published *The Golden Nightmare* (1952), an anti-Communist suspense mystery. After moving back to New England he worked as a journalist in Willimantic, Connecticut, for a number of years. He died there in 1973, not long after reconnecting with his leftist commitments.

Wallace Stevens (1879–1955) grew up in Reading, Pennsylvania, and was educated at Harvard and New York University Law School. Had Stevens not existed—a lifelong insurance executive writing some of his country's most insistently metaphysical poetry—it would hardly have been plausible to invent him. Yet Stevens had actually committed himself to writing poetry before taking a position with the Hartford Accident and Indemnity Company; the job was a way to earn a living. He began publishing poems in magazines in 1914, but his first book, *Harmonium,* did not appear until 1923.

His poems are so captivating in their rhetorical inventiveness—the play of words deployed for their sound, the almost palimpsestic thickness of imagery, the wit—that one can easily miss Stevens's regular (if abstract) engagement with the issues of his day, but it is nonetheless a continual feature of his work. Debates about public events and contrasting philosophical or cultural positions occur throughout his poems.

Genevieve Taggard (1894–1948) was born in Waitsburg, Washington, where her parents taught school. Her parents were also active members of the Disciples of Christ, and, when Taggard was two, they became missionaries and headed to Honolulu to teach. The family left Hawaii in 1914, at which point Taggard enrolled at the University of California at Berkeley, meanwhile joining the socialist political and literary community in the San Francisco Bay area. She graduated in 1919, having edited a Berkeley literary magazine and deepened her commitment to the radical Left. The following year she was in New York. It was a decade when the socialist and communist Left was in intense conflict and when revolutionary sentiment was entangled with artistic experimentation. Taggard edited the *Measure: A Magazine of Verse,* married the writer Robert Wolf, and participated in radical causes. By the end of the decade she had begun college teaching and eventually taught at Mount Holyoke, Bennington, and Sarah Lawrence. A Guggenheim year in Europe enabled her to see Majorca, a memory that would be important when the Spanish Civil War broke out a few years later.

In 1934 Taggard was divorced and married Kenneth Durant, who headed the American office of Tass, the Soviet News Agency. This placed her at the center of Left politics in the "red decade" of the 1930s. Tass employed several Spanish Civil War vets, including poet Edwin Rolfe, in the 1940s, and Taggard came to know them well. Her politics would be most evident in the growing political eloquence of her poetry, notable in *Calling Western Union* (1936) and *Long View* (1942).

Leslie Ullman (1947–) was born in Chicago and educated at Skidmore College and the University of Iowa. She has taught at a number of colleges, including most recently the University of Texas at El Paso, where she directs the master of fine arts program. Her first book of poems was *Natural Histories* (1979); it was followed by *Dreams by No One's Daughter* (1987) and *Slow Work through Sand* (1997). She lives on ranch land in southern New Mexico.

Mona Van Duyn (1921–) was born in Waterloo, Iowa, and educated at the University of Northern Iowa and the University of Iowa. Typically a formalist poet, she often works in long lines with varied meters. Sometimes taking up philosophical topics, she also writes about the commonplace events of ordinary life. She has taught most recently at Washington University. Her 1982 book, *Letters from a Father and Other Poems,* included the poem "Madrid, 1974."

Byron Vazakas (1905–87) was born in New York. When his father died in 1913, the family moved to Chicago for a short time and then settled in Lancaster, Pennsylvania. Vazakas's formal education ended with the eighth grade, after which his family moved again, this time to Reading, Pennsylvania. He began publishing poetry in magazines in the late 1930s. William Carlos Williams wrote a preface for Vazakas's first book of poetry, *Transfigured Night* (1946); it was followed by *The Equal Tribunals* (1961), *The Marble Manifesto* (1966), and *Nostalgias for a House of Cards* (1969). At the time of his death he had returned to Reading, Pennsylvania.

David Wojahn (1953–) was born in St. Paul, Minnesota, and was educated at the University of Minnesota and the University of Arizona. His books of poetry include *Ice House Lights* (1982), *Glassworks* (1987), *Mystery Train* (1990), *Late Empire* (1994), *The Falling Hour* (1997), and *Spirit Cabinet* (2002). He is also the author of *Strange Good Fortune: Essays on Contemporary Poetry* (2001) and the coeditor of *A Profile of Twentieth-Century American Poetry* (1991). He currently teaches at Indiana University, where he directs the program in creative writing.

James Wright (1927–80) was born and reared in a steelworker's family in Martin's Ferry, Ohio. He joined the army after high school and was sent to occupied Japan. After returning, he studied with John Crowe Ransom at Kenyon College and Theodore Roethke at the University of Washington, where he earned a Ph.D. He taught at the University of Minnesota, Hunter College, and the University of Delaware. In his first two books Wright used regular meters and rhymes and often celebrated the social outsiders of the small towns and farms near where he grew up. Then, on a Fulbright in Austria, he discovered the associative and sometimes partly surreal imagery of the poets Georg Trakl and Theodor Storm. A visit to Robert Bly back in the United States helped give a name to this impulse and a rhetoric with which to bring it to realization—poetry of the "deep image." He adopted free verse forms based on colloquial American speech and constructed as a series of evocative images leading toward moments of epiphany. At the same time some of his poems became more political, including some written in protest against the Vietnam War, and the outcasts he depicted were more often victims of American history.

ACKNOWLEDGMENTS

Below is publication information for the poems in this volume. Grateful acknowledgment is made to those individuals and publishers that granted permission to reprint selected poems in this book. I have made every effort to contact copyright owners to obtain permission to reprint these poems, but in a few cases my best efforts have been to no avail. I welcome further inquiries as appropriate.

Ai, "They Shall Not Pass," from her *Sin: Poems* (New York: Houghton Mifflin, 1986). © 1986 by Ai. Reprinted with the permission of Ai.

John Bensko, "García Lorca and the One-Legged Schoolteacher," from his *Green Soldiers* (New Haven, Conn.: Yale University Press, 1981). © 1981 by John Bensko. Reprinted by permission of Yale University Press.

Alexander F. Bergman, "To Eugene J. Loveman," from his *They Look Like Men* (New York: Bernard Ackerman, 1944). © 1944 by Bernard Ackerman, Inc.

John Berryman, "Nineteen Thirty-Eight" (first published in the *Kenyon Review* [1938]), from *Five Young American Poets: Mary Barnard, Randall Jarrell, John Berryman, W. R. Moses, George Marion O'Donnell* (Norfolk, Conn.: New Directions, 1940). First Series. © 1940 by New Directions Publishing Corp. Reprinted by permission of New Directions Publishing Corp.

Alvah Bessie, "Buried Alive," "The Dead Past," "For My Dead Brother," "Technicality," and excerpts from unpublished poems, from "The *Free* World and Other Captive Verse," unpublished manuscript, 1952, in possession of Sylviane Bessie. "The Dead Past" was published in the *National Guardian* in 1952, and "For My Dead Brother" was published in *Masses and Mainstream* in 1953. Reprinted by permission of Sylviane Bessie.

John Malcolm Brinnin, "For a Young Poet Dead in Spain," from *Salud! Poems, Stories and Sketches of Spain by American Writers*, edited by Alan Calmer (New York: International Publishers, 1938). © 1938 by International Publishers Company.

Olga Cabral, "To Spain," from *Masses and Mainstream*, June 1953.

Robert Bhain Campbell, "Among the Fallen," from his *The Task* (New York: Farrar and Rinehart, 1945). © 1945 by Farrar and Rinehart.

Hayden Carruth, "The Spanish Civil War," from his *From Snow and Rock, from Chaos: Poems, 1965–1972* (New York: New Directions Publication Corp., 1973). © 1973 by New Directions Publishing Corp. Reprinted by permission of New Directions Publishing Corp.

John Ciardi, "Reply to S. K." and "To a Young American the Day after the Fall of Barcelona," from *The Collected Poems of John Ciardi,* compiled and edited by Edward M. Cifelli (Fayetteville: University of Arkansas Press, 1997). © Ciardi Family Publishing Trust. Reprinted by permission of the trust.

Joy Davidman, "Elegy for García Lorca," from *Seven Poets in Search of an Answer,* edited by Thomas Yoseloff (New York: Bernard Ackerman, 1944). © 1944 by Bernard Ackerman, Inc.

Joy Davidman, "Near Catalonia" and "Snow in Madrid," from her *Letter to a Comrade* (New Haven, Conn.: Yale University Press, 1938). © by Yale University Press. Reprinted by permission of Yale University Press.

Barrows Dunham, "Neutrality," from *Presbyterian Tribune,* January 5, 1939.

Martín Espada, "The Carpenter Swam to Spain" (first published in *Volunteer for Liberty* [October 1999]), from his *A Mayan Astronomer in Hell's Kitchen* (New York: W. W. Norton, 2000). © 2000 by Martín Espada. Used by permission of W. W. Norton & Company, Inc.

Kenneth Fearing, "The Program" (first published in *New Masses* [1938] and in *Salud! Poems, Stories and Sketches of Spain by American Writers,* edited by Alan Calmer [New York: International Publishers, 1938]), reprinted from Fearing's *Collected Poems,* edited by Robert Ryley (Orono, Maine: National Poetry Foundation, 1994). © 1944 by the National Poetry Foundation. Reprinted by permission of the National Poetry Foundation.

Lawrence Ferlinghetti, "Into Darkness, in Granada," from his *Landscapes of Living and Dying* (New York: New Directions, 1979). © 1979 by Lawrence Ferlinghetti. Reprinted by permission of New Directions Publishing Corp.

Sol Funaroff, "The Bull in the Olive Field," in *The Heart of Spain,* edited by Alvah Bessie (New York: Veterans of the Abraham Lincoln Brigade, 1952). © 1952 by Veterans of the Abraham Lincoln Brigade, Inc. Reprinted by permission of Veterans of the Abraham Lincoln Bridgade, Inc. "To Federico García Lorca" (first published in *Poetry* [1938]), from *Exile from a Future Time: Posthumous Poems of Sol Funaroff* (New York: Dynamo, 1943). © 1943 for Sol Funaroff.

Margaret Gibson, "From a Single Center," "Madrid," "Maria," and "Retreat to the Future," from her *Memories of the Future: The Daybooks of Tina Modotti* (Baton Rouge: Louisiana State University Press, 1986). © 1986 by Margaret Gibson. Reprinted by permission of Louisiana State University Press.

Don Gordon, "Spain," from *The Heart of Spain,* edited by Alvah Bessie (New York: Veterans of the Abraham Lincoln Brigade, 1952). © 1952 by Veterans of the Abraham Lincoln Brigade, Inc. Reprinted by permission of Veterans of the Abraham Lincoln Brigade, Inc.

William Lindsay Gresham, "Last Kilometer," from *War Poems of the United Nations,* edited by Joy Davidman (New York: Dial, 1943). © 1943 by Dial Press.

Barbara Guest, "All Elegies Are Black and White," from her *Poems: The Location of Things* (Garden City, N.Y.: Doubleday, 1962). © 1962 by Doubleday, a division of Bantam Doubleday Dell Publishing Group, Inc. Used by permission of Doubleday, a division of Random House, Inc.

Robert Hass, "Rusia en 1931," from his *Human Wishes* (New York: Ecco Press, 1989). © 1989 by Robert Hass. Reprinted by permission of HarperCollins Publishers, Inc.

Langston Hughes, "Air Raid: Barcelona" (first published in *Esquire* [1938]), from *The Collected Poems of Langston Hughes* (New York: Alfred A. Knopf, 1994). © 1994 by the Estate of Langston Hughes. Used by permission of Alfred A. Knopf, a division of Random House, Inc. "Hero—International Brigade" (first published in the *Daily Worker* [November 14, 1937]) and "Tomorrow's Seed," from *The Heart of Spain,* edited by Alvah Bessie (New York: Veterans of the Abraham Lincoln Brigade, 1952). © 1952 by Veterans of the Abraham Lincoln Brigade, Inc. Reprinted by permission of Veterans of the Abraham Lincoln Brigade, Inc. "Letter from Spain," from *Volunteer for Liberty,* November 15, 1937. "Madrid," from *Our Fight,* July 1938. © 1973 by the Estate of Langston Hughes. Reprinted by permission of Harold Ober Associates Incorporated. "Moonlight in Valencia: Civil War," from *Seven Poets in Search of an Answer,* edited by Thomas Yoseloff (New York: Bernard Ackerman, 1944). © 1944 by Bernard Ackerman, Inc. "Postcard from Spain," from *Volunteer for Liberty,* April 9, 1938. "Song of Spain," from *International Literature,* no. 6 (1937).

Rolfe Humphries, "A Gay People" (first published in the *New Republic* [1939]) and "Lines Written for the Occasion of a Sale of Manuscripts," from *Collected Poems of Rolfe Humphries* (Bloomington: Indiana University Press, 1965). © Indiana University Press. Reprinted by permission of Indiana University Press.

Randall Jarrell, "For the Madrid Road" and "A Poem for Someone Killed in Spain," from his *The Complete Poems* (New York: Farrar, Straus, and Giroux, 1969). © 1969, renewed 1997 by Mary von S. Jarrell. Reprinted by permission of Farrar, Straus and Giroux, LLC.

Robinson Jeffers, "Sinverguenza," from *The Collected Poetry of Robinson Jeffers,* vol. 3, edited by Tim Hunt (Stanford, Calif.: Stanford University Press, 2000). © Jeffers Literary Properties; © transferred 1995 to the Board of Trustees of the Leland Stanford Junior University. Reprinted with the permission of Stanford University Press.

Bob Kaufman, "Lorca," from his *The Ancient Rain: Poems, 1956–1978* (New York: New Directions, 1981). © 1981 by Bob Kaufman. Reprinted by permission of New Directions Publishing Corp.

The Collected Poems of Thomas Merton (New York: New Dimensions, 1977).
© 1944 by Our Lady of Gethsemani Monastery. Reprinted by permission of
New Directions Publishing Corp. and Laurence Pollinger Limited.

Edna St. Vincent Millay, "Say That We Saw Spain Die" (first published in *Harper's* [1938]), from her *Collected Poems,* edited by Norma Millay (New York:
Harper and Row, 1956). © 1939, 1967 by Edna St. Vincent Millay and Norma
Millay Ellis. All rights reserved. Reprinted by permission of Elizabeth Barnett, literary executor.

Martha Millet, "Women of Spain," from the *Daily Worker,* September 14, 1936.

James Neugass, "Before Battle," "Es La Guerra," and "The Word Is Twilight,"
from *War Poems of the United Nations,* edited by Joy Davidman (New York:
Dial, 1943). © 1943 by Dial Press. "Give Us This Day," *Story* 13 (November–
December 1938). All reprinted by permission of Paul Neugass.

Kenneth Porter, "Harvest: June 1938" and "¡Salud!" from his *No Rain from
These Clouds* (New York: John Day Company, 1946). © 1946 by Kenneth
Porter.

Mike Quin, "How Much for Spain?" from the *Daily Worker,* August 8, 1937.

Kerker Quinn, "Gautier Visited Spain," from *Poetry,* July 1938.

Kenneth Rexroth, "Autumn in California," "Blood and Sand," and "Requiem
for the Spanish Dead," from his *The Collected Shorter Poems* (New York:
New Directions, 1967). © 1944 by New Directions Publishing Corp. Reprinted by permission of New Directions Publishing Corp.

Edouard Roditi, "Lament" (first published in *Poetry* [1939]), from his *Poems,
1928–1948* ((New York: New Directions, 1947). © 1947 by New Directions
Publishing Corp. Reprinted by permission of New Directions Publishing Corp.

Edwin Rolfe, "Brigadas Internacionales," "City of Anguish," "Death by Water,"
"Elegia," "Elegy for Our Dead," "Epitaph," "A Federico Garcí Lorca," and
"First Love," from his *Collected Poems,* edited by Cary Nelson and Jefferson
Hendricks (Urbana: University of Illinois Press, 1993). © 1993 by the Board
of Trustees of the University of Illinois.

James Rorty, "Elegy for the Spanish Dead," from *Modern Monthly,* September
1937. Reprinted by permission of Richard Rorty.

Norman Rosten, "Journey to Madrid," from his *Selected Poems* (New York:
George Braziller, 1979). © 1979 by Norman Reston. "The March" (published
in *New Masses* [1937]), from *Salud! Poems, Stories and Sketches of Spain
by American Writers,* edited by Alan Calmer (New York: International Publishers, 1938). © 1938 by International Publishers Company, Inc. "Spanish
Sequence," from his *The Fourth Decade and Other Poems* (New York: Farrar
and Rinehart, 1943). © 1942, 1943 by Norman Rosten.

Muriel Rukeyser, "Letter to the Front," nos. 4, 5, 6, "Long Past Moncada,"
"Mediterranean," "Neruda, the Wine," "1/26/39," and "Word of Mouth,"
from *The Collected Poems of Muriel Rukeyser* (New York: McGraw-Hill,

INDEX OF POEMS AND POETS

CARY NELSON is Jubilee Professor of Liberal Arts and Sciences and a professor of English and Criticism and Interpretive Theory at the University of Illinois at Urbana-Champaign. He is the author of *The Incarnate Word: Literature as Verbal Space* (1973), *Our Last First Poets: Vision and History in Contemporary American Poetry* (1981), *Repression and Recovery: Modern American Poetry and the Politics of Cultural Memory, 1910–1945* (1989), *Shouts from the Wall: Posters and Photographs Brought Home from the Spanish Civil War by American Volunteers* (1996), *Manifesto of a Tenured Radical* (1997), *Revolutionary Memory: Recovering the Poetry of the American Left* (2001) and the coauthor of *Academic Keywords: A Devil's Dictionary for Higher Education* (1999). His edited or coedited books include *Theory in the Classroom* (1986), *W. S. Merwin: Essays on the Poetry* (1987), *Regions of Memory: Uncollected Prose by W. S. Merwin* (1987), *Marxism and the Interpretation of Culture* (1988), *Edwin Rolfe: A Biographical Essay and Guide to the Rolfe Archive at the University of Illinois* (1990), *Cultural Studies* (1992), Edwin Rolfe's *Collected Poems* (1993), *Higher Education under Fire: Politics, Economics, and the Crisis of the Humanities* (1994), *Madrid 1937: Letters of the Abraham Lincoln Brigade from the Spanish Civil War* (1996), *Disciplinarity and Dissent in Cultural Studies* (1996), *Will Teach for Food: Academic Labor in Crisis* (1997), *The Aura of the Cause: A Photo Album for North American Volunteers in the Spanish Civil War* (1997), and *Anthology of Modern American Poetry* (2000). He is vice-chair of the Abraham Lincoln Brigade Archives and vice president of the American Association of University Professors and has served on the executive council of the Modern Language Association.

The American Poetry Recovery Series

The University of Illinois Press
is a founding member of the
Association of American University Presses.

Composed in 9/13 Meta Normal
with Meta display
by Jim Proefrock
at the University of Illinois Press
Designed by Copenhaver Cumpston
Manufactured by Cushing-Malloy, Inc.

University of Illinois Press
1325 South Oak Street
Champaign, IL 61820-6903
www.press.uillinois.edu